A Mystical Friendship
in Letters

A MYSTICAL FRIENDSHIP
IN LETTERS

My Year with Henry David Thoreau

Cynthia Fraser Graves

Mellen Poetry Press
Lewiston, New York
mellenpress.com

Library of Congress Cataloging-in-Publication Data

Library of Congress Control Number: 2023939304

Graves, Cynthia Fraser
  A Mystical Friendship in Letters: My Year with Henry David Thoreau /
Cynthia Fraser Graves.

1. Literary Collections—Letters. 2. Body, Mind, & Spirit —Subjects &
Themes. 3. Body, Mind, & Spirit—Mysticism.
     p. cm.
  Includes bibliographical references.
  ISBN-13: 978-1-4955-1082-3 (softcover)
  ISBN-10: 1-4955-1082-4 (softcover)

  I. Title.

hors série.

Copyright   ©   2023   Cynthia Fraser Graves

All rights reserved. For information contact

The Edwin Mellen Press
Box 450
Lewiston, New York
USA 14092-0450

Printed in the United States of America

To order books, telephone 1-716-754-2788
or
go to mellenpress.com

Dear Cynthia

I, too, am waiting, waiting for you to gaze over your shoulder on these early mornings when you take up writing, waiting for you to slow down and notice that I am leading or following, no difference as there is no position or direction where I am.

In this new kind of seeing, you experience some of what I saw but meld it with your personal vision, expanding and contracting the mystery according to Cynthia. I have seen you twinkling out there, a star by any other name…

I am joyous to be enfolded again in the fizzing energy of the Earth plane. I have never really left, only rescinded my human form, become the draft, the thought in the mind, the emotion sweeping the heart, coming from nowhere, but there is nowhere I am not…

-Henry David Thoreau, August 29, 2015

Contents

Dear Cynthia	**5**
Prelude One: In The Labyrinth	**15**
Prelude Two: Why Me?	**15**
Summer 2015 - July	**16**
July 1, 2015 - Day One	17
July 2, 2015 – The Scarf Of Light	18
July 3, 2015 – Delight Of Discovery	19
July 4, 2015 - Independence Day	20
July 6, 2015 - Green Beans	23
July 7, 2015 – To Walden Pond	23
July 8, 2015 – A Day On Walden Pond	23
July 11, 2015 – The Black Prince	24
July 17, 2015 - Solitude	25
July 20, 2015 – The Hollyhock Clock	26
July 22, 2015 – Queen Anne's Lace (Daucus Carota)	27
July 22, 2015 - The Places We Write From	28
July 25, 2015 – The Heart Of Now	29
July 30, 2015 – August Arrives	30
July 31, 2051 - A Walk On Walden Pond	31
Summer 2015 - August	**31**
August 9, 2015 – Finding Love In All The Right Places	32
August 10, 2015 - Lace Of Shadows	33
August 11, 2015 - Holding On For Dear Life	34
August 12, 2015 - Campfires	35
August 13, 2015 - Rocks And Other Characters	36
August 17, 2015 - The Road Home	38
August 18, 2015 - The Smallest Town In Maine	40
August 21, 2015 - A Moment's Play	41
August 23, 2015 - Going Somewhere	42
August 26, 2015 - A Light At Sea	42
August 28, 2015 - In Your Hands	43
August 29, 2015 - Listening And Hearing	43

Fall 2015 - September   **44**

September 1, 2015 - Stasis   44
September 2, 2015 - Entertaining Angels   45
September 3, 2015 - Wild Apples   46
September 4, 2015 - Dear Cynthia   47
September 5, 2015 - Sunflowers   48
September 7, 2015 - I Will Go A-Graping   49
September 9, 2015 - Kennebunk Blueberry Plains   50
September 10, 2015 - Manifesting 101   51
September 12, 2015 - Dear Cynthia   52
September 17, 2015 - Let Us Rise   53
September 18, 2015 - A Bee-Loud Glade   55
September 21, 2015 - The Cliffs Of Moher   57
September 23, 2015 - The Neighborhood   56
September 24, 2015 - Berries And Light   57
September 25, 2015 - Berries Redux   59
September 26, 2015 - The Neighborly Rocks   60
September 28, 2015 - Landscape   61
September 29, 2015 - Puritan Time / Irish Time   62
September 30, 2015 - Sunset   63

Fall 2015 - October   **64**

October 4, 2015 - The Famine Walls Of Maghery   65
October 5, 2015 - A Peat Fire On The Hearth   66
October 6, 2015 - A Fresh Perspective Every Hour   67
October 7, 2015 - An Irish Wake   68
October 8, 2015 - A Morning Walk In Pamplona   70
October 9, 2015 - A Fly On The Empire State Building, NYC   71
October 10, 2015 - After Collecting Wild Fruits, The Road Home   72
October 15, 2015 - On The Cusp   74
October 20, 2015 – The Imaginal Realm   75
October 22, 2015 - On This Earth Day   76
October 23, 2015 - The Sound Of Hope   77
October 26, 2015 - All Souls Walk   78
October 29, 2015 - The Transparent Eyeball   79
October 30, 2015 - All About Your Light   80

Fall 2015 - November   **82**

November 1, 2015 - The Same Garden? 82
November 3, 2015 - Creation And Creators 84
November 5, 2015 - Meetings 85
November 6, 2015 - Kyrie Eleison 85
November 7, 2015 - Moonrise 86
November 9, 2015 - I Love Nature 87
November 10, 2015 - November Litany 87
November 11, 2015 - Sky Painting 88
November 12, 2015 - To Seasons In New England 89
November 13, 2015 - Gaia 90
November 13, 2015, Again - Walking 91
November 14, 2015 - The Walk Taken 92
November 15, 2015 - Seeing Paris 11/13 93
November 16, 2015 - Soul Cakes: Small Comforts 94
November 17, 2015 - The Last Manuscript: Wild Apples 95
November 18, 2015 - Woodsmoke 96
November 20, 2015 - Rangeley, Maine: Height Of Land 97
November 21, 2015 - Into The Wild 98
November 22, 2015 - A Maine Morning 99
November 23, 2015 - The Surprise Of The Sacred 100
November 24, 2015 - The Sound Of Water 101
November 25, 2015 - Simplify, Simplify 102
November 26, 2015 - Thanksgiving 2015 103
November 27, 2015 - Everything Waits 105
November 29, 2015 - Allowing Loss 106

Winter 2015 - December **107**

December 1, 2015 - Tree Hugger In A December Wood 107
December 2, 2015 - Acquaintance Among The Pines 108
December 3, 2015 - The Yellow Brick Road 109
December 4, 2015 - Looking Behind As You Leave 110
December 5, 2015 - Crow Season 111
December 7, 2015 - Hawkeye 112
December 8th, 2015 - The View From (T)here 113
December 11, 2015 - One Hundred And Sixty Years Ago Today 114
December 12, 2015 - Tableau, A Dream Poem 115
December 14, 2015 - Henry, We Hardly Knew Ye 116

December 16, 2015 - A Powerful Idea Is Born 117

December 19, 2015 - A Windy Day Here 118

December 22, 2015 - A Moment In Time: Winter Solstice 120

December 24, 2015 - A Magic Night 121

December 25, 2015 - The Christmas Full Moon 122

December 26, 2015 - The Twelve Days Of Christmas, Day One: The Kiss Of A Conscious Earth 123

December 27, 2015 - The Twelve Days Of Christmas, Day Two - Two Pennies 124

December 28, 2015 - The Twelve Days Of Christmas, Day Three: Frankincense and Myrrh 125

December 29, 2015 - The Twelve Days Of Christmas, Day Four: Four Things You Can't Recover 126

December 30, 2015 - The Twelve Days Of Christmas, Day Five: Five Golden Rings 127

December 31, 2015 - The Twelve Days Of Christmas, Day Six: Six Crows a Cackling, The Turn of the Year, 2016 128

Winter 2016 - January **129**

January 1, 2016 - The Twelve Days Of Christmas, Day Seven: Happy New Year 130

January 2, 2016 - The Twelve Days Of Christmas, Day Eight, Day Nine: My Error Revealed 130

January 3, 2016 - The Twelve Days Of Christmas, Day Ten: Ten Cows a Jumping for Joy 131

January 4, 2016 - The Twelve Days Of Christmas, Day Eleven: The End Is In Sight 132

January 5, 2016 - The Twelve Days Of Christmas, Day Twelve: The Lonely Drummer 133

January 6, 2016 - Epiphany Station; All Aboard 133

January 7, 2016 - Venus And Saturn 134

January 8, 2016 - The Pond In Winter 136

January 9, 2016 - Waveless Serenity 137

January 10, 2016 - Wood Heat At Walden 138

January 11, 2016 - The Great Snows 139

January 12, 2016 - Earthing 140

January 13, 2016 - The Path To Walden 141

January 15, 2016 - The Huckleberry Baron 142

January 16, 2016 - Chains 143

January 17, 2016 - "The Day Is Forever Unproved" 144
January 18, 2016 - "Jove Nods To Jove From Behind Each Of Us" 145
January 19, 2016 - Way Leads On To Way 146
January 20, 2016 - Silence Baying At The Moon 147
January 21, 2016 - Earth Time, Up In The Eastern Predawn Sky 148
January 22, 2016 - Traces Remain 149
January 23, 2016 - Come For A Walk, Henry 149
January 24, 2016 - January's Full Wolf Moon 151
January 26, 2016 - Winslow Homer's Journal 152
January 27, 2016 - Lessons Of A Starling Murmuration 153
January 29, 2016 - The Journals 154
January 31, 2016 - The Power Of Now 155

Winter 2016 - February **156**
February 2, 2016 - Reflections 156
February 4, 2016 - Green Surrender 158
February 6, 2016 - A Journal 158
February 7, 2016 - A Morning Song 159
February 8, 2016 - The Song Sparrow: Emily Dickinson 159
February 9, 2016 - A Competent Witness 161
February 14, 2016 - Heart Day 162
February 15, 2016 - Monday Meditation 163
February 16, 2016 - Shades Of The Biblical 164
February 21, 2016 - Dear Cynthia - The Advent Of Spring 165
February 22, 2016 - Early Spring 166
February 23, 2016 - Believing Is Seeing 167
February 24, 2016 - Written Word 168
February 25, 2016 - Where Things Come From 171
February 26, 2016 - A Red Song At Dawn 172
February 27, 2016 - A Walk At The Society Of The Four Arts 173
February 29, 2016 - A Rare Day; Look About You! 174

Spring 2016 - March **175**
March 1, 2016 - The Beginning 175
March 2, 2016 - The Prevailing Winds 176
March 3, 2016 - Wind People, Part Two 178
March 4, 2016 - Visiting Royalty 180
March 5, 2016 - These Fleeting Moments 181

March 6, 2016 - Thoughts Become Things	182
March 7, 2016 - Falling Through To Silence	183
March 9, 2016 - With The Power Of The Sea	184
March 10, 2016 - A Point In Space	186
March 11, 2016 - The Evolution Angel	187
March 12, 2016 - The Full Definition Of Joy	188
March 14, 2016 - A Walk About Under The Moon With Henry	189
March 16, 2016 - The Full Moons Of March	190
March 17, 2016 - Knowledge Of Star Songs	191
March 18, 2016 - The Concord River Today	193
March 19, 2016 - Blue Curls	194
March 20, 2016 - Plant Your Dreams	195
March 21, 2016 - The Open Road	196
March 22, 2016 - To Sing You On Your Way	197
March 24, 2016 - Fire Rainbows	197
March 24, 2016 - Quiznos, Concourse C, and Nick's Tomato Pie	198
March 26, 2016 - Holy Saturday Of The Triduum	199
March 27, 2016 - Easter Vision	200
March 28, 2016 - A Plain Monday	201
March 29, 2016 - Ecosystems Plus One	202
March 30, 2016 - John Farmer	203
March 31, 2016 - Robins And Poetry	204

Spring 2016 - April	**204**

April 1, 2016 - Julia Cameron	204
April 2, 2016 - Amy Lowell	205
April 3, 2016 - Walt Whitman	206
April 4, 2016 - Sue R Morin	207
April 6, 2016 - William Wordsworth	208
April 7, 2016 - Stephen Spender	210
April 8, 2016 - Bob Dylan	211
April 9, 2016 - Rumi	212
April 10, 2016 - Robert Frost	212
April 12, 2016 - Carl Sandburg	214
April 13, 2016 - Edgar Lee Masters	215
April 14, 2016 - Wendell Berry	217
April 15, 2016 - Edna St. Vincent Millay	217

April 16, 2013 - Mary Oliver ... 219
April 20, 2016 - Tomorrow ... 219
April 21, 2016 - Poem in Your Pocket Day ... 220
April 22, 2016 - Earth Day ... 222
April 23, 2016 - The Time Is Now ... 223
April 24, 2016 - The Pink Full Moon ... 224
April 25, 2016 - A Knocking Mood ... 224
April 26, 2016 - Dark Nights, Bright Dawns ... 225
April 27, 2016 - The Nick Of Time ... 226
April 28, 2016 - The Road Home: Day One ... 227
April 29, 2016 - The Road Home: Day Two ... 227
April 30, 2016 - The Road Home: Day Three ... 228

Spring 2016 - May ... **229**

May 1, 2016 - Arrival In Kennebunk Just Ahead ... 229
May 2, 2016 - The Trees Are All The Right Height: Home ... 229
May 4, 2016 - A Gray Wood ... 231
May 5, 2016 - To Stand Up Through It All ... 232
May 6, 2016 - Dear Cynthia, Perspective And Lilacs ... 233
May 7, 2016 - A Bell, Struck ... 234
May 8, 2016 - Being In Good Company ... 235
May 9, 2016 - All Things Held To Be Good ... 236
May 10, 2016 - Short Shrift ... 237
May 11, 2016 - In Florida Again ... 237
May 12, 2016 - In Memory ... 237
May 13, 2016 - Better To Keep It Simple ... 239
MAY 15, 2016 - Heading North...Polaris ... 240
May 16, 2016 - Road Trip Continues ... 241
May 18, 2016 - Newton's Third Law ... 242
May 19, 2016 - Wool Gathering ... 242
May 20, 2016 - The Commonest Sense ... 243
May 21, 2016 - Dear Cynthia, The Eternal Society Of Woolgatherers ... 245
May 22, 2016 - Lilac Dusk ... 245
May 23, 2016 - Spring Seeding ... 247
May 24, 2016 - The Wind Writes A Note ... 248
May 26, 2015 - Now You See It — The Powers Of Heaven And Earth ... 248
May 27, 2016 - Two Crows, Joy ... 249

May 28, 2016 - Kiuna Opens Today 250
May 29, 2016 - The Qualities Of Innocence 251
May 30, 2016 - Earth Time 252
May 31, 2016 - A Perfect Day For A Perfect Day 253
Summer 2016 - June **254**
June 1, 2016 - An Empty Calendar 254
June 2, 2016 - The Wood Thrush Is Singing 255
June 3, 2016 – Book Ends 256
June 4, 2016 - Rhubarb Season 258
June 5, 2016 - Grandfather 259
June 6, 2016 - Advice 261
June 7, 2016 - A Tide Of Iris 262
June 8, 2016 - Back To Walden Pond 263
June 9, 2016 - A Letter To Mr. D.R. 264
June 10, 2016 - Acorns Abounding 265
June 11, 2016 - The Summer Solstice Window 266
June 12, 2016, Earth Time - Dear Cynthia 268
June 13, 2016 - Sea Rose And Sea Lavender Season 269
June 14, 2016 - Cranberries, Pigs, And Flag Day 270
June 15, 2016 - Rhode Island Road Trip And Inspiration 271
June 16, 2016 - Our Thoughts Are Prayers, And We Are Always Praying 272
June 17, 2016 - Expectations 273
June 19, 2016 - The Strawberry Moon Lights The Solstice 274
June 20, 2016 - Dear Cynthia, Sacramental Time 275
June 21, 2016 - Half As High As My Head 277
June 22, 2016 - Meadows 278
June 24, 2016 - In Memoriam 279
June 25, 2016 - Stillness 280
June 26, 2016 - Sheltering 280
June 27, 2016 - Retrospective 282
June 28, 2016 - Industries Of The Wind 283
June 29, 2016 - The Morning Star 285
June 30, 2016 - Dear Cynthia, In The Beginning 286
July 1, 2015 - Day One, Again 287
Summer 2016 - July **287**
July 7, 2016 - The Perfect Summer Day 288

Summer 2016 - August ... **289**

August 28, 2016 - Postscript ... 289

August 29, 2016 - The Angelus Rings ... 290

August 30, 2016 - Red Gems ... 290

2017 And After - Tatters Of Letters ... **291**

November 26, 2018 - Phantom Geese ... 291

November 29, 2018 - November Winds ... 293

December 2, 2018 - Nativity ... 293

December 7, 2018 - Winter Solstice Begins ... 295

April 1, 2022 - In Chartres This Morning ... 296

April 2, 2022 - God, The Iridescent Love Cloud ... 297

April 3, 2022 - All About The Light ... 298

May 10, 2022 - There Truly Is No End, Henry ... 299

Prelude One: In The Labyrinth

I am in the Labyrinth bookstore: the famous store on Nassau Street, in Princeton, NJ. It's a pleasant day, sunny and warm. I am in the state of openness that comes when you have no goal in mind but that of an observer enjoying the aura of all these books.

I walk past a display of books set out on the aisle and notice the book nearest me has a cover photo of Henry David Thoreau. I quickly have the feeling that I know him well from my reading of Walden, and from the years I prepared for classes in American literature at Westbrook High School. The transcendental ideas he and Emerson espoused found a natural fit in me and have grown with passing years. I pause in front of the book to look fondly at this hero of mine. Perhaps I pick the book up, I don't remember; what is very clear is that I hear someone say out loud and clearly, "*Write to me!*"

I look up quickly to discover the source of this command, turn around a time or two searching, but there is no one near me. When I look down again, the image of Henry in front of me brightens, the gaze between us warming. In a little burst of panic, I decide to put the book down and move on, letting the words I heard dangle in my wonder.

After a turn around the abundantly stocked shelves and tables, my interest in what has happened does not fade. I walk back toward the front of the store to the book, still within the thrall of the encounter. (At this point, I must reveal my personal knowing that all, ALL matter is energy, and all energy vibrates in the great space of presence that is waiting for what is wished. Finding oneself in this perceptible field of energy not visible but felt happens all the time.)

I regard your image, and again, I hear, "*Write to me!*" The voice and message are so beyond doubt, I look up to see if anyone else has heard this, is looking my way. I know you have issued a request, and, though your voice was gentle, there is an urgency to the tone, "*Write to me!*"

When I leave, all I am able to think about is the warm, buzzing effect of the meeting; the light, buoyant, interesting idea of being able to write to Henry David Thoreau, of knowing his address. This powerful new intention walks with me towards Wheatsheaf Lane.

From that day on, I know you are waiting, and, as Marley said to Scrooge, "*No space of regret can make amends for one life's opportunity misused.*" I know a rare opportunity is offered me, *especially* me, and though it will take courage to take up the task, and to believe I am worthy; the delight of that prospect is enough to make me all for it!

Prelude Two: Why Me?

Looking back to those precious days centered in his presence as if holding hands, I ask myself how I dared launch such an endeavor? To declare that I, Cynthia Fraser Graves, a blue-eyed girl with Acadian ancestors standing behind her all the way to the Great Expulsion at Grand Pre, was to begin a conversation with someone of Henry Thoreau's natural genius and literary heft required a bit of cheek along with intense courage. The cheek I claim, the courage came harder. Letters began to spool out from my mornings obviously connected with someone unique, fine, and sacred.

Our relationship was, and is, above the ordinary experiences of this life. I gave myself permission to believe Henry when I heard him say, "Write to me!"

In the wake of that request, excitement gathered, and trust built that I could do just that: write to Henry Thoreau in real and tangible communication.

The experience has been thrilling, refreshing, and rejuvenating.

The depth of knowledge and excitement I felt as I approached each morning could only have been because you, your incorporeal self, was my partner in this correspondence. I knew I could bridge the space between earth and the seemingly close precinct of heaven and be in his presence in a twinkling.

Did I have trust in myself that I could pierce present energy modulations to visit with the boundless, compassionate Spirit being that he is now? Could I put aside my fear and doubt to speak back to the Speaker who he had so obviously spoken to me? I said "YES!"

The letters I received from you during our time encompass both of us within one voice. Considering your precious and adept listening and responses, and the flow of time and consciousness between us, how could I ever be lonely again?

As I write the above, I know it's as simple as can possibly be. I have always been a child of the wind, a believer in magic, seer of the invisible. In this voyage of heart-unto-heart knowing, there was never a moment of doubt. We are a pair, you, and I, for you never doubted me either.

For those limited by what we think we know in this life on earth, this account might sound preposterous. To think Henry David Thoreau would wish to or could engage in correspondence with me—he, American essayist, poet, philosopher, abolitionist, naturalist, tax resister, development critic, surveyor, and historian and most excellent of men, who died in 1862—might give some pause.

That he left the Earth plain on May 2nd, at the age of 44 is a fact. I have stood by the cabin site of Walden Pond, and at his grave in Concord, Massachusetts. I have seen the monument the world makes of both earthly sites; the precious tokens left in both places. I felt the hand of fate touch my shoulder there. I take up this task of sharing our letters with humility and joy and ask you to be with me in this correspondence as we offer it to the planet.

Summer 2015 - July

In preparation for my first day of correspondence, July 1, 2015, I read constantly from texts written by and about Henry Thoreau. I thought I knew a good bit about him but, as I went to write to him, I had no surety of what I would say. As inspiring and eloquent as his words were, it seemed a very unsure and daunting thing for me to address him as a pen pal.

In the beginning, the letters I wrote were written on trust—trust that this correspondence could take shape, substance, and voice if only I kept going, writing faithfully and with faith, without doubting my readiness for such an undertaking.

The first morning of July, 2015 was my seventy first birthday. I sat down at the computer, encouraged by my previous experiences in the imaginal realm, and by my belief, Henry, that you were there with me at my desk in the writing room on Warren's Way in West Kennebunk, I began…

July 1, 2015 - Day One

Dear Henry,

We will walk on our own feet; we will work with our own hands; we will speak our own minds… A nation of men will for the first time exist, because each believes himself inspired by the Divine Soul which also inspires all men.

-Henry David Thoreau

When I was slogging away in my high school classroom day after day, struggling to instill an appreciation for the genres, writers, and concepts of the American literary canon, the clouds always parted and the sun came out when I arrived at Transcendentalism. The air in the classroom became charged with new, hopeful energy and interest. During one year, I took on the task of being your spokesperson, and a prescient group of students boycotted the lunch line because of the inequities that had been exposed there by the tenets of the living art of you and Ralph Waldo Emerson. I got into trouble on your account, Henry, and I relished being your stand-in deeply.

Your words have life within. "*God is Omnipresent, Man is divine, Intuition lives within us.*" Simply saying them aloud challenges any dogma to the contrary, making rules unbearable. I was christened a devotee in those days and remain one today; these inspiring beliefs making a great difference in my life then, and now.

Henry, you didn't surprise me on that Sunday stroll in Princeton, NJ, when I came upon your image, and you spoke to me. The glimmer of encouragement lit your literary stare from that cover, and I heard your invitation as clearly as if you had been standing beside me. I smiled my acceptance, and that is the trust upon which I now act.

For tomorrow's blog, I will include a story I would tell you, eyes alight with discovery, over a cup of tea on a drizzly summer afternoon. I know, Henry, in some way unimaginable, you will hear me here and now in West Kennebunk, Maine, on this warm July afternoon.

My pledge is made. My intention set. I will drop a missive into the ethers every day for one whole year. 365 days. The rest, I trust to you.

With great affection,
Cynthia

P.S.
Tomorrow: The Scarf of Light.
Writing for a daily blog is a new experience for me, not to mention the inscrutable process needed to post this letter on a blog site. It took many drafted letters to feel comfortable with the writing platform and to be anywhere near satisfied with the results.

In the beginning, I worried about what I would find to talk about each day.

I needn't have; each afternoon, as hours proceeded toward evening, the next day's topic would arrive.

I immersed myself in your Journal and essays looking for connections between your experiences and mine. Before long, I felt the ground under my literary feet become a conjoined world where we both existed. I began thinking of you, me, and our conversation constantly.

July 2, 2015 – The Scarf Of Light

Henry, it happened that same month we were introduced: June 2015, in Princeton New Jersey. That same weekend, after a wonderfully rich breakfast, my family and I went for a morning walk along the Raritan Canal. There was no hurry, no destination, no tasks to attend, and I found myself sauntering in nature— echoing the sauntering of which you were so fond. Lagging back a little from the group, I was thinking over the possibilities of my new vow of correspondence with you, one that was to begin in a few weeks. Wide open to and absorbing the natural environment, silence descended around me, and my companions moved further along the path.

That whole walk, Henry, I felt your love for a good walk. I was quiet, expectant, and—when I saw the impossible take shape before my eyes—I said aloud, "Henry, do you see that? What on earth is it?" I was aware that the scene—along with our meeting the day before—was obviously prescient territory: the imaginal realm.

Twelve feet from where I stood, mystery unfolded in the air. Where the canal waters backed into a spot on the edge of the path, they formed a small tributary that pooled close to me. A random branch lay bridging one bank to the other, a broken limb protruding up into air several feet from the ground.

In some sleight of hand, Henry, light was coalescing, dropping from this limb, and becoming visually solid, unfurling, undulating. This light had the dimension of a square of filmy cloth blowing in a breeze that I could feel, ruffling like the thinnest silk. And, Henry, the subtle design it made of dappling shade and patches of sun around me created a scarf of light. I walked around this chimera looking to discover the source for this mystery; nothing could explain it.

I was the sole viewer; I did not call anyone to corroborate my experience. There would be no interpreting this sight; I didn't want another's doubt or contorted logic contaminating the holy instant.

Since then, the memory has returned many times to make me smile. I am grateful to have been there, at that spot, at that moment. I even suspect the vision was for me—unless it was for you, Henry, and those who might read of the event.

The experience reminded me of you, Henry, and of miracles you found in Nature daily. It has led me to want to revisit the path you cleared for us believing someone would follow you there.

I will go there Henry.

With great affection,
Cynthia

P.S.
With Day Three dawning, the demands of this pledge have kicked in. Every time I finish one letter, I have a few hours of equanimity; I can breakfast and sail along with my daily chores and pleasures. But, by noon, I feel something is being left undone and I need to search for the morning's topic.

I would farm (a metaphor you would like) your words as well as those of your colleagues and friends—whether your era or mine (I'm sure you know how extolled you are now)—looking for a seed to plant. And, on most days, I expect I will be rewarded with the grace and joy of finding I am in tandem your spirit; that we walk hand in hand:

July 3, 2015 – Delight Of Discovery

Dear Henry,

Dawn has come, strewing dappled light about quietly after a deluge of crystal rain yesterday. I imagine this to be the kind of morning where you could not bear the inside of a house, the kind of morning that sent you out, alone, the soft sound of your boots on worn paths, your rapt attention perceiving music in the amphitheater of the beginning day.

Henry, I am here too. I feel the hugeness of trees, birds, clouds written on air...all performing their dance of love for you and me.

Your awareness is spacious enough to understand what we have only begun to suspect today: that possibility is always the river we travel in the canoe of our particular being, a possibility to be collapsed to the particular by the vision of the seer/creator... and as we walk with you Henry, we get glimpses of the Divine, just ahead walking with us, companion in a sacred co-existence, co-creation; Walker and Power knowing of each other within a dance of energy. The delight of this discovery was the engine that inspired and confirmed so many of your society of Transcendentalists, ignited your dinner discussions, and inspired your daily rounds with passion and hope, hope in all possibility for all men, regardless of class.

I am envious of your society, Henry.

Cynthia

July 4, 2015 - Independence Day

When first I took up my abode in the woods, that is, began to spend my nights as well as days there, which, by accident, was on Independence Day, or the fourth of July 1845.

-Henry David Thoreau, Walden

Dear Henry,

Today is Independence Day in America, one hundred and fifty-four years since your leaving us. The morning is bright, warm, and pleasant here in Maine. Parades are scheduled in cities and towns all over America. Dusk will hold great plumes of sparkling fireworks. Topographically, the country is almost the same as when you traveled it. That being said, you would not recognize the place. Cities have been built up at a crazy pace and many forests and groves have fallen to those inert worlds of cement and steel.

Separated, as we are by 154 years, a pittance in time really, I have set out to follow the imprint of your footsteps, believing I will find you on some path, somewhere, in some time. Those I share this Present with, for the most part, think me daft to persist in this belief that your notice is attainable. They are so sure that a corporeal person, once relieved of his/her shell, is removed entirely from this dimension. That's the going belief, but I don't concur.

I believe that if I come each day to the doorway of your domain, you will hear me and respond in a way that is discernible to me. The link between us might be in thoughts that bloom, a notion or idea that I do not recognize as my own, a contemplation that has the elegance and complexity of yours, Henry. Or, it might be a sudden understanding, a veneration of the natural, a privileged peek inside some truth curled tight, then unrolling like the young fern frond, from your energy to mine, beautiful and unique, infused with splendor.

I take encouragement in synchronicity that has begun to pepper my days, showing up as encouragement, telling me "*You are on the right path... Just keep going, I am not far ahead.*"

Take, for example, your Journal entry for June 4th, 1853. In this entry, you visited the clerk's office in Concord to read grants of land. You pronounce the names of these grants, savoring their sound—*Nutt Meadow, Willow Swamp, Goose Pond*— expressing surprise to find *Walden Pond* recorded and named as early as 1853. On that day, you were unaware that Walden Pond and your experience in the cabin you were about to build would become a model of heaven come to earth for countless numbers in my world—a place where you inhabited a different dimension of human experience within Walden's silent, winter-swept woods.

Your understanding and communion with Nature rose in the sap of that year, sharing age-old counsel written in the book of Seasons, published anonymously. Squirrel, deer, fox, and all manner of birds, sensing your gentleness, crept near you with trust. The darling, green rise of bean seedlings in brown velvet gardens provided elegantly for you from the hands of the Creator, in fact, overwhelmed you.

You taught us so much, your brave mind casting ahead the idea that Divinity pervades and inhabits all of nature.

Here in West Kennebunk, in this year of 2015, in echo of you, I speak names of many roads and fields I travel: *Old Alewive Road, Winnow Hill, Old Thompson Road, Kennebunk Blueberry Plains.* Their history is hinted at in the sound of their names. Old Alewive Road follows a stream that once bristled with alewives— herrings to those who fished them—mostly gone today because of the dams erected on the Mousam River.

Winnow Hill still exists as a small rise above the gently swelling land of West Kennebunk, an old farm, king of a small mountain, but high enough for fall winds to blow chaff from crops, or, it might be that the person who named the road meant to separate themselves from the crush of living, freeing themselves from an advancing tide of development as ubiquitous as it must have been a hundred or more years ago.

I pass Winnow Hill and an air current of ancient peace and usefulness flows over me. I see shadows of men in straw hats raking and lifting bouquets of dried grasses saluting the fecundity of land. By the side of the white farmhouse on the crest of the hill, a New England housewife shakes out her wash, pinning it to a line for the sun to dry, explosions of meaning shaking into air as wind enlivens the clothes. The farmhouse keeps its distance from town but quivers on the edge of the tide of development advancing from Kennebunk into the hinterlands.

Old Alewive Road is now only a byway, narrow and winding—no traffic lights allowed. It follows the Mousam River as it veers off main roads to wander into the countryside toward the small towns of Lyman, Dayton, and Alfred. In these places the past is traceable. Large colonial houses with porches, shuttered windows and barns stand quiet in once planted fields.

I am encouraged. All possibility exists; the old informs the new. Happy Fourth of July, Henry, and an appropriate poem...

New England Women

I love New England Women who
put the light on in the kitchen
under dark January skies and make soup.

I love New England Women who
gather berries on summer hillsides
white clouds above in blue skies.

I love New England Women who
hang out wash and read prophecy in sheets,
sweaters pushed up on strong arms.

I love New England Women who
shun despair in the dead of January
to wash a floor, bake bread, or knit.

I love New England Women who
feel the wind with their body and dance
the kitchen when no one watches.

I love New England Women who
walk a March storm down to the farm
under spring apple trees to hear them singing.

I love New England Women who
stop clocks and cover mirrors
to sit with Death like a relative who needs no talk.

-Cynthia Fraser Graves

Even the fragments of our letters held interest...

July 6, 2015 - Green Beans

What I want to talk with you about today is that the green beans planted in the community garden are coming into flower! This growing season here in Maine has been cold (next door to freezing, really) with downpours daily, suffering the lack of sun and infestations of scores of insects; all of this we have endured, survived, and it has brought us (gardeners all) closer each to each.

After a welcome wave of warmth, blossoms are opening all over the garden. Summer squash, tomatoes, eggplant…not the winter squash yet, but we are encouraged. Like you, my beans here in my own 'Concord' *"attach(ed) me to the earth, and so I got strength like Antaeus"* (Thoreau, 1854, "Walden").

The garden is the ground of being, a floor for transformation of both physical and spiritual dimensions, and this flowering of food is for it!

How fortunate to have no corporate interests at all. All for all, beans for me and for you, a harvest of good, giving all, taking nothing but my labor and interest. Lucky me!

Tomorrow, I travel to Concord to trace your footsteps for one day.

With affection,
Cynthia

July 7, 2015 – To Walden Pond

And so, we travel to Walden Pond, driving along Maine's artery to the south, I-95.

At a certain point, I begin to recognize names of places that sang off your tongue: Assabet, Concord, Lexington… and at last, Walden Pond.

July 8, 2015 – A Day On Walden Pond

Dear Henry,

Do you know how many people visit this site of your cabin looking for what you found here or left behind in these quiet woods? Do you know that the now shadow village in which you tramped out your shining path with illustrious friends has become a labyrinth for those of us in search of the meaning and joy you found in life?

The sound of a gentle breeze and water waving into the shore. In the distance, children laugh and play at the beach. Someone runs on the path that you once walked, footsteps sounding then dying out. Just ahead is the site of your cabin, but your memory is in the very air here. It is the same in all important qualities as it was, though two hundred years have passed.

We amble up the humble path you walked so often, looking down to read the hearthstone. *Go thou my incense upward from this hearth.* Your wish is granted, Henry. Rising with the smoke of your lonely fire, your words have become as common and exquisite as the eloquent air.

As we leave and walk away from the stone cairns and notes left by those who love you, a little girl is reading your Declaration aloud to her school group, her clear, lovely voice rings in your woods charming us all. It was easy to see you in her young heart. She echoes you...

I went to the woods because I wished to live deliberately, to front only the essential facts of life, and see if I could not learn what it had to teach, and not, when I came to die, discover that I had not lived.

A little further along the path a pure, white dove rests in a thicket. Are there really doves in these woods? There are today. This one does not fly or even move away but watches us approach. I am not surprised.

As ever, in friendship,
Cynthia

P.S.
And, oh Henry, The Black Prince has set fruit...

July 11, 2015 – The Black Prince

Dear Henry,

I planted a strong, royal, tomato seedling in the rich brown velvet of my garden. Its given name is "Black Prince." I am enchanted with the possibilities of this green guest. In its maturity, it will be a tomato of rusty color; the taste of which will surely brighten my days. My imagination is stirred by this addition to our garden: He guards His community of vegetables. May that be true! Since planting, this Prince has come along and is now three foot high, bejeweled with hardy fruits. Dark green and beautiful, He is the keeper of the peace in the garden, talking sternly to all the neighbors (especially the squash).

In your Journal, dated June 2,1853, you tell us you were awake by 3:30 AM, listening to the rise of birdsong; by 4:00 AM, you were out and gone, walking to the river in a *sea of fog, level and white.* You walked until the land clouds thinned in the advance of a sun rising. You watched the green meadows seep through this gossamer and until the sparkle of brooks appeared in the last entrance on the stage of this play.

You were thirty four years of age as you made this entry. If one were to attempt to retrace your steps in this century, walk your morning journey, they would be disappointed. The green of meadows and sparkle of clear, pure water has been dispensed with for gain in the topsy-turvy world risen around Concord, as with most inhabited land.

Ownership has triumphed…

July 17, 2015 - Solitude

Dear Henry,

There is no one left on earth who had the experience of seeing or knowing you when you walked Concord. The best we have of you are your words. I continue to read from Walden, from your journals, from the mountain of material about you.

You write much of the environs around Concord and adjacent lands in your travels. Every now and then, you lift away from describing and commenting on solid ground to the enlightened air of transcendence. I offer below a paragraph from Walden:

This is a delicious evening, when the whole body is one sense, and imbibes delight through every pore. I go and come with a strange liberty in Nature, a part of herself. As I walk along the stony shore of the pond in my shirtsleeves, though it is cool as well as cloudy and windy, and I see nothing special to attract me, all the elements are unusually congenial to me. The bullfrogs trump to usher in the night, and the note of the whip-poor-will is borne on the rippling wind from over the water. Sympathy with the fluttering alder and poplar leaves almost takes away my breath: yet, like the lake, my serenity is rippled but not ruffled. These small waves raised by the evening wind are as remote from storm as the smooth reflecting surface. Though it is now dark, the wind still blows and roars through the woods, the waves still dash, and some creatures lull the rest with their notes. The repose is never complete.

If ever there were an experience of your friend, Ralph Waldo Emerson, to plumb the depths of, you have it here, or it has you.

As Emerson penned:

All aspects of nature correspond to some state of mind. Nature offers perpetual youth and joy, and counteracts whatever misfortune befalls an individual. The visionary man may lose himself in it, may become a receptive "transparent eyeball" through which the "Universal Being" transmits itself into his consciousness and makes him sense his oneness with God.

The trick is to remember that the experience of the transcendent moment is hidden in each moment, for each traveler on this path called life on earth.

I have a stand of poplar trees near my house. They watch me come and go, leaves wagging messages down to me, offering whatever I need, solace, comfort, congratulations, but always they remind me that the ripples and waves on the surface of my life do not reach the still waters of my soul. I think you knew the language they speak well.

With Gratitude,
Cynthia

P.S.
Well, Henry, twenty days into this new life of mine and I look each day to find the gifts you have left for me. I am never disappointed.

Often, on summer afternoons when clouds noiselessly skim across the saucer of blue sky turned upside down over my home, I sit on the front porch in quiet. The light rises and falls, shadows of leaves bow on a soft wind. I feel the presence of a whole other kind of time: a broad, deep existence, peace drops down. At times like this, I can hear my garden.

July 20, 2015 – The Hollyhock Clock

Dear Henry,

The hollyhocks in my garden are measuring sticks of summer. They reach for the sky as they break the cool earth in spring. A year's digits in blossoms rise on strong stalks, the first opening early in July.

This is, of course, relative to the growing zone one lives in. Here in southern Maine, we are the slower end of Nature's great push of green and must attune our living to this timecard.

As the hollyhocks open their stalks, one to another, I can see the advance of summer, read time's march, and take heed. Each time I look to my garden from the front porch, I hear hollyhocks ticking like a timepiece; I see the blooms, like faces, looking back to me telling me time is passing. It takes me up short sometimes, Henry, when I realize how quickly we live.

Today is Monday, another Monday in the wheel of weeks, added to the string of months and years I have gardened my life here. Your noble work asks me to look at what I have laid by for the following winter in terms of my living on earth. You ask us to live truly, harmlessly, each aware of our life as a gift.

In any weather, at any hour of the day or night, I have been anxious to improve the nick of time and notch it on my stick too; to stand on the meeting of two eternities, the past and future, which is precisely the present moment; to toe that line.

-Henry David Thoreau, Walden

And what can I do better this day, knowing the swiftness of time's flight?

Be quiet, be alone (oh how you loved solitude) and let the great tide of air wash in the presence of all that is.

This is your advice, Henry. Your best discovery.

Be quiet and listen to the hollyhocks…

With great affection,
Cynthia

July 22, 2015 – Queen Anne's Lace (Daucus Carota)

Good morning, Henry,

It's just rising six and I must be about my business. This pledge, desire, aim (I am not sure what to call it) to write to you every day for one year has become part of my day as surely as my meals and my sleep. I find myself looking about in the progress of my day to see what might be of interest to you and, therefore, what I might pay attention to.

Today, I imagine that I walk out to Walden Pond, knock softly at your door and—if you are at home and willing—you invite me in for a small time to converse about this or that. This, for me, is a real thing, an actual relationship.

The month of July has moved ahead of me on the trail. She is calling flowers to decorate the air of her reign, to become visible and bask in the strong sun.

Today, our star is Queen Anne's Lace, foaming up from the fields and roadways all over New England, ubiquitous loveliness in every stage from the woven basket of the early flower to the full lace doily of the mature plant.

Folklore tells us about the red at the center of the second year's flower; that it is a drop of red blood from Queen Anne as she wrought lace with her needle. Though there are two possible namesakes for the flower—Queen Anne of Britain and her great grandmother, Anne of Denmark—this red center attracts insects to the plant.

Anne's Lace is like poison hemlock; any gathering should be done with great care. If gathering for food, the carrot root is edible only while young, but quickly becomes too woody to eat, classified as a beneficial plant when paired with tomato and lettuce.

As substantial as these facts seem, I am not a person for facts. The beauty and grace this humble plant lend our summers and falls is without measure. Any patch of ground will do for its effort. These earth's diadems take to the air in fields, stretching under the hot sun for miles and miles—good season or ill—and sprout around discarded equipment in forgotten yards, around anything classified unsightly. They are as forgiving as they are lovely.

Who has not had their spirits lifted by a chorus of this waving lace under a blue sky on a summer day?

I feel connected to you in my devotion to this flowering root. I know you loved the Daucas Carota, Henry, how could anyone not; I hear the name on your tongue. And you would approve of the thrift of such a multitude.

I will be out lace hunting before long. The season is upon us.

With affection,
Cynthia

July 22, 2015 - The Places We Write From

My 'best' room, however, my withdrawing room, always ready for company, on whose carpet the sun rarely fell, was the pine wood behind my house. Thither in summer days, when distinguished guests came, I took them, and a priceless domestic swept the floor and dusted the furniture and kept things in order.

-Henry David Thoreau, Walden

Dear Henry,

Here in my village, the day has begun to walk about. We are rounding the corner of July. The noble, queenly aspect of August rises on the horizon, the month of plenty. If I let go of my sense of this modern world I inhabit with its immediacy everywhere, I feel around me the lonely circle from which every writer writes. Time slows, minutes stretch; I step outside for a moment to look back at the Whole. You wrote from this circle as well. We are neighbors here.

On August 1st, I will go to Hermit Island for a week, off the ease of the electric grid. No electricity, no heat or easy food, no diversion. On this island cell phone connection (a gadget that allows constant chatter, you would hate it) is not available—nor are television screens. Rather, campers put up tents, gather wood, light campfires, and circle up under the stars, or else enjoy the solitary experience of an island washed by the cold Atlantic. There are many who still desire this experience.

On Hermit Island the hours drift like small waves rolling in at ebb tide to the beaches, one like the other. There are no appointments, no conveniences, no noise, and one is left holding the responsibility of their own life in a new way, a way of presence with what is around.

It takes a day or two just to slow down enough to feel it.

And so, Henry, I prepare to leave West Kennebunk for a week on my island— but before I go, this new energy, new level of communication has begun to unsettle me in ways that I know were familiar to you.

What will I find in the Woods?

July 25, 2015 – The Heart Of Now

Dear Henry,

What's in the Woods?

Write while the heat is in you. The writer who postpones the recording of his thoughts uses an iron which has cooled to burn a hole with. He cannot inflame the minds of his audience.

-Henry David Thoreau

Driving through my village yesterday, I felt uneasy, discontent, suspicious of what, in the recent past, seemed fine, recognizable, usual. The life I thought I was busy living was the life of errands in the great job of being alive and present in this society; juggling balls in the air, so to speak.

As I drove slowly through West Kennebunk, a disparate echo of your voice sounded in my head, asking this question of me:

Didn't you know that immersing yourself in ideas of this potency and power would disrupt your balance in the self-constructed prison you have built to keep your attention off what Is?

After hearing that, I parked and sat for a while, highlighting and itemizing my great and profound waste of time. From that vantage point, I allowed this personal audit to continue to multiply the collective waste of time, village to city, city to country, country to continent, and continent to globe. It was distressing in the extreme.

Ideas, politics, fashion, television, news, education, broadcasting, cuisine, Wall Street, too many to list here deconstructed before my eyes as what they really are: diversions, many harmful to minds and hearts that attend and mistake them as a living creed that offers to substitute ennui for the simple joy waiting prepaid for all who arrive in the heart of now.

Henry, I am ignited by the truth and the simplicity this change of direction offers. When I began this conversation with you, I hadn't bargained on transformation, but now that is in play. What will I do with its lit flame?

Have I left my village behind? What really IS in the woods?

Mighty questions.

Thank you, Henry, for your part in this. And Mr. Emerson as well.

July 30, 2015 – August Arrives

Dear Henry,

Royalty approaches. In this opulent month, let us imbibe the bounty provided each day. This gift given to everyone carries with it the fragrance of time's passing and the allure of winter ahead, allowing the earth to lie fallow a while. Make haste. Walk in the halls of August. Do not waste a precious hour.
How often you have offered the same sentiments.
I will let my poem speak.

Cynthia

Clarions of August

August approaches, month of gold,
of amethyst, of sapphire.
lace flowers, woven on looms of charged air
foam in fields and waysides.
August burnishes everything, sets fire to the seen
as the unseen rises.
Donning her eternal crown of blue,
August clouds skitter in delight,
tracing rivers running below,
shadow-racing to the edge of the horizon.

Bouquets blow in breezes,
wildflowers bow low before royalty.
Counterpoint of golden filigree under foot
as endless as the grasses proclaims allegiance from earth.
Swallows escape July's humid court
to leap and roll,
their joy burning in small bodies,
amazing those who look up to the circus ring
to have the bluebird's blue streak test their faith.

Color spills out…in forms that spin
bright smudges on air.
August laughs at the fun. The kind monarch
takes the throne.

July 31, 2051 - A Walk On Walden Pond

Dear Henry,

I am signing off. We leave for our island adventure early tomorrow morning.
I will have my journal with me, as well as your Journal. Each day, I will observe the trinkets Nature strews before me with close attention. You may rely on me to give you a good account of my week when I return. Who knows what I will see and hear?
I will be back and writing to you again daily on August 9th—or at least a new version of myself will.
In Life Without Principle, you say:

We should treat our minds, that is ourselves, as innocent and ingenuous children, whose guardians we are, and be careful what objects and what subjects we thrust on their attention. Read not the Times, Read the Eternities.

I am for that Henry!
Where I am going, that will be my text.

With Affection,
Cynthia

Summer 2015 - August

August's amethyst gown is spread over a landscape that simmers in sweetness. Her breath is the delicious scent of ripening berries, apples, and golden corn. There is a fathomless, invigorating clarity deep within that imparts strength and beauty. August demands boldness, fleet action for her nights begin to chill. Her voice is that of Time itself. The earth crowns her with a diadem of shimmering turquoise skies, coral sunsets, and starry nights.

-Cynthia Fraser Graves

The week on Hermit Island drifted by. The days were spent in silent conversation with you, my new and ever-present friend, escaping as speech often, out loud in wonder at what I experienced myself. I kept true to my journal, made notes of what I thought might interest a man of your soul-driven seeing in Nature.
The first letters of this month's leger came straight from my experience suspended on that rocky isle in the soughing, slate-hued Atlantic.

August 9, 2015 – Finding Love In All The Right Places

Dearest Friend, Henry,

I have returned from my week on the Island.

The sights and sounds of Maine are deep in my cells: fragrant tapestry of evergreens, gray of rocks, humble brown of sand, slate blue of ocean, fire of sun and moon, all are fused as threads, tints enhanced by the clearest air. All this beauty is now within me, memory and emotion, a map.

This week's letters will stand as a record of my journey. There were wonderful moments, moments that rose from the ordinary to lift into a zenith of discovery, and from there to the signature voice of Spirit leading me in renewal of the original energy. The knowing that Divinity lives in all of Nature was as surely confirmed on Hermit Island as pennies found scattered, full moonlight on ponds of crystal, mood swings of powerful Maine weather flashing over the jagged spit of land, inner doors opening, gifting new understanding. One had to be Present to receive the gifts. There is always a price.

We are now striding into the heart of August. Nights are cool. Air is clear, dry of the humidity left behind by July. Sleeping on the earth, as we did, offers a unique perspective to those willing; during the night, I heard the heartbeat of the Earth. On one of our sleeps, an owl perched nearby called out its lovely question. Wind, always music, we had as well. Wind lifted from the green instruments of evergreens, a counterpoint swelling up to join the aria from waves on the shore. Always, the bell on the water in the harbor rang with the tide; the composer's message enfolded us.

This earth which is spread out like a map around me is but the lining of inner most soul exposed.

-Henry David Thoreau, Journal

I like thinking that a heart etched and painted in the bark of a tree I once came upon during a hike told me many things all at once; the impulse of its maker was love, giving love to those on the path it marked. It was a way the great Universe could signal its affection for all my fellow travelers and for me in our journey here.

But most wonderfully, it is my signaling to myself that love is in me, for me, whenever I look. And still the days turn.

Until tomorrow,
Cynthia

August 10, 2015 - Lace Of Shadows

Dear Henry,

My sentiments are yours as August's cool breath heralds fall. Your Journal records this notice on August 7, 1854. You are 37 years old, rambling in nearby fields, only five years from your death.

It is inspiring at last to hear the wind whistle and moan about my attic, after so much trivial summer weather, and to feel cool in my thin pants. Do you not feel the fruit of your spring and summer beginning to ripen, to harden its seed within you? Still autumnal, breezy with a cool vein in the wind; so that, passing from the cool and breezy into the sunny and warm places, you begin to love the heat of summer. It is the contrast of the cool wind with the warm sun.

As I walked one of the few roads that intersect that craggy, cliff-riven spit of land, I looked down to see the reverse print of shadows, trees as shade flowers on the road beneath me, so much like the Queen Anne's Lace blooms I wrote of lately. The dirt of the road had become imprinted in fractal repetitions, never ending patterns, repeating all the way down the road as simple designs.

We share this noticing, you, and I, of what is around us. What do these patterns mean? Are they embellishment or text? I believe, like you, Henry, they evoke an inner lexicon of knowing.

I watch Lace Shadows on these roads, wondering at the beauty that is literally cast upon the ground; pennies to be gathered.

In this letter, Henry, is the clearest picture of what this tandem project of ours is becoming. I found the term 'recursion' recently. It is for us!! We—you and I—are recursions, surfaces of two mirrors paralleling each other's seeing, concurring images in different time localities, understanding each other clearly, together, here, now, somehow.

How wonderful is that?

Until tomorrow,
Cynthia

P.S.
Walking Hermit Island, my eyes seek to find the zenith in blue sky and clouds, to look out on the enchanting sea, waves crashing onto rocks, birds soaring, calling… But one had better look down at tree roots under foot. With no depth of soil on the cliffs, the gnarled, knobby fingers spread everywhere for a hold. Storms with wild winds, deep snows, certain rivers of ice and rain always present. The trees hold on for dear life…

August 11, 2015 - Holding On For Dear Life

But nothing could exceed the toughness of the twigs—not one snapped under my weight, for they had slowly grown. Having slumped, scrambled, rolled, bounced, and walked, by turns, over this scraggy country, I arrived upon a side-hill, or rather side-mountain, where rocks—gray, silent rocks—were the flocks and herds that pastured, chewing a rocky cud at sunset. They looked at me with hard gray eyes, without a bleat or a low. This brought me to the skirt of a cloud and bounded my walk that night. But I had already seen that Maine country when I turned about, waving, flowing, rippling, down below.

-Henry David Thoreau, The Maine Woods

Dear Henry,

Trees dig into the earth with roots, snarled holds that stretch ten to fifteen feet away from the center pole of a tree. Gnarled and tough, these roots will not give in the most wicked of weathers that blow in off the Atlantic. As I hike the path on this clement August day, they are everywhere under foot, some older than the presence of humans here. One must pay good attention to each footfall as the sharp cliffs are only feet away. Plummeting over the edge is not an empty fear.

As you remarked…

But nothing could exceed the toughness of the twigs—not one snapped under my weight, for they had slowly grown.

-Henry David Thoreau, The Maine Woods

These roots are as veins of a great hand holding on to earth, gathering needed nourishment from the unending Source—and being, just being. Lovely in color, strength, and form, they play their part in the realm of Forest; the tree they hold aloft breathes the air and therefore gives us oxygen and shade and a place to harbor in a storm to those beneath it.

Henry, I read the record of your assent to Mount Katahdin in which granite rocks became sheep and clouds, skirts of moisture that blew around you; below you solid land waved, flowed, and rippled as your vision pierced and played with what, for others, seemed commonplace.

A great gift.

More Hermit Island tomorrow,
Cynthia

P.S.
And I would not be worthy of you and our conversation if I spoke not of the campfires blooming like flowers as dark descends.

August 12, 2015 - Campfires

Dear Henry,

The fire is the main comfort of the camp, whether in summer or winter, and is about as ample at one season as at another. It is as well for cheerfulness as for warmth and dryness.

-Henry David Thoreau

We now no longer camp as for a night but have settled down on earth and forgotten heaven.

-Henry David Thoreau

Campfires on Hermit Island begin to glow from four o'clock in the afternoon. Smoke rises in aromatic plumes, flames brightening as night lowers. No electricity available, campers experience conditions as from centuries ago. Families draw close to get through the night in spite of anxiety about food, shelter, safety, things now taken for granted.

Soon all of us are reassured by the light and warmth given up from the collected wood, faces reflect the rosy flames. Then, the Stories begin, small circles telling of their lives, or making up scary scenarios with ghosts and demons that might be behind the dark trees watching in the woods, only to laugh when the telling is done.

The Island is alight with these fires, two hundred plus hearths when the campsites are full. I wonder what it looks like from above. Maybe it becomes a small galaxy with stars blazing and twinkling in the dark. Gathering around the fire is important, the camaraderie extant, all looking back with recognition to each other, then looking up to stars. Is someone looking back?

Things are never what they seem.

Until tomorrow,
Cynthia

P.S.
So, Henry, I am going to wax playful now. It occurred to me that a light-hearted entry could work wonders…

August 13, 2015 - Rocks And Other Characters

Good morning, Henry,

I ask your indulgence. I have written a play with characters from my time on Hermit Island; a rock, a fir-tree, the sea, and with myself as interloper. In my lexicon, the synonym for energy could be life, therefore the title: *The Life Of Rocks*.

Taking into consideration that everything in existence *is* energy and information, when we set an intention, waves of energy create movement to become that intention.

Before our intention setting, be it conscious or unconscious, this energy is ready and waiting to become our thoughts. Subconscious intention setting is the real fly in the ointment...always ongoing, silent, smooth, and hidden, events play out coming from this shadow side of ourselves.

This scenario attempts to illuminate this idea. We interplay unknowingly with matter in the daily scenes of our lives...

The Life Of Rocks
A Play in One Act

Setting: Hermit Island, Small Point, Maine, late morning, a path leading to the sea.

Characters:
Woman, of some age
Companion, man of some age
Rock, grey granite
Tree, evergreen-pine
Sea, full tide but calm

Act One:

Tree (annoyed): Hey, you two. People are coming down the path. They are expecting to see a peaceful ocean, gray rocks, slate blue seas, sun on waves. Take your places... Stop flitting and bouncing around, settle down. We don't want the word getting out that we are anything but what they think we are. Rock, stand still, look solid, don't move.

Rock: I will if you will. The woman expects you to be waving your dark green boughs in the wind. I can't do this all by myself. Shape up!

Sea: What about me? What are my stage directions? I could have a storm. What does she expect me to be? Could I crash on the rocks?

Tree: By the feel of the energy, she thinks we are peaceful and soothing, so soothe, Sea. She has a camera. She's going to take our picture. Arrange yourselves, Maine Coast! Smile everybody!

Woman (obviously charmed with the scene): Dear, what a beautiful place. I want to take a photo from here and keep it on my desk through the winter to remind me of this day. It will keep me peaceful. Sturdy granite stone, calm sea, waves, and the lovely green of that tree. What angle should I shoot from? It is so beautiful.

(Several clicks of camera)

(Sounds of steps retreating down the path)

Rock: I'm glad that's over. OK everyone, back to flowing until the next interruption comes our way. Yippee!

The End

Forgive me, Henry, for my obvious masque; I was inspired by your words about life inherent in all things. I'll tone it down tomorrow.

Playfully,
Cynthia

Just for A Moment…

Stand with me,
Here on an Island in Maine.
Let the softness of everything in,
Before we leave Hermit Island behind…

Sounds of Silence

-Cynthia Fraser Graves

Could a greater miracle take place than for us to look through each other's eyes for an instant?

-Henry David Thoreau

August 17, 2015 - The Road Home

Dear Henry,

Last weekend we took a short trip to New Haven, and traveling both ways we were stalled by a river of traffic that left us mired in stops and slowdowns, forward motion becoming a thready pulse, causing anxiety in the small universes of cars all around us.

Life on Earth today would be such a shock to you. There is nothing in your time that could prepare you for the projectiles of automobiles traveling in dizzying channels of roads at speeds that would frighten the citizenry of your day.

We are used to it in most ways. Used to the mental and physical anguish that driving those projectiles—while avoiding hitting each other—entails.

So, it was as we hurtled towards Connecticut from Maine this weekend, air-conditioned cool seeping from vents as the temperatures rose into the low 90's, when I happened to spy the small sign telling me we were crossing the Assabet River in Massachusetts, one of your beloved waterways.

Because of my ever-widening acquaintance with you, my friend, a clear, fresh image of you in your boat, floating down this river with a great smile on your face rose into my mind and, may I say, I smiled with you. The noise and threat from the parade of steel and aggression I was riding in momentarily stopped. I breathed a deep breath, letting go my travel angst.

He who hears the rippling of rivers in these degenerate days will not utterly despair.

-Henry David Thoreau

Even now, I hear the ripple of those sweet waters through the doors of the vehicle, feel the brush of a breeze and warmth of the sun. What a treasure your work is!

Thank you, for this knowledge of rivers, and for so much! The image of you on a peaceful waterway, no asphalt, may even be an image that takes us within ourselves where the real journey begins.

With gratitude,
Cynthia

The Assabet River

(For Henry Thoreau)

The Assabet runs high tonight,
her tributaries glinting, etched in brown
earth as she runs for the sea under the full solstice moon.
When I think of you on your boat, Henry,
quiet and sharp,
floating beneath a trusting night sky
on waters pure and alert,
waters that gift the silver heft of fish into hands,
waters that wash away meanness,
then I am with you, Henry, breathing the air you breathe.

Though I span your river this night in a steed of metal
under a sky that may not be trusted
where fish choke on the dregs of greed,
I am with you, in your time…
filled with a loneliness so precious,
so full,
it is enough for one life.

-Cynthia Fraser Graves

P.S.
It seems appropriate, Henry, to acquaint you with the town I write from most days.
As Concord was to you, so West Kennebunk is to me…

August 18, 2015 - The Smallest Town In Maine

Dear Henry,

In this year, 2015, I live in West Kennebunk, Maine, a few hours travel by car from your Concord, Massachusetts. At least, I used to. In the past few years, someone has been busy switching things around until at this time the only actual place that bears the name and zip code (a modern mailing numerology device) of West Kennebunk is a white clapboard building by the side of Alfred Road, a two-lane road that runs up through Dayton and out to Alfred, the seat of York County.

For the more than the forty years that I have been here, West Kennebunk has been a place where people lived, worked, and came home from school. It was one of the three Kennebunks: Kennebunkport, Kennebunk Village, and West Kennebunk.

West Kennebunk was mostly rural, rolling hills and stretches of land with open fields abounding, the old farm perimeter of the Village featuring Blueberry Plains, streams lacing lovely vistas with old farmhouses every few miles, herds of cattle and goats. I can remember when the half-mile out of Kennebunk to West K was festooned by stretches of wild day lilies beside the road as summer bloomed.

As of the 2000 Census, there were 809 people, 316 households in West K. The population density was figured at 233.1 people per square mile with the racial makeup: 97.90% White, 0.12% African American, 0.25% Native American, 0.87% Asian, 0.12% Pacific Islander, and 0.74% from two or more races.

In those 316 households, 37.3% had children under the age of 18 living with them. The median income for a household was $42,125, and the median income for a family was $47,333.

Well, it's all disappearing. I don't mean the land itself, although that is being subdued under construction of new subdivisions, submitting to growth of business and Kennebunk's need for more room. I mean the whole idea of living in West Kennebunk, the small townlet of years past, is disappearing.

The lovely land itself still presents itself as one drives the roads of the region. Fields stretch under the summer sun and under the snows of a Maine winter. The citizens of the little town still meet at the PO and shake their heads about the change. The sacred circle of the Blueberry Plains enfolds you as you drive up to Sanford on Rt. 99—but what is changing is the idea of West Kennebunk.

Kennebunk proper kept nudging borders until West Kennebunk lost political clout and its identity and became just more Kennebunk. It happened quietly. No votes, no options, it just was.

Those living here still think of themselves as residents of West Kennebunk, still remember the "old days", still try to hold onto the history and image of the small village. They hold an annual West K Day. But the tide has turned. The only place that IS West Kennebunk is the Post Office, and that is slated to disappear soon as well. The rest of what was once West K now registers as 04043, Kennebunk.

It's now the smallest town in the world by my account.

A little digression.

Thanks for listening,
Cynthia

August 21, 2015 - A Moment's Play

Dear Henry,

I am here on the coast of Maine for a final summer visit. The Atlantic rises and falls at my feet breathing, softly filling the small cove to my right with tide the color of jade and seaweed, swaying to music unheard. Around me ancient junipers and other low bushes take a stand, though whittled, stunted by the ice and winds of the winter months. A flag, intermittently full then slack, waves in a gathering wind. I am lulled by the repetitive slap of small surf down at the beach.

When I open my eyes, the weather is changing. Out over the water, the cloud deck thickens and lowers, moves toward me as I watch. Ripple patterns on the tide meet and combine creating a tapestry of light and shadow.

Two kayakers glide by in silence, their motion marking time that otherwise is invisible.

A pair of ospreys begin some game I don't understand, calling to each other from the tall signal pines around the cove, one flies out of sight, then comes back, the other goes, calling all the while. Seems much like a human game to me. Suddenly, one of the birds flies up and spirals down, plunging into the water to rise with a fish. Such accuracy and purpose is to be admired.

The wind comes up again, blows through the screens of the cottage behind me, through trees in bursts, stronger now, ruffling the halyard on the flagpole, the sound of which rings out in quiet over the sea.

There is nothing to do about anything here, observing is the game. Observing and allowing, this completes the circle.

Fog seeps down to land as a white gauze, erasing detail, consuming everything visible; quiet is everywhere.

(Henry, you so loved observation, I dared to offer this to you.)

With gratitude,
Cynthia

August 23, 2015 - Going Somewhere

Dear Henry,

When I travel up to Biddeford for shopping, part of the appeal of making the trip is the road I drive. At one point, the narrow two-lane road turns a corner to break out from the wooded, occluded view and climbs to the top of a hill where there is a clear mile or more of perspective.

At the top of the hill, the road bisects an old farm. The barn—an old, faded red, sagging structure not used for much anymore—rises on one side, the farmhouse on the other. Both buildings sit very close to the edge of the road. You get a sense that the road was once a path for the cows to come home at night.

Before you reach the farm, in a field of wildflowers on the left rests a small cemetery dating to the middle 1800's. It bears the name of the family interred. The whitewashed fence enclosing it is there keeping no one in or out. Its poignancy sings out as I pass, giving rise to nostalgia for my own departed.

Driving through this scene always affects me. The peace in the air reaches through the car's metal barrier, encouraging me to stop. So, yesterday, I did. It was a brilliant late August day. The Daucus Carotas (Queen Anne's Lace) were basketing up, getting ready for the thrill of autumn winds and the ride they will take to fields of possibility.

When I took out my trusty phone (forgive me Henry) to capture an impression of the area, the most evocative image was of a man with a stick walking at the edge of the flower-thick field, the lovely lace blossoms offering a wave, trying to slow you down, recommending that you savor the moment and reminding you to be carefull. Who knows what is around the next corner?

In my heart, the man walking with the stick became you, Henry, hiking mile after mile, translating all you saw, gloriously happy in the doing.

With gratitude,
Cynthia

August 26, 2015 - A Light At Sea

Good morning, Henry,

It's the fifth day in a chain of muggy days, days that portend the change of seasons. We will wander back and forth, in and out of the doorway, temperatures dropping degrees at time until we are subsumed by Autumn and her gorgeous clear season.

August 28, 2015 - In Your Hands

Good morning, Henry,

It is very cool here in Maine this morning. The humidity has fled leaving us with crystalline Canadian air full of the energy of the great, green northern forests. Today, it will warm to almost eighty degrees with pleasant sun. We are grateful.

In my reading last night (I am reading the biography by Walter Harding, The Days of Henry Thoreau) before sleep, I heard about all of the company you had out there in your little home by Walden Pond. It seemed, especially at the beginning, that you were not allowed much alone time.

According to one visitor, a family walked out to see you, and, during their visit, you called *"your little family"* in to see them. With the use of a language of chirrups and bird calls, you sent out the invitations and in they came: a woodchuck, a pair of gray squirrels, several birds including two crows, one of the flocks nestling on your shoulder. You proceeded to feed them from your hands, and they were very content and fearless in the presence of the human company. When the visit was over, you sent them off with the same sounds that called them in. Everyone was amazed. So was I!

These pets of yours could feel the touch of love and caring in the energy transmitted to them. Your great patience in the observation of natural things was a player as well. We all touch others with our energy in deeper ways than we know. How do we use it? Do we put our hand on other shoulders in support and caring, or give the flip of dismissal, or worse, disdain?

You showed us what love can do.

Thank you, Henry,

P.S.

At last, the day dawned that I heard back from you. When I settled at my computer, I lit a candle and took a few moments to center myself... Then, feeling a shift in the room, I asked...

August 29, 2015 - Listening And Hearing

Dear Henry,

Something tells me that I am in your presence. This lit flame creates a new space, a new room, a room of light. I wait here.

You promised, remember?

Cynthia

Dear Cynthia,

I, too, am waiting, waiting for you to gaze over your shoulder on these early mornings when you take up writing, waiting for you to slow down and notice that I am leading or following, no difference between them as there is no position or direction where I Am.

In this new kind of seeing, you experience some of what I saw but meld it with your personal vision in different ways, expanding and contracting the mystery according to Cynthia. I have seen you twinkling out there, a star by any other name...

I am joyous to be enfolded again in the fizzing energy of the Earth plane. I have never really left, only rescinded my human form, become the draft, the thought in the mind, the emotion sweeping the heart, coming from nowhere, but there is no where I am not.

Words, my words, your words play leapfrog with each other, one idea leaping out, my words that you take and empower to go beyond my experience, color with your time, your vision and I am present again in a new way all these years into the future.

All of this is born of WILL, your will to look beyond the symbols that surround you seeming oh so solid. These are but suggestions of the glory and grandeur of Truth that hovers behind them, echoes of what IS waiting for you outside of your human experience.

I like your image of the listening tree, it means something; all of your creation is listening to hear your slightest thought, to bring it back as a gift to you, to weave your world around you on the loom of energy according to your thoughts. Think bold, think good, think beautiful, think holy.

Oh, the power you have to Create. It is no less than was mine. And I am here.

In friendship,

Henry

Fall 2015 - September

September closes August's door. A slow Sister, she is satiated with the fruits of summer's labor. Cricket song and the first whispers of the loneliness to come swirl in her winds. Her tone is deep and hushed with rustling dried grasses in warm fields. As she casts her glance about, the green world bows and subsides in compliance.

-Cynthia Fraser Graves

As September of 2015 took over the calendar, a surprise was waiting for me. When at a local hairdresser's, the operator—one Shaun Patrick from Donegal, Ireland—stopped in the middle of the haircut, regarded me in the mirror we occupied together, and said, "Would you be interested in a month's house swap in Ireland?"

Now, Henry, Shaun is the real thing; red haired and with that pleasant Irish lilt embedded in his accent. Once he asked the question, I simply investigated our reflected images and nodded my head in an affirmation in acceptance of the opportunity, sight unseen.

This is the reason that, in mid-month, my letters began arriving from Ireland.

I stayed true to my pledge even though I had moved to another part of the world. Each morning, in Donegal, I would carry out my coffee routine, signaling my time with you, settling down to my keyboard—the one that was connected to your environs.

September 1, 2015 - Stasis

Dear Henry,

We have stepped into September, toes in anyway. It is still warm here in Maine, summer warm, and will probably stay that way for the first week of the month. Often a gracious month, September provides plenty of sun to enjoy the flowering earth around us, a stasis period of balance or equilibrium when the forward motion of seasons pauses to mirror the balance of the hours of light and darkness which are equal at this point.

In the terms of seasons and celestial spin, patterns seem eternal, though we know they are not. The design of our lives is much more malleable.

In human terms, CHOICE can disrupt patterns, send us on new paths, or set us back on the path we are on with new vision and enthusiasm. Living into your choices takes clarity and courage. We rise above where we stand to find which direction the road we follow will take us.

These moments of clarity are like this stasis, times between change, as change is ongoing.

The question is, can one take charge of this new vision, give it intention and energy?

It takes courage to step onto a higher road, but always, the voice within gives direction and encouragement.

Will we listen?

Change will happen each day.

Who is in charge?

I know you agree wholeheartedly, Henry.

Cynthia

September 2, 2015 - Entertaining Angels

Dear Henry,

It seems that your small house at Walden Pond was a way station for anyone passing by. You certainly had company! Your door was always open to those who stopped in, and you welcomed most (there were a few exceptions) with your hearty handshake, the offer of a chair (you had just three) and your attention. No invitations needed. If they arrived at dinner time and could be fed by the food you were preparing, you shared.

And people came, people curious about a man who would deliberately move to the woods, disconnecting himself from the protection and distraction of a community to live among. Although you got your wish to live deep within the presence and silence of Nature, the great metaphor of surrender and rebirth in its seasons, you were not disconnected from "folks".

One of your preferred guests was the Canadian wood chopper, introduced as being *...so quiet and solitary and so happy withal; a well of good humor and contentment which overflowed at his eyes. His mirth was without alloy.* His naive intelligence gave you both pleasant hours of discovery, like companions without pretense.

Your list of visitors included children a-berrying, railroad men in clean shirts taking a walk on Sunday mornings, fishermen and hunters, poets and philosophers, an enslaved person who had escaped, all who came out to the woods for freedom's sake.

And you were there to offer welcome.

All the while Walden Pond shimmered through the passing days and nights, watching you.

May we all be as welcoming, as interested, as present to the visitors in our lives. Even though modern life is more complicated in so many ways, we can be present for our visitors and receive their gifts.

There are two angels visiting with me right now.

I am grateful.

See you tomorrow,
Cynthia

September 3, 2015 - Wild Apples

We are wont to forget that the sun looks on our cultivated fields and, on the prairies, and forests without distinction. They all reflect and absorb his rays alike, and the former make but a small part of the glorious picture which he beholds in his daily course. In his view the earth is all equally cultivated like a garden.

-Henry David Thoreau, Walden

Dear Henry,

The apple trees in Maine are bearing fruit, boughs being heavy enough to bring them to earth. The red gems gleam from under still green leaves on both cultivated trees in orchards and myriads of wild apple trees in secret, trees sewn by birds and wind. On walks into woods, on old, now-fallow farmlands, forgotten trees offer a harvest of wild apples to whomever is sharp enough to value their gift.

Certainly, the true inhabitants of the land take advantage. Deer, woodchucks, birds, all come to feast on the sweet nourishment of these trees. Even winter apples, frozen under trees in the circle where they fell, offer food during the long winter.

Harbingers, forerunners, heralds, signs of seasons' advance, crimson apples border a lane that ambles down to the sea. Above them, geese lift off the marsh, practicing a traveling formation that will take them south for the winter. Not yet, but soon, the Arrowed V will depart these skies.

In quiet forgotten orchards, red orbs bob in an atmosphere made of the union of earth, air, water, and that invisible wild substance that unwound the seed into this sacred gift. Let us not walk by blind and dumb, but see and offer gratitude as we take one and bite in.

These apples have hung in the wind and frost and rain till they have absorbed the qualities of the weather or season, and thus are highly seasoned, and they pierce and sting and permeate us with their spirit. They must be eaten in season, accordingly—that is, out-of-doors.

-Henry David Thoreau, Wild Apples

I see that you agree, Henry.

Until tomorrow,
Cynthia

P.S.
I was ecstatic when your second letter landed in my mailbox.
The gift portended that you were listening to me.
Oh! Wonders of wonders, could it be so?

September 4, 2015 - Dear Cynthia

Dear Cynthia

As I collect and cast my memory back to those days at Walden, what comes most clearly are the moments when all the "doings" of mankind drifted away like morning fog in the wind and I sat on my doorstep in precious undisturbed Presence to the light rising and falling with the passing hours. It was there, it was then that I heard the heart of Nature beating. Every hour I sat infused in my new lessons; my life was all I needed, my life uninterrupted by the measurement of time or accomplishment. I heard the forest grow around me.

I would take amusement in my chores. Emptying my room of its furniture, I let the desk, bed, and chairs compliment the pinecone strewn floor of the forest—pen, and paper ready on the desk for a woodchuck to take up and render his thoughts. The wood of the chairs and tables remembered themselves as trees then.

With the help of sun and wind, I would clean my floor with pond water and sand, wash the walls in the living air, making the room ready for my meditations. And, in the depths of the new quiet in the so cleaned room, I heard the bells of surrounding towns call, reminding me they still existed. I had forgotten that for the duration of this spell. This was where I lived best.

Value your life, give it room and silence to grow unobstructed by distraction. Walk in the woods, walk by the sea, listen for the sound of Creation. The tenets of existence are in the wind.

Henry David Thoreau,
with blessings.

September 5, 2015 - Sunflowers

Dear Henry,

Thanks so much for your note of yesterday. In this quest of mine it is helpful to hear back from you. I was with you in your day back there on Walden, felt the sun on your shoulders, heard the silence around you. When you began your chores, the joy of motion and purpose was in your words.

As the bells from surrounding towns pealed, reminding you they were still out there, it put me in mind of how it feels to be in the garden here in West K on a warm late summer day with no one around but the birds flitting to and from the little houses around the garden, the vegetables smiling up from where they are planted, and sunflowers, sunflowers that now reach fifteen or more feet into the blue sky.

A gardener can get lost in the garden, find themselves talking to the tomatoes and squash, railing at the pests that threaten their kingdom. Hours pass before they straighten up and recognize where they are. In those hours, hands thrust into the warm, brown earth and there is a harmonizing process, a learning that has no words. I always return to my day changed, peaceful, charged with new energy and clearer sight.

The sunflowers are standing perfect, strong, faces following the trail of sunlight like a savior. I thought, too, you might enjoy one of my poems.

Oh, didn't I tell you that I am a poet as well? I will wager that you knew that.

This poem was written for friends who were retiring from careers, stepping into unknown territory after a life of work, but it could also be for a person as they rise out of bed on any given day, the world of possibilities before them—or it could be for you, Henry. As I read more and more of your work, you light my way and reassure me of the nobility of the human heart and of courage.

Cynthia

A Moving Day

So, is this door closing or opening?
Is the glow in the windows of this room
dusk or dawn?
There is so much light in here with you,
light that has become you,
that you now light your own way and
the way for others.
As the familiar faces here ebb,
a wave of new ones turns toward you
to be discovered by you
as you turn toward them.
Curious who they will be to you,
the hearts of these people want to know you.
They long to hear the music of your voice.
If you don't go through this door,
they will be bereft
and never know why.

-Cynthia Fraser Graves

P.S.
There are still many things that distress one in the world of 2015. I could enumerate them, put them out for inspection and approval, but that would serve to dismay and discourage us all. What I know about co-creation on the Earth plane tells me to disregard the seeming blockade of things that are not as we would have them be. Each breath is imbued with creation and what we are thinking and feeling guides the form of what arises.

September 7, 2015 - I Will Go A-Graping

Henry, Dear,

Imagine my surprise yesterday, on a Sunday's excursion out of West K over to New Hampshire, to be walking an everyday dirt path between a barn and the riding ring at horse farm and seeing the royal purple flash from under large, protective leaves of a woody grapevine. There, stretched along a fence, was a universe of glowing fruit in perfect readiness for picking and, as I discovered, tasting.

Since beginning my dialogue with you, so much of what I see goes zinging back to what I know of your experience in life.

(Let me stop here and thank you. As a person who writes a bit, I know the loneliness of the empty page, the desire to fill it with what you see as you see it and to offer it as testimony. You are a superstar in that department.)

Today, when I saw the grapes, Concord grapes (so named in 1849 because they abounded in and around Concord, Massachusetts), I heard your words in the air around the lovely display.

They are a noble fruit to the eye. I pluck splendid great bunches of the purple ones with a rich bloom on them and the purple glowing through it like fire.

-Henry David Thoreau

And I could see you, the boat you built with your brother John, bow filled with sweet globes of fruit, the scent of it wafting over you paddling the Concord River, smiling in the nourishing exchange between you and your beloved nature.

From my stance on this earth of 2015, I feel a ripple of connection. I take a sweet grape and standing in the warm sun, I let its warmth dissolve in my mouth with all the sweetness and goodness intended for me, relishing this gift of perfection. I pluck this royal purple thread to weave it into the tapestry of my life today, letting the jewel toned color tint everything that comes after it. My day is enchanted by the hue and savor of the grape.

Because of the ever-increasing pace of communication as we leave the age of the written word behind and sprint into a crystalline exchange of thoughts embedded in the very air, these grapes take shape and I offer the experience at lightning speed, images of my discovery as gifts.

I would bet you hear me where you are.

Cynthia

September 9, 2015 - Kennebunk Blueberry Plains

Dear Henry,

The Kennebunk Plains, a barren grassy circle created by a glacier over 14,000 years ago, is composed of gravelly soil—an area very unlike the woodsy coastal Maine ecosystem around here. The region supports many rare species of plants and animals.

This stark landscape waits just a few miles up the road from West K. Driving west on Rt. 99, the trees diminish, and open space engulfs from both sides. The vista takes attention, displaying the often-dramatic cloud scapes of New England, letting the sunshine directly through rather than filtering past the leaf-cast we are more used to. Entering this space is an emotional experience and one is called to stop the car, leave it behind and come into this clarity physically and spiritually.

I now go through my daily chores and pleasures with my copy of Walden beside me. Today I happened onto a description in "The Village" which describes for us the joy you had in walking through the pitch dark back and forth to Concord:

It was very pleasant, when I stayed late in town, to launch myself into the night, especially if it was dark and tempestuous, and set sail from some bright village parlor or lecture room, with a bag of rye or Indian meal on my shoulder, for my snug harbor in the woods…

My thoughts drift this morning into the wonder of landscape and the courage it requires to enter it. Here you are, dark as pitch, winds, snow, rains falling and still you glory in the opportunity, take it passionately even, to enter the dance of matter in motion, though you cannot see what is ahead. Your write of finding your way home by the touch of certain trees and the feel of leaves under your feet. Oh, Henry, how amazingly brave you were!

When I see the Kennebunk Plains open in loveliness, I feel the invitation. I often drive by eyes on the next thing on my list, a thing I think is vital. Today, I will not drive by, I will stop and walk out to the land that is always calling. Time to wake up!

Every man must learn the points again as often as he awakes, whether from sleep or any abstraction. Not till we are lost, in other words not until we have lost the world, do we begin to find ourselves and realize where we are and the infinite extent of our relations.

-Henry David Thoreau, Walden

I wonder what I will discover.
Thank you for your courage, and your delight.

Cynthia

September 10, 2015 - Manifesting 101

Dear Henry,

In your short-lived years on Earth, you were a Way Shower, one who did not take the confines of what had come before as the pattern for what your life would be. There was a deep knowing within you that a truer, lighter, more natural, and loving path was available, not only to you, but to all men. The walking of that path was your gift to all of those in your time, and all who walk behind you. This living cost you much, but what it gave to you is the great charm of yours and millions of other lives. You discovered that the connection to the All is possible—and showed the wonder of what that connection can offer.

In our time, there are many Way Showers; we are fortunate. Going further ahead on the path you cut, we now know that we are the architects of our lives, that what we think becomes what IS. Wayne Dyer is a bright, constant light on this path, even more so now that he is passed on to your new world. His reading, writing, and seeing in Manifestation, the art of creating your life, is revolutionary.

In his youth, Wayne met the rigid, often thoughtless, and unproductive codes of conduct established in schools (meant to keep great numbers of people docile and malleable) with clarity and courage.

Dr. Dyer, just plain Wayne at that time, refused—for substantial reasons—to comply with a class requirement. I won't give the particulars here, suffice it to say, you would have been at his side waving flags in his defense; in fact, you were! During his penance (an in school suspension) someone placed or left a copy of your books, Walden and Civil Disobedience, on the bench where he was to sit for hours each day.

Henry, he read them both, all, there and then. You might know this; he became a devotee of yours and said he felt you at his side when he had to plead his case to the principal. He talked with you, as I do, and heard your voice in reply giving guidance and caring support—in his life going on.

Plain Wayne, now Dr. Dyer, went to Concord, the resting place of your memorabilia and talked the guard into allowing him to sit at your desk, to recline on your bed. Your words inspired and changed his entire life, validated the knowing you and he shared, that the current of your life is a dance with yourself and Source, and is in your hands.

Wow!

A single gentle rain makes the grass many shades greener. So, our prospects brighten on the influx of better thoughts. We should be blessed if we lived in the present always and took advantage of every accident that befell us.

-Henry David Thoreau, Walden

Cynthia

September 12, 2015 - Dear Cynthia

Dear One,

"Many an object is not seen, though it falls within the range of our visual ray, because it does not come within the range of our intellectual ray, i.e., we are not looking for it. So, in the largest sense, we find only the world we look for."

-Myself, Journal, 2 July 1857

I begin with a statement from my musings when I walked the paths of the Earth School. I, too, was subject to all the conflicts and considerations that any human is; emotions roiled within me, pushing me thither and yon in search of balance. The great quest for happiness consumed me as well as my brethren, but there was a difference in my seeing, a difference that was lived in my good fortune to meet Ralph Emerson and become part the group that honestly and bravely believed that all mankind has knowledge within themselves, knowledge that transcends what is seen by the naked eye or felt by the senses. One can trust themselves as the authority of their lives rather than be ruled by the fear and distraction of society.

This knowing is available through intuition and imagination more than through the great god of logic. The divine awaits your notice in the silence within. From there, you invest your every moment on earth with the bliss I found walking my verdant paths.

Wayne Dyer was/is indeed a friend of mine. We are all here in the swirling presence of love and support, constantly at your side. Let those who sneer do so at the risk of missing the portal open to them as well, the portal to joy.

I see you there, at your work, dawn into morning, struggling to con sentences in which to lodge the discovery of this miracle. Bravo! Work on but take time while you are in it to revel in the wonder you feel and see and that sees you as you step further into my woods.

I am ahead. Be brave!

Henry

Henry, the scene from my windows has utterly changed. Yes, I'm still on Earth, but New England has disappeared and I am in Dublin, Ireland. I told you about this trip I had been invited on… Well, here I am!

Driving into Dublin from the air terminal, a green of every hue rose to color the air.

September 17, 2015 - Let Us Rise

Dear Henry,

The great appear great because we are on our knees…Let us rise.

-Jim Larkin

Jim Larkin was a man who contributed indirectly to the Easter Rising of 1916 by highlighting the lack of social justice and the plight of workers in the current system. He also made a direct contribution by establishing the Irish Citizen Army, becoming a soldier in that fight.

I am in a coffee shop on O'Connell Street in the fine old city of Dublin, Ireland. An avenue of people passes by, all ages, all races. The blue eyes and red hair of the Irish people are to be seen in profusion, but the cosmopolitan nature of this city presents every possibility of people. Somewhere on the street someone is playing a bagpipe, the reedy notes sweeping up into a strong breeze. The air is fresh, temperatures cool, sun shining through a gauzy cloud deck lending everything the silvery island sheen. In other words, just wonderful!

Despite the celebratory face of this city, it is not the Dublin I thought I would find. In tours of the town, I have stood within shrines where the great fight for Irish independence was won, though the cost was—as it always is in the battle for Freedom—heavy in loss of life.

Most impressive of these sites is the Kilmainham Gaol, the scene of the execution of the leaders of the 1916 Easter Rising; the place where thousands of men, women and children were held captive—some for stealing food for their families in the face of sure death by starvation and exposure to Ireland's damp cold. The Gaol is a museum today, a museum dedicated to the suffering endured here. The execution of the men of the Easter Uprising—men who dared think of Freedom for Ireland from British subjugation—planted the Seeds of Independence. When they were executed cruelly, the people of Dublin awoke and dared the fight to finally win in 1922 with the signing of the Anglo-Irish Treaty.

William Butler Yeats, a Dubliner and a pillar of 20th Century poetry, encouraged this fight for Independence. Stirred by the righteousness in the martyrdom of these men he wrote:

Easter, 1916

I write it out in a verse–
MacDonagh and MacBride
And Connolly and Pearse
Now and in time to be,
Wherever green is worn,
Are changed, changed utterly:
A terrible beauty is born.

-WB Yeats

Being here, walking the cobblestone streets of Old Temple Bar, the story of this long battle is still sung by folk artists echoing from the pubs nightly, the pathos of their history alive in their words. O'Connell Street, the grand thoroughfare in the heart of Dublin, hosts the statues of the heroes in this struggle. Freedom is in the national character here.

I know, Henry. We have not talked of this before. The preferred setting for you (and me) would be the woodsy path, bird calls leading us on, the fragrance of pine and cedar on the breeze. We would go in our own directions, stepping in time to the drummer of our discoveries. Our fight for Freedom was fought by those who came well before us. We sing of their bravery and commitment in our ballads as well.

You walked us all forward on the trail of Freedom, Henry, so I must not fail to comment on the bravery, dedication to, and love for freedom in these Irish folk. It has grown with the years between them and the sacrifices of their liberators. It is in the air here.

Until tomorrow,
Cynthia

September 18, 2015 - A Bee-Loud Glade

Dear Henry,

It is afternoon here in Dublin town. I visited the W.B. Yeats Exhibition currently on display at the National Library of Ireland. After a cappuccino and scone, both superb, I went to the many-faceted montage.

The exhibition was housed on the bottom floor of the historic old building. As we entered the quiet space, the Poet himself was speaking his words, reciting his many poems. Yeats is one of the foremost figures of 20th century literature, a great name in Irish literature winning the Nobel Prize in Literature in 1923, the first Irishman to do so.

But Henry, in coming upon the poem below, The Lake Isle of Innisfree, I drew a breath of wonder and heard, within the poem, your words Henry. I was walking into Walden Woods with you, listening to you breathe.

The Lake Isle of Innisfree

I will arise and go now, and go to Innisfree,
And a small cabin build there, of clay and wattles made:
Nine bean-rows will I have there, a hive for the honey-bee;
And live alone in the bee-loud glade.
And I shall have some peace there, for peace comes dropping

slow,
Dropping from the veils of the morning to where the cricket
sings.
There midnight's all a glimmer, and noon a purple glow,
And evening full of the linnet's wings.
I will arise and go now, for always night and day
I hear lake water lapping with low sounds by the shore;
While I stand on the roadway, or on the pavements grey,
I hear it in the deep heart's core.

-W.B. Yeats

Can it be that as you were dying in Concord, Massachusetts, a poet was born in Ireland to take from you the torch of your philosophy to brandish it forward into the next generations?

In a letter written to John O'Leary, Yeats declares: *"The mystical life is the center of all that I do & all that I think & all that I write."* His belief in the existence of the spiritual component of all life echoes your emphasis of the discovery of the sacred in the commonplace.

He has you, Henry, even down to the green beans.

I must cut this letter short as we travel up to Galway and the Cliffs of Moher early in the morning and I must sleep.

I just had to tell you that you are here in Ireland, in the words of an Irish Poet of great love and respect, like yourself.

Till Tomorrow,
Cynthia

September 21, 2015 - The Cliffs Of Moher

Dear Henry,

After a long bus trip on tour from Dublin to Galway, we boarded the vehicle again driving an impossibly switching road up, up, and then, again up. At times, it seemed the driver turned the bus in thin air. Finally, the door opened onto a landscape so awesome and unique in aspect it took your breath away. The scope of the Cliffs of Moher rivals the Grand Canyon of America in majesty. Way, way below, on the five mile stretch of time sculptured rock, waves of a familiar Atlantic crash and spray, pushing into rock caves that are so large and so dramatic they provide the backdrops of disaster and challenge for current films such as Harry Potter and the Half Blood Prince and The Princess Bride. I can't help but think you know of what I write since there is no time where you are.

I apologize for always talking of developments that were not seen by your generation, or the next, but that were right around the corner in the flow of time. The world of film would amaze you. A person steps right into the lives of others sitting in a darkened room. The question here is, as always, what is the purpose of the experience? When the lights go back up, what is the effect on the soul? Can one take up the reins of their own life again with more hope and courage, or has the film darkened one's outlook?

Today, I want to offer you the experience of being on the edge of those monumental rock formations, to let their grandness fill your senses. Wildflowers tremble in the wind that is always blowing on their edge. This very year alone, 13 people have met their death at the Cliffs of Moher either by accident or on purpose. Our bus driver, a very knowledgeable fellow called Anthony, told us this and warned us off parts of the path that were unguarded.

In the ancient Gaelic language, the word Mothar means "ruined fort"; a fort in 1st century BC stood where Moher tower now stands. Although there is no trace remaining of this two-thousand-year-old fort, it lingers in the name of these cliffs visited annually by almost one million people.

Tina Mulrooney, the Cliffs of Moher musician, was playing her harp there on the edge for us. While she took a break to talk with some visitors, her harp was left on a rock wall nearby. I stood near and heard wind playing an original song in the strings.

Loveliness lives in all landscapes. Sometimes it is devastation and ruin... But the land is forgiving. The landscape of Ireland is the ultimate experience of this loveliness.

Cynthia

September 23, 2015 - The Neighborhood

Dear Henry,

The fog is as thick as cream this morning; a large mountain in the backyard has vanished, and the wee, ragged road passing by runs off into a pool of silver mist. Aye, it is a wild place this Dungloe, Ireland. Not like your accommodating village of Concord, this place splays out on miles of rock-strewn moors, decorated with heather, blackberries, fuchsia full-grown into wild bushes, ambrosia (an orange yellow lily-like flower), and low-slung junipers, whittled to the earth by wind.

Wind is a crop here. As I write, it howls down the chimney, sings around the corners of the cottage, pulls open all the doors. Never has there been a more apt place for a Wind Farm, but change comes very slow here, and is generally not welcomed. Folks like this place just the way it is.

Yesterday was a bright day; the sun fired all beneath, warming us up. We walked the one road inching off whenever we saw or heard a car. Though it may sound impossible, the roads in most of the area are not wide enough for two cars to pass each other. The drivers each perform a dance maneuver and the pedestrian must run out of the way.

We didn't notice, as we walked, that we were going downhill sharply; when we turned to go home, the climb was a gym workout doubled. The blackberries we found bobbing and weaving by the thousands in the sunny air, dark jewels washed by the intermittent rain that is a constant of Irish weather, kept us distracted. The bright taste of the fruit broke over our taste buds, fueling a very good walk indeed.

I can't account for how much I love blackberries; the symbol of abundance spoken in the language of earth, better than jewels and for free. We picked and ate as we walked, smiling at such luxury. At home, a little plastic container of berries picked who-knows-how-long-ago are very pricey.

I want to tell you about the peat bog that stretches for miles at the bottom of our road. I will have to save that for another time. I mustn't let these letters get too long. I'm not sure of the postage between us. Suffice it to say that a peat fire glows on the grates of our hearth just now, wind singing all around. I find so much in this new landscape, and not just about any one place, discovery at its finest.

When this batch of weather clears, I believe we will go a 'gathering again.

Cynthia,
With affection

September 24, 2015 - Berries And Light

Dear Henry,

This morning dawned amethyst-hued, streaked with promise of a sunrise on one side of the cottage while a driving rain from gray lumbering clouds doused the other. Even in this little time I spend collecting my thoughts, pouring my coffee, and starting my computer, the sun has risen over our craggy hills and light spills into the wild landscape on powerful winds. This is a land of great contrast. Not at all like the constancy of New England, where pastoral fields dotted with villages, houses clustered around the white spires of churches, was the predominant view. Here, a few cottages huddle around each other, small, low structures, usually made of stone, looking much like sheep.

Henry, as you walked the forests and fields, you discovered natural environments, but you found nothing like the stark glorious diversity of northwest Ireland, the Donegal land. Here, little pockets of cleared land rise among the multitude of rocks bearing cows, sheep, horses, chickens, all looking like the day

God created them, healthy, content, and in the free air. They chomp on lush grass the color of emeralds, placidly eyeing their observer, calm greeting in their gaze.

These creatures provide basic ingredients of the diet; meat—most assuredly—and eggs, the thickest cream I have ever poured, milk, butter, as well as wool for the famous knitters of Ireland to fashion into sweaters against winter's cold. It is all organic here, food and fabric and people. Everything is poured through with pure air off the Atlantic and clean water that runs in freshets down from the mountains. Somehow, Ireland's grass grows untreated, as it has done for centuries in the clearest of sunlight.

Wheaten bread nourishes with grains grown in the area; heavy, dark, slightly sweet... Heaven when slathered with the rich gold of Irish butter, gluten free be damned! (Sorry about that!)

More about those crown jewels: berries. In late September, blackberries rule the land, peeking from roadsides everywhere here in Donegal. We went berrying yesterday and picked a quart or more in 20 minutes. Very encouraging indeed. Not like the little Maine blueberries we are used to spending a day to collect. The taste of these black gems is deep, dusky, sweet to tart delight. Despite the seeds, a bowl of them with clotted cream will be remembered for a long time.

I will close for today. We are having internet problems so this letter will post a bit later than usual. We must get into the car and drive into town for an internet connection.

Until tomorrow,
Cynthia

September 25, 2015 - Berries Redux

Dear Henry,

We are way out here! Even as I say that I pause to wonder what I mean. Really, we are way IN here, way into landscape that wows you every half hour with a display that stops you and pulls you to a window to watch. Yesterday alone, we saw three rainbows arc over the valley below us, one of them a double. We are into a quiet so deep it has weight; you feel it drop around you like some sort of new vision, allowing you to see how things are connected and interconnecting you with all you are seeing.

Today, out of my windows here in Dungloe, a full-circle vista is painted silvery gray with strong, bright rays from a hidden sun piercing the clouds, moving like spotlights over the land saying, *"Look here, now, here. See the glory within all these simple things?"*

Yesterday, we took an up close and personal tour of the rugged Atlantic coast on roads that don't appear on maps, roads that are memory lanes existing in some sort of spectral landscape that is not shared with those from away.

Our tour guide, Ulric, a man of great generosity, showed us the perspective of goats cresting a mountain top, then up again to a higher peak. I was holding on for dear life as the Land Cruiser we rode (few other cars could manage this terrain) pitched and waddled on roads that were really paths. Again, the only word that fits my experience is awe. Everything was inspiring in its beauty. People built houses on the edge of this coast—snug cottages, a few clustered together into a tiny village—with views that would cost millions if we were to levy a price, but are, in fact, priceless. The people living here accept hard travel each day for space to breathe and nature their neighbor.

In your era, living by the sea was for the poor. These days, it has become the neighborhood of the rich. Here in Dungloe, it is for anyone who will take the trouble to pursue it.

Cynthia

September 26, 2015 - The Neighborly Rocks

Dear Henry,

Land in Ireland—in general, and in this area—is almost treeless. On our five-hour bus ride from Dublin to Donegal, the view disclosed neat, bright green plots of uniform size land enclosed by walls of either low bushes or rocks. By the hundreds, these green squares stretched on and on, abutting each other neatly.

As the counties ticked by and we approached the northwest coast, the lushness diminished steadily and we entered a new landscape, one of rocky hills that rose into mountains abruptly, leaving little room for the neat patchwork quilt effect of central Ireland.

They grow rocks here—rocks that were gifts from the glaciers, left as calling cards as the ice melted. Looking out from my window this morning, the dear rocks send their ancient energy to me, visible in every nook and cranny and yet, in little pockets of green between the crags, cows and sheep prosper. These animals look out at you with such an innocent, curious attention to stop their cutting and chomping just long enough to fix their gaze on the passerby. Rarely do they bleat or moo; they just stare.

A few days ago, one very large cow escaped its pasture and was in the road as we tried to pass. The driver of our vehicle nonchalantly got out of the car to open a gate down the road a little, the gorgeous animal eying him suspiciously, but, as soon as the gate was opened, he trotted into the opening with a lovely, fluid energy, looking back at the man standing by the gate with thanks. This was a conversation of some sort going on, one that took years to understand.

Sheep live here in great numbers as well. They, too, want to know what you are about as you pass by their postage-stamp sized pastures. They can be found out on impossibly inaccessible areas, standing on rock outcroppings as we pass, giving the same attention we felt from the cows.

The products from these locals are very important to those whose home this is: wool for the wonderful sweaters here, rich cream and milk which becomes delicious cheeses of hundreds of varieties, dung—very important to any agriculture—and, of course, meat.

I know, Henry, from my reading of your later works, that you went off meat and advised all to think carefully about doing the same to put an end to causing the suffering of animals for our needs. This is a country that has known starvation and famine. Vegetarianism gets nothing but a laugh on the streets here. All will be in good time, Henry. You were so far ahead of us in so many compassionate ways.

Thanks, and love from Ireland.

Cynthia

September 28, 2015 - Landscape

Dear Henry,

The wind riffles through the ubiquitous gorse—green now and past its bloom— singing in the rocks, sweeping down from abrupt mountains, pushing clouds along quickly and buffeting at windows, playing games of hide and seek with me. This landscape is a changeling. Time is all different here, longer, deeper. There are few distractions from the present moment. Everything I see feels like a part of me.

I am so far from home. A Cancerian, I love home. The shape of home is etched on my heart, not so much as a Place but as a Feeling. There, I can walk out of my door and years of experience walks with me. In Maine, as was the case with your Concord, the past and future are bound up with the present, burdening its buoyancy some with the weight of memory, but allowing all to see the path they have walked and to have some idea what is ahead (although we never really know).

Here, on this lake strewn land of peat bogs and rocky meadows, I am in new country, without any path to follow, without references. Only large-scale guidance (GPS) works. No more am I Cynthia, a woman of some age from Maine, mother, teacher, friend, sister, partner; here, I am only woman, human, and then, spirit. The one path to follow is intuition and experience.

What will I learn here? As the days tick by, I hope to learn to allow what comes to me to happen without encumbering the experience with the past or future, just let it be what it is Now. Let it be enough.

You traveled from Concord, but always returned to the warmth of your welcoming family, bringing your experiences with you to ponder and pen into lovely words that brought the whole world along on your internal and actual journey. It was always what you learned—taken within and transformed into new perspectives—new paeans that reordered all you were. I wonder if you had any idea of the magnitude of what you were about. Did you know of the great wave of freedom you were about to set in motion as you set up housekeeping on Walden Pond? I bet not.

So, today, I will take courage on these unknown paths I tread. I will be an agent of kindness and curiosity as I walk the moors and streets. Yesterday, my friend and I went to Mass at the local Catholic Church in Dungloe. During the Peace greeting, people looked at us with curiosity and fear as we were unfamiliar. I felt the connection as we smiled back into those Irish-blue eyes with clarity and love, just what such a moment calls for. It was a good feeling. It was enough.

Until tomorrow,
Cynthia

September 29, 2015 - Puritan Time / Irish Time

Dear Henry,

This morning's face is sunny, light still diffused through the banks of Irish mist off the sea, not a clear sun, radiant but gauzy. The air is mild, very mild. Today is supposed to be the warmest of the week, temperatures rising to 17 or 18 C, that would be almost 70 on our scale. No wind, really, no wind! The neighbors keep telling us that we don't know how lucky we are to have this weather instead of what would be more probable: rain, lashing winds, and cold. Well, I think we are lucky as well.

A week or so ago, a friend brought us to Huidy Baegs Bar just past Croithlí or Croichshlí (anglicized as Crolly), which has one convenience shop slash restaurant and one petrol station and one public house, Páidí Óg's. As you might guess, finding your way around here on these wee tiny roads with names in Gaelic, and at night to boot, is no little challenge. The reason for the trip was a spontaneous gathering of musical talent in this area at what is named the Monday Music. Last night, determined to record some of it, we went again, with my equipment this time.

Now, there is a bit to say about how folks go about living here. It is not on Puritan time, Henry. As you know, in New England, we are born into many beliefs, one being that a day starts early, 6 a.m., and that time is to be used for providing the necessities to life. Long ago, this was borne out by the fact that all food, clothing, and shelter were produced in the region where they were needed. This great endeavor took all day and more, to end for this day only when the sun went down with sleep fast on its heels. Over here, that just isn't so.

To be present for the spontaneous band, or any music in the numerous pubs in Ireland, one goes out at half-ten, buys a pint of holy water—Guiness—and waits for the doors to open as the participants stroll in one by one, settle in seats, and begin in initial improvisational sounds, rising in harmony, decibels, and cooperation until, around midnight somewhere, THE music is fully present. The band plays until the wee hours, keeping well-watered, achieving magic along the way but only for those who can hang in there. The music is the thing; these are the doorways for the notes to enter the room.

Last night we had a bagpipe, two guitarists, an accordion player, a flute, two drums, and a keyboard. I'm afraid my Puritan time had me leaving at midnight, so I didn't see the after-hours magic. We still had to drive 16 k back to our cottage, so we were careful.

There is music for everyone here in Ireland —for the cost of a pint if you can stay awake. Toes will tap as folk sitting around bask in the lilting, ancient sounds that have been played here for centuries. It's another way to speak Irish.

Cynthia

September 30, 2015 - Sunset

Dear Henry,

I ran out to catch the indescribable sunset over the mountain a few days ago, aimed carefully, clicked, and was disappointed when I looked at the results.

The yellows that overlay the pink were really a glowing apricot in color, the whole canvas of sky simply vibrating with color and texture. This picture was a dumbed-down version of what we can see each morning and evening as the sun lifts from or sinks behind mountains that cup this valley in protective—but sometimes causative—hugs. These same mountains in winter months provide a funnel for winds off the sea exceeding 90 mph, the power of which create waterspouts in the lakes dotting the valley floor. The folks here abouts have seen these monster spouts with their own eyes. When they talk of them, it is with the same dread we speak of hurricanes or tornadoes in our country.

Last evening, we were invited for dinner to the home of an exceedingly kind man, King Of The Mountain, as his house is built on the highest ground around here and has a view that cannot be put into words. At night, the lights of his lovely house shine like reassurance that all is well. His friendly horse, Jebel, gallops up over the edge of land, giving anyone watching the thrill of seeing his flying mane and his exuberance.

There were others from the valley invited to this tasty feast, and we sat over our dessert coffee, the conversation went here and there, meandering, but, when it turned to politics and America on the world stage, the bitterness that our history has spawned among these people became clear. The words that best describe the way this gathering saw America's actions in the last ten years would be expressed as 'blind belligerence'. The pairing of America's weaponry and the dubious leadership of this past decade has made for serious damage to the world and its people on many levels, as well as deep distrust of the motives of all Americans, but it does not originate wholly within America; this misunderstanding of each other is primal as well, and universal. I felt the sting of this view as I sat in their midst.

They spoke and waited for a response. I know what you thought of that; each person's responsibility for the actions of the whole was your mantra. I wish you had been there Henry, to speak, fueled with your passion and illumination of the nature of Freedom, to change the focus of that discussion from an onus on the sins of government to the integrity of the individual. I know that my part of this lies in my respect and compassion for each person in my path each day, no matter what the rules are. It comes down to that for all of us.

Cynthia

P.S.
And on that somber note, I will close out the month of September 2015. The host of our dinner was evidently following YearWithHenry, our blog. Reading of my discomfort with the dinner conversation described above, it didn't take him but a day to be at our door with a gift and an apology. So much appreciated.

Fall 2015 - October

October

O hushed October morning mild,
Thy leaves have ripened to the fall;
Tomorrow's wind, if it be wild,
Should waste them all.
The crows above the forest call;
Tomorrow they may form and go.
O hushed October morning mild,
Begin the hours of this day slow.
Make the day seem to us less brief.
Hearts not averse to being beguiled,

Beguile us in the way you know.
Release one leaf at break of day;
At noon release another leaf;
One from our trees, one far away.
Retard the sun with gentle mist;
Enchant the land with amethyst.
Slow, slow!
For the grapes' sake, if they were all,
Whose leaves already are burnt with frost,
Whose clustered fruit must else be lost—
For the grapes' sake along the wall.

-Robert Frost

Henry, there is no better way to step into the month of October than the poem of the same name by Robert Frost. The sweetness of the sun as it approaches its trail to winter skies, the soft dying grasses rasp, flowers, leaves... Each willingly letting go of the perfection so apparent in summer. Even though I am in Ireland, the same rusty ennui is overtaking the fields and meadows.

October 4, 2015 - The Famine Walls Of Maghery

Good morning, Henry,

After three mornings of dull weather with no wind, this morning dawned clear and bright. The sun lifted into waiting skies, no clouds. Weather is always the topic for conversation and, here, its ever-changing nature keeps the talk fresh. As I look out on the valley from my computer, the air simmers with the characteristic silvery tinted illumination so unique to Ireland.

Days ago, my friend and I made a journey to search out the Famine Walls of Maghery. We are slowly getting comfortable (that might be too strong a word) with tilting along on the small, curving roads, ever ready to engage the brakes as cars approach us; talk about the eye of the needle. And all this needs doing while driving on the opposite side of the dashboard.

On this day, we drove from Minnah Crosse to the Maghery Coast, approximately ten miles. The air, pure crystal, seemed electrified. Everyone was somewhere else and the roads were empty. Following a map, our attention was often diverted from our search by the stunning beaches and surf as we rode along.

Famine Walls appear in many places in Ireland, but especially here in the northwest, County Donegal, the most northern of the counties. During the 1600s, the British confiscated land that was farmed and owned by the Irish for hundreds of years. Families became dependent on landlords who forced them to pay rent they did not have, often evicting them in the dead of winter.

The Famine Walls began to be built in 1845, during the infamous Potato Famine, and were built by starving, impoverished, despairing men, women, and children. The laborers were paid in small amounts of food, a desperate scheme operated by local churches and landlords. The Irish are a proud people and would not take charity without work so they built these stunning walls. While this was the main reason for the Famine walls, it was not the only reason. The walls also served the practical purpose of clearing local soil of stones so land could be farmed. Today, fields are strewn with boulders and stones of all sizes. Farming has never been possible on a large scale here.

The sight of the Walls stops you in your tracks. Eight to ten feet in height and three feet wide, this triangular base stabilizes them. No cement or fixatives were used when first erected; the Walls stretch for miles over this region. Here, in Maghery, they are three hundred yards in length. Some reconstruction has been done in the present to help them stand the over a hundred mile an hour winds that often blow off the Atlantic. They have been standing for almost two hundred years.

As you walk their distance, you notice holes built into the structure at intervals. These holes have attained historical and cultural importance as they were designed for one purpose… Fingers. Fingers were to be inserted ceremonially in and through reaching to someone on the other side: tribesmen, chieftains, families of a betrothed… Both parties were to slip fingers through and touch one another in sacred, meaningful manners. Pacts, weddings, agreements, and contracts, all were made legal and binding in this way.

No one was about but us on this walk. We stood in quiet regarding the walls, imagining their era when they rose into the sky, constructed by hungry, oppressed people who somehow found the strength to do what was needed to survive. It was humbling and inspiring all at once. These walls are a reminder of the history of this long suffering, brilliant country.

They put me in mind of the stone walls of New England, Henry. There is a story there as well. The early settlers possessed the endurance and resolve to create a homeland in the wilderness, clearing fields for crops and animals. Concord is stitched with these stone walls, each a memorial to where we come from and on whose shoulders we stand.

Until tomorrow,
Cynthia
And more of Ireland

October 5, 2015 - A Peat Fire On The Hearth

Dear Henry,

Traveling on the bus a few weeks ago from Dublin, the landscape appeared to turn from the patchwork pastures in all shades of green to an expansive ocher shaded land that put one in mind of Scottish moors. Craggy, rock strewn fields awash with purple heather and yellow gorse, hovered in the shadow of stupendous mountains lifting off earth sharply. The land in northwest Ireland bears little resemblance to its green neighbors in the south.

Living here for these last weeks, I am discovering what lies beneath one's first cursory view: peat. Peat, also known as turf log, is an accumulation of partially decayed vegetation or organic matter uniquely found in either blanket or raised bogs. The cutting and drying of peat is a serious industry here as peat is burned for heat in colder months and all season when the rainy cold sets in.

Once burning, it's a fine fuel with an earthy odor that is not unpleasant. On a cold day, any town you visit will have scents of peat smoke in the air. In this area, along with a bit of coal, peat keeps folks warm as it has done for centuries. Once free for the digging, it now costs about half as much as wood. At present, Ireland pays a penalty in the vicinity of 30,000,000 euros yearly for its use of peat because of the pollution caused by burning the fuel. (I learned this from the neighbors.) Conservationists are also alarmed by the rapid disappearance of these wetland habitats. According to the BBC, almost 40 percent of Ireland's bogs were destroyed between 1995 and 2012. Peat takes a long time to form, and once the bogs are damaged, it can take up to 100 years to regrow.

Facts fade when sitting before a blazing peat fire. Letting the warmth wash over me, I imagine folks in cold, damp, stone cottages, this heat all they had between themselves and the elements. No indoor heating systems here.

It has begun raining, Henry. Time to set a fire and gather. When you were in your cottage on Walden Pond, you gathered fuel from your earthy yard and sat dreaming while the winter winds blew and snow pelted the small roof you were under. The fire is the thing, here and there; then and now. I'll put the kettle on for some tea.

There is so much interesting about this place.

Cynthia

October 6, 2015 - A Fresh Perspective Every Hour

Dear Henry,

I had this advantage at least, in my mode of life, over those who were obliged to look abroad for amusement, to society and the theatre, that my life itself was become my amusement and never ceased to be novel. It was a drama of many scenes and without an end… Follow your genius, and it will not fail to show you a fresh perspective every hour.

-Henry David Thoreau, Walden

Thank you for the words above. They ring true this morning. From my windows looking to the east and south, the sun rises tinting mountains of gray clouds with mauve and pink, then rolling them past. Now the sun breaks through. All this in ten minutes. Entertainment indeed!

The value of daily experience rests with the observer. Who is the person watching? Is it the little "I" of my particular gender, ethnicity, etc., the one who will take for granted the great gifts that are offered only to return to the small world of ego and its problems, or is it an eternal being who recognizes the dance of love played out before them, the elements of earth as dancers? Everyone must choose.

Things happen fast. Landscapes and people-scapes change in a matter of moments. It helps to have a secure, loving home within oneself as a refuge during the challenges of living on earth. You advise us, Henry, to *"follow our genius, and it will not fail to show you a fresh perspective every hour."* I think the word "fresh" is key. Once we uncouple ourselves from the idea that we are students learning in the Earth school, each lesson created just for us and our needs in this moment— we can relax into trust and appreciation for the gift of our lives and become the "genius" observer of our own uniqueness. Things, people, events, all become fresh.

All this from watching the sunrise up on Minnah Crosse in Dungloe, Ireland. You saw this in your woods at Walden Pond and spoke it to me today, generations later.

Thank you, Henry. My words are not able to convey my gratitude.

Cynthia

October 7, 2015 - An Irish Wake

Dear Henry,

I am up early this morning here in Minnah Croise and have stepped outside for a breath of air. Directly above me a fragment moon looks toward bright Venus as it pales in the rosy glow at the edge of the mountains. The air is as pure as it comes, the Atlantic within sight below. It will be a stunning sunrise; there are just enough clouds to catch tints of the morning.

Henry, I seldom know what I am to write about from day to day. I have a queue of ideas, but what I settle on usually comes as a surprise to me. Yesterday, I literally collided with this day's subject.

As we drove away from our cottage headed for Donegal Town, we came to the crossroads about a half mile down and were stopped by a queue of cars parked the length of the road, both directions and spilling up the hill. People moved briskly toward the small Catholic church here at Minnah Croise. The skies had taken on a gray which suited the black coats of many walking to the church. Backed up to the church doors, a hearse waited for pall bearers to take their place and escort the casket into the funeral mass.

The impassable road had been shrunk down to a walking path by the number of cars parked. We managed to squeak by, feeling strong reverence lifting from the crowd. There were over one hundred people walking silently to the church, some holding hands, some in tears, all respectful.

An hour or so later, I was in conversation with a wonderfully helpful agent at the tourist center in Dungloe when I mentioned the funeral we had seen and asked about Irish ceremonies regarding death. She shared with me the story of her Father's wake, a ceremony that is much honored in Ireland. The Irish Wake is really for the whole village, for everyone who knew the deceased, or the deceased's family. And in these villages, everyone knows everyone. It is an event meant to include all.

This woman's father died in hospital and was taken to the morgue for restorative work as he would be exposed for the next three days—an echo of the time Christ was in the tomb. When the man was ready to be taken home, a mile-long queue of cars accompanied the hearse with his daughter's car in the lead. Before that, an army of neighbors and friends came into the house to give it a "Spring cleaning" (she was very strong on my knowing that the house was spotless), to prepare food, to move furniture for the coming solemnities, and to await the arrival of the departed. Traditionally, candles are placed above the decedent's head and boots are placed at his or her feet to make the journey through purgatory easier. Out of respect, clocks are stopped, blankets placed over mirrors. (She didn't disclose this, but it is tradition.)

The father was taken into the living room where he was to be waked three days and two nights. These times are fixed, the third day being the funeral and committal. The term "wake" was used since family members stay with the body at night, making sure its spirit didn't come back to life and evil spirits do not claim it. Though the idea of evil spirits has lost credibility, the wake goes on. During these days, the house is open from nine in the morning until eleven at night, all are welcome, no matter if they knew the deceased personally or not. In a small village, everyone is connected and everyone feels each other's life events deeply.

Food and conversation flow all day, people coming and going all the while. The women of the village simply take over the kitchen, making and serving food, doing dishes, keeping order so those visiting may sit with the departed. It is a ceremony full of emotion, sadness and joy mixing together in the way it does in life. Joy for a life well lived and sadness for those who must go on without this person's presence. If the loss is untimely, as in the case of a young person, or tragic circumstances, the wake takes on that aspect with keening (an audible display of sorrow) and weeping. There is strong drink available as well as tea and coffee. (Prior to the mid 1900's these events turned into large celebrations partly because men were not otherwise allowed to congregate, for fear of planning rebellion against the British government.) The deeper the connection with the departed, the longer one stays, even sitting with the body as the night hours tick by so that the person will not be alone. When we talked of the sweet presence of her Father in her home for those three days, tears slid down her cheeks. I felt the gratitude she had for this time with him before his image disappeared from earth.

As the third day dawns, another army of friends and relatives arrives ready all for the funeral mass at the local church. This mass is attended by the whole village, as with the committal following; friends bear the casket into the church, and out again and to the graveyard.

Most villages have a social center which is open for a luncheon when all is completed. By the time it is finished and the family of the departed reaches their home, the house is as it was before the wake, cleaned, back to order, symbolizing life resuming for those that live, the memory of the deceased being all that is left.

American funerals could take a lesson, and they are doing so. The need to focus on the departed soul and what they brought to us is being addressed by families taking over the perfunctory funerals of the past. I am curious about the funeral tradition in your time, Henry.

Until tomorrow,
Cynthia

October 8, 2015 - A Morning Walk In Pamplona

Dear Henry,

The sky is all yellow glow, hills turning smudgy blue as the sun rises. When I first step out to survey, the quarter moon has slung itself on the bow of Venus along with another star I can't identify, ready to be shot, straight and fast, into the zenith. The sun nears the edge of the mountains, and fields around take on detail, rocks emerge, gorse, fences rise that were sunken under the dark of night.

Yesterday we went for a walk on the road in front of the house enjoying the mild, fresh air and nibbling blackberries as we walked. The great handicap with blackberries is that your fingers stain purple with the sweet juice until you can't touch anything. We passed a pasture on our left and stopped to admire a herd of bulls, very large, very healthy, contained in a small lot. They stopped chomping on Irish green to regard us as we regarded them. Beautiful animals, a few pure black, some shades of white and gray as well. After a decent minute or two, we turned back to our walk up the hill ahead of us, leaving the bulls behind.

So employed were we on this wee road that we were surprised when we heard a bellow, then louder bellows behind us. We turned to see that the bulls we thought we had left behind were out into the road and now ambling in our direction, the biggest bull, the black one, in the lead.

Suddenly, that wee road seemed very small indeed, flanked as it was on both sides by high, extremely prickly gorse bushes allowing no way off. Luckily, the bellowing herd was as interested in the blackberries as were we, and paused to enjoy them. Their keeper, unaware of us (maybe) was intent on moving them down this very road to a different pasture.

Everything I ever heard about bulls being dangerous came zinging into my mind; don't run, don't wave anything colorful, find an escape route, stay calm! At that moment, the road might have been the alley in Pamplona and those bulls as threatening as a stampede. We took on a mighty pace up and down the hills just ahead of the bellowing travelers behind. Just when I thought I had outwalked them, they would come over a rise trotting as fast as I was. I knew that they were being herded, but that didn't make any difference when I looked into the eyes of the leader of the pack.

In the end, all was well. They got to their new pasture and—though they loved the freedom of the road—were coaxed to go behind the gate after a bellow or two. The grass was much greener there really.

The upshot of this, Henry, is discovering fear. I was surprised at how fearful I was; fear that came from old ideas. Not that I'm going to go pat that bull, but now I can take another look at myself. Though there are no bulls in my Maine neighborhood, there is always fear and its effects, fear that I recognize as unnecessary.

An interesting observation from Minnah Croise, Dungloe, Ireland.
Only a few days left before we return to New England,
The sun is up and blazing away.

Gratitude, Henry.
Cynthia

October 9, 2015 - A Fly On The Empire State Building, NYC

Dear Henry,

Whenever I attempt a description in depth of Donegal County, I put it off for another day, hoping I will find a way to convey what we have experienced here.

Last week, in Adara—the village known for Irish sweaters, especially hand knit sweaters from the Aran Islands in the Atlantic blue—we took a wrong turn searching for waterfalls and found ourselves on a road that aimed up and up again scaling mountains of enormous proportions that rose over a magnificent, green floored valley dotted with white sheep and thatched cottages. The view was straight from a scene of Lord of the Rings, one of my favorite films.

We continued driving up and up, and then up again, anxiety increasing in the small car as we went. The road became a thin ribbon of gray twisting its way on rocky land just at the edge of open space. The immensity of this land took our breath away.

A man was nonchalantly pounding fence posts into a patch of grass that seemed to hang off the side of this mountain. We stopped to ask him where we were, as we had arrived here by taking the road to the waterfall.

He laughed at our folly. We were on the road to the highest cliffs in Europe, the Sileve League cliffs. These rocks, he told us, rise 1972 feet above the Atlantic Ocean, making them nearly three times higher than the Cliffs of Mohar I told you about a few letters ago, and were once watchtowers for threats of invasion to Ireland from many enemies, Napoleon among them. The man tried to encourage us to go all the way up as if it were a little drive to the grocery.

We will never know the view from the top of Sileve League in any other way than in photos. The sheer terror that overtook us on that ride, even up to the halfway mark as we had done, was enough to encourage us to turn around and come down. The front of the car was out in nothing but air as we turned to leave.

That is truly what this landscape has you doing, holding your breath with the grandeur it presents—then one must address the power that could create something so unspeakably beautiful. A fly on the Empire State building, Henry, our car to that mountain was in that proportion. Since you could not be aware of the Empire State building, let me try for a comparison you would recognize. Ah, I have it! The great Mt. Katahdin in Maine. Our drive up that mountain was like crossing the Knife's Edge—but five times greater in height, with a searing wind off the Atlantic. Maybe that begins to deliver what we felt in that little car.

With affection,
Cynthia

October 10, 2015 - After Collecting Wild Fruits, The Road Home

Dear Henry,

The value of these wild fruits is not in the mere possession or eating of them, but in the sight and enjoyment of them. The very derivation of the word "fruit" would suggest this. It is from the Latin fructus, meaning "that which is used or enjoyed." If it were not so, then going a-berrying and going to market would be nearly synonymous experiences. Of course, it is the spirit in which you do a thing which makes it interesting, whether it is sweeping a room or pulling turnips.

-Henry David Thoreau, Wild Fruits,

The road home is opening before us. Before we step foot on it, I can't help but turn and look behind me—although that sort of thing is not recommended in general. There can be heavy consequences for looking behind for too long, especially when moving forward, and we always are moving forward, whether we know it or not. Someone once said, *"You can't drive a boat by watching the wake."*

Well, I'll risk it. I am in The Cope, a small restaurant in Dungloe, Ireland, a cup of coffee beside me. The Cope offers blessed free WIFI and has big windows onto the street. It is a lovely place to sit, to watch, and to write. The room is full of women on a shopping break, friends having a 'cuppa' and a chat, students out on lunch break. One threesome is listening to an old Irish storyteller and laughing at his quips.

I am invisible here. The lilting brogue fills the small space in conversation. We seem interested in the psychology of common day events. The "he said that she said that he heard what he said when she said…" and on and on. As I don't know anyone, I surf the sound, comforted that personal relationships are the same the world over. I am getting nostalgic about the rhythms of my own life in my own place, West K' Maine.

There is so much of value in your words, Henry. *"Of course, it is the spirit in which you do a thing that makes it interesting, whether it is sweeping a room or pulling a turnip."* Everything we have seen and done here gives us new ways of seeing how others live. The things we take with us will be gratitude for the endless kindness and friendliness of the Irish people, and the memory of the staggering beauty of their country. We see sadness as well for suffering imposed on them from so many overlords, though they are stronger in character and deeper in wisdom for all of that. We take the new friends we have made as well, gifts of great worth.

Our little cottage in Minnah Croise poised on the rocky meadow looks down to the sea ready for whatever will come; hurricane winds, waterspouts, pelting rain and snow, sun, strength within its thick stone walls. There is always a warm fire on the hearth and the melody of wind playing all around. The neighborhood is alive, everyone connected in their living. People drop by for tea or coffee, invite us here and there, make sure we see what there is to see, and there is too much to see for one visit.

We are grateful in full measure for their kindness. The golden road to this cottage is gone wild with gorse, yellow and fragrant in spring. A prickly, tough evergreen, it is almost indestructible, much like the people of the land on which it flourishes. When cut back, it will regrow with great vigor. In the recent past, it was used as fuel or to thatch a roof against the nearly constant winter rains. The top of our cottage becomes visible above the flowering gorse as one climbs the hill to home. Many seasons will come and go before we come back here, if ever we do. We are grateful for the wild fruits of this place.

And thank you for your words which are light for us all.

Cynthia

P.S.
Tomorrow, we travel to Dublin to catch a ride home.
And so, we leave Ireland behind us...but Ireland never leaves the memory.

October 15, 2015 - On The Cusp

Dear Henry,

Voyage accomplished! After a long flight I write to you from my little room here in West Kennebunk. It was interesting to be embedded in throngs of travelers. Every face turns here and there, looking at those who appear in front of them, exercising judgement in terms of what they think but, not knowing anything about that person really. Shoes, handbags, coats, clothing seems like badges of who this person is, when the real reflection of a person is in their eyes; we do not dare look there. I encountered several people at the different ports who were in tears, so downhearted I wanted to put my hand out to them. I dared look into the eyes of one woman as she got my coffee. I felt her surprise when someone looked at her, wishing her well wordlessly. It was a fine moment.

As we drove the Maine turnpike beginning the final twenty plus miles to our driveway, trees blazed with fall color on each side of the road. We listened to the news (we had heard nothing of America in Ireland) as it aired. The commentator said that the great Leaf Peeping weekend had arrived and that this is it, color in the state was between 75 and 100 percent possible. It was easy to see that he was right. Candles of oak, maple, ash and birch glowed on the altar of earth, green fir between and around to show them off. The sun was sinking in the west, its light golden, glazing everything around a honey hue.

Exiting the turnpike, the underside of Maine-gray clouds, a deep indigo, caught a special light turning azure-yellow with a unique tint only seen now and then. This cloud floated over our house as we drove down the drive. We got out to observe the beauty commanded to do so by the colors.

The news commentator also told us that this day coming, today, would be one of the last of this fall splendor as we were in for wind and rain; the leaves would surely come down.

Full disclosure here that this day, this cusp day, is my favorite of the year. Well, one of my favorites. I also love showers of blossoms in May, and the first fall of snow, but let's stick with leaves today. It's Cusp Day! The *"right point of view,"* as you say Henry, will render for us beauty in and around everything.

We are always on the cusp of discovery and transformation, seasons turn into seasons, we turn into our next best vision of ourselves. I know that you exist as love, Henry. You left this energy to guide us.

Your returned pen pal,
Cynthia

October 20, 2015 – The Imaginal Realm

Dear Henry,

Today, I am with you on your morning walk around Walden Pond. I wait for you sitting on a rock by your cabin door. It is October 20, 1846...

The door of your cabin swings open. You step out dressed in shirtsleeves, pants and boots, no jacket, though the air is cool. Yawning and stretching, you look up through trees into the brightening sky, turn round to get the whole of it, smiling just a little. After a few moments of quiet observation, hands on hips, you go back into the cabin for your coat and hat, putting them on as you close the door behind you. The smoke of your hearth flies from your chimney, perfuming the beginning day's breeze with the sturdy smell of wood smoke.

Your energetic pace aims to the water's edge, air around you laced with the call of waking birds. You stand listening to the net of their language as it falls to the earth, and you laugh out loud in delight. Walden Pond simmers, steams in cold air, mist rising from the surface. It is a mirror reflecting a sky waiting for the sun's arrival. There has been a frost already, and the trees are weeping leaves. As the breeze thickens, smaller trees begin their dance, letting their colored rags of leaves fly. It is a beautiful morning; so much happening in each little space.

But you are out for exercise. Quickening your pace, you enter the path you have cut for your morning walks, watch for the landmarks of trees, leaves, rocks, and plants you have made acquaintance with, noting their growth and decline in the fine language of leaves and flowers. Once or twice, you bend to look closer, to touch gently the object of your interest. Perhaps you pluck a seed or two, tucking it into your pocket to record tonight in your journal.

As you walk a renewed stride, the wind blows in greeting, playing in the lyre of trees, deepening tones to symphonic. The gale does not deter you, but rather, inspires you onward, hands raised to feel the current. You engage in a dance step every now and then, letting the energy around you dance you.

Halfway around the orbit of the pond, a path rises up through which you can see down into the wind ruffled water's surface; stopping, you turn your focus east.

Here, you allow yourself to stand still for many minutes. The rising of the sun takes the sky, bidding you to wait for it. And you do.

Now, the living light of the sun washes over you; the first ray enters your body with a potent greeting. Henry, you turn and twirl in the sweetness of this encounter. The original energy of creation is yours at this moment, and you are first, here, at its most potent state. Rewarded by the confirmation of what you already know: the beauty of this encounter is Divinity, is a gift to all for the taking. Your ecstasy will later be couched in the words of your enlightened work, Walden Pond. It began here!

There is no one to witness this encounter but me. The horizontal line of earth time has crossed the vertical ray of this morning's light, and, in this synapse I see you within my own time.

I am there with you.

With Gratitude,
Cynthia

October 22, 2015 - On This Earth Day

Dear One,

Good morning my Defender, my Translator. I see you here as well, a point of light among millions of others, scurrying on beautiful planet Earth, choosing moment to moment what you will do. I watch your brilliance grow with the love you accept from the waiting storehouse of the present, and see you strew that precious energy around you, enlivening those you touch. I see, too, the dampening of that light when confusion, doubt, fear, or anger dulls your vision.

If only you could see the tapestry of this light as it rolls out on the grand scale of the whole of human existence, you would know that, in spite of darkness in some places, this light is sweeping the planet, growing swiftly. Darkness cannot win. No matter what the news broadcasters say on the electric square of the television; it is a foregone surety that Love will win. It already has.

It would be helpful if these never silent talkers on TV realized they are sewing fear in the fertile fields of the human mind and the effects of this are poisonous. My old argument with acquiring wealth at the expense of your real life was a valid one; in your time, you are selling your children for cheap as they sit to their daily measure of murder and cruelty. The Darkness in these moments is a heavy burden and leaves young minds crippled, and their parents with them as they take the prescribed dose of cruelty with their favorite shows; lives turn cruel because of it. I feel the old human anxiety building, and I desist. I will use words from my life to sum all this up.

"However mean your life is, meet and live it: do not shun it and call it hard names. Cultivate poverty like a garden herb, like sage. Do not trouble yourself much to get new things, whether clothes or friends. Things do not change, we change. Sell your clothes and keep your thoughts. God will see that you do want society."

When I whispered to you on that street in Princeton, I hoped you heard me. And so you have. Myself, having been in the place you are now, a human who resists the tide of what they see around them with the words and actions they have, I encourage and support you from here. Be brave. You are running a race you have chosen, and it is a good thing for all.
Thank you for coming with me on my morning rounds in Concord; I felt you there; it was good. I look for you again at some moment when we are able to meet.
Count on me to listen for you in the ether between us.

-Henry, with affection

October 23, 2015 - The Sound Of Hope

Dear Henry,

Your words to me yesterday were pure inspiration. Each morning the empty space of the letter for this day weighs heavily on my mind. What can I offer of interest to one such as yourself, or anyone else who stumbles upon this place we both share? I take my daily meeting here with you as something I am meant to do. The idea that you see me on the path of my life gives a new and bright perspective; I relish that. Thank you for your part in this mission of mine.

I stop for a moment on my way to my writing room and, coffee cup in hand (I am aware of your opinion of coffee and tea, but no one is perfect) and open the front door to step out on the porch. I like it best when the weather is wild, and, so to speak, in your face. Windy gales are my favorite, even better when the rain— spinning inside wind somehow—is on the verge of becoming ice and clinks and clatters on windows, hissing, piling up on the drive and lawn. This is not to diminish the delight of a blizzard, its palette of grays and browns on white, dark green in between, is so restful to the soul. "No need to go out today", the weather shouts, nowhere to go. Everything vanishes in the spinning white web of snow. Sit instead by the fire and dream. Oh, I love blizzards! I know that you do as well. Many of your assemblages of words let us see you enthralled by the energy displayed in these storms, walking out into them on purpose.

My neighbor's car has just backed around and driven out to our street on their way to a day's work. This sitting here to talk with you, this is my work. The mystery of what will show up each morning that is of interest to you has reordered something within me. Everything we do changes the world and changes ourselves as well. Yours and my correspondence is a lovely change for me. You have assured me it is interesting to you as well. That is a great incentive for me to continue. I find myself wondering what you would think of this or that as I walk my days. I wonder, too, what you meant in the quote above by *"these degenerate days"*. I will have to think on that.

As I opened the door this morning, it was to a quiet, pale blue, almost gray, sky day with a few clouds of a darker hue sailing above the circle of trees in the front yard. But now, the wind has begun stirring the trees all around into a swaying dance. Fall colors are still bright though the leaves are trailing down through the clear air with greater enthusiasm and purpose now. It will be a lovely day here on Earth. I can only imagine what goes on where you are.

Thank you for your part,
Cynthia

P.S.
Henry, in my village there is a surprisingly visionary event that has been enacted for the past ten years or so. It takes place just as October turns the corner into November, during the All Saints and All Souls venerations here in New England. This time of the year, we here on the unyielding Earth are encouraged to look back to our lost loved ones, to pray (that language without words), and to endeavor to remember that life as we know it on terra firma has a seeming end and we are so warned... Although you and I know differently, Henry.

October 26, 2015 - All Souls Walk

Dear Henry,

Monday has arrived again here in West K. The weekend was full of activities in the advance of All Hallows Eve, or Halloween. As I write this, it occurs to me that you probably didn't call Saturday and Sunday the weekend, and that you may not be familiar with Halloween. It was a date on the first liturgical calendar and is now on the calendar of holidays (read holy days) of our year, right up there with Christmas and Easter.

In my little village, Halloween has become a big celebration. Spiders and ghouls, witches, headless creatures of all sorts appear on front yards that have become cemeteries for effect. Death is the big scare. There is a competition among folks about who can create the scariest scenario. Need I say it, it is also very good for business in the local establishments.

Ten years ago, the town of Kennebunk created the All Souls Walk: a rather bizarre event at sunset in late October. It is said that at this time that the veil between the worlds is thinnest while the visible world is dying, i.e. from fall into winter.

So, what happens on All Souls Walk?

A group of willing specters, whoops, I meant spectators is led by a Guide who is supposedly able to speak with the dead. At the first of these "tours", the Guide holds a lantern lit with a candle into the very graceful and beautiful Hope Cemetery beside the old Unitarian Church in the center of Kennebunk.

There, as the participants wend their way through grief-carved gravestones, the more prominent or interesting of Kennebunk's dead wait, standing or seated, in full costume of the period of their lives. When the group arrives at the grave, the waiting soul begins an explanation, a monologue about their life and the conditions of their death—not in a morbid or spectral way, but in present tense and in the simple language of their time. The message left behind with the watchers is, *"Beware, Time Is Passing, And We Know Not the Season."*

This event has become very popular and is enacted each year. It is a sight to behold—the cemetery peopled as if on a stage, the embodiment of inhabitants all waiting to welcome the living who, fascinated with the theater of the moment, walk paths that wind about the village of the dead.

On one of these walks, I signed onto the last hour's group just as the skies darkened and opened in a sudden, wild snowstorm under the old, tall trees thrashing overhead in the unexpected gale. It was grand theater. It sent chills up my spine to see those departed ones in the snow shivering, waiting for us to arrive at their stone. Need I say that in the doing, I passed the grave of my departed love; he did not rise to speak to me here, but I hear him all the same.

Henry, would that they had an All Souls Walk at Concord's Sleepy Hollow, and that you were waiting to speak to us as we wound our way up the avenue of authors in whose company you were laid to rest. Only thank God, you left yourself behind for us in your writing.

Enough for this letter. There is so much to love.

Cynthia

October 29, 2015 - The Transparent Eyeball

Dear Henry,

Could all the depth and ecstasy of experience felt by your friend, Ralph Waldo Emerson, be ours for the taking within a simple walk across a snowy field at twilight? If so, then let the experiment begin! Let us go into the world with new eyes.

I mean to turn sleuth, to walk abroad looking for moments when this reality in which *"the transparent eyeball posits a vision wherein the eye sloughs off its body and 'egotism,' merging with what it sees"* appears.

I will be going to Princeton, NJ, for a family visit. I leave you with the stirring verses from Emerson's Nature which you had the good fortune to hear in original tones from Mr. Emerson himself. It is an invitation for all of us to see in a new way.

Cynthia

Nature

Crossing a bare common in snow puddles, at twilight, under a clouded sky, without having in my thoughts any occurrence of special good fortune, I have enjoyed a perfect exhilaration.
I am glad to the brink of fear.
In the woods, too, a man casts off his years, as the snake his slough, and at what period soever of life is always a child.
In the woods is perpetual youth.
Within these plantations of God, a decorum and sanctity reign, a perennial festival is dressed, and the guest sees not how he should tire of them in a thousand years.
In the woods, we return to reason and faith.
There I feel that nothing can befall me in life—no disgrace, no calamity (leaving me my eyes), which nature cannot repair,
Standing on the bare ground—my head bathed by the blithe air and uplifted into infinite space—all mean egotism vanishes.
I become a transparent eyeball;
I am nothing;
I see all;
the currents of the Universal Being circulate through me;
I am part or parcel of God.

-Ralph Waldo Emerson

October 30, 2015 - All About Your Light

Dear Henry,

I'm waking up in New Jersey today. I won't get to take that walk in the woods with Emerson for a few days yet. It is just ahead though.

In the meantime, here is a poem I wrote for a departed friend upon hearing of her death. When I did, inner doors opened and she was in the room with me. In reviewing the poem recently, I found you within this image as well. I offer it to you today.

I think of you,
Cynthia

All About Light

Your priesthood is shattered, broken into shards of light,
broken as you stepped through the curtain
with which
death veils its chosen ones.
Your beauty touched us all, beauty
you lent us as we walk the circle of earth.
And your loveliness grows, grows like the endless
seconds since your departure grow into minutes,
and your absence will grow
into the hours and days of years we must
spend hidden from your now perfect sight.
Just behind the air, you are watching and,
if, as the seers say, No Where is Now Here,
then, you are here with us,
available as breath and thought,
dreams and love, those things that reach through
the fabric of time and place, wanting to set us free.
You dance on the point of my pen as I write,
smiling the deep-eyed joy you loaned my soul.
Your earthly shadow called home,
you are free to shape shift into geese overhead
tracking south on this fall day,
into fireflies mimicking God playing hide
and seek, or into me, as I reach out
to someone in need, reading their heart
and singing courage and love into a shawl
to cover them or write a poem in memory of
one who could not be contained by time for long.

-Cynthia Fraser Graves

Amen! Henry. On to November, the somber month.

Fall 2015 - November

Henry, this month of November is a somber one, inviting us all to shelter around inside fires... Assessing our year in a backwards glance, knowing winter nears.
I include a poem that is full of that backwards glance's perspective.

November Litany

The razorbacks of islands surface through
the pewter mirror... morning, low tide,
November, the somber month of remembrance.

Walking out a rosary of steps, I count ten by ten,
stamp prayers into the hard packed cold sand.
I pray for those whose step once mirrored mine,
whose hearts warmed the cold air I breathed.

My footsteps vanish behind me,
erased by the gray wind off a rising sea.
There will be no trace, no telling
I was ever here.

Out on the horizon, the islands have disappeared
beneath the relentless regularity of tides.

-Cynthia Fraser Graves

November 1, 2015 - The Same Garden?

Dear Henry,

On this first day of November 2015, I include an essay I wrote years ago. It seems to fit here as it tells of the approach of winter.

Cynthia

The Winter Garden

This garden rises every year in the same place, green plants of the current season taking root in the same brown earth as the many gardens of the past.

Eventually though, this year's population will cease growing and sink, some gracefully, some more awkward and indecorously, back into the brown soil that waits outside my windows while winter passes.

I try keeping the garden orderly, rearrange seeds into rows, tie things up onto poles and such, but plants have a mind of their own. Though I have new ideas about location, when I plant them there, they (the vegetables and flowers) seem to remember themselves from past years and go about looking as they did in last year's neighborhood, a notion I have noticed we humans have some affinity for as well. Though we transform and advance in stages to fruition, we look back to the previous flowering version of ourselves.

Tomatoes are strictly patrolled; I execute search and seizure operations to find the little vagrants wherever they pop up while silently setting down roots. Just what they think they are doing is beyond me. It may be that other neighborhoods of the garden are more racially diverse, more cultured, or less leafy, more upwardly mobile. Perhaps they want to hobnob with the eggplants wearing their purple robes or fling themselves at the basil in a frenzy of Mediterranean passion. That may be what they are up to; in the end though, as a rule I win. They settle back with their own kind and mature.

Some plants are more romantic than others. I would appreciate it if you didn't tell them I said that. They compete for the attention of their caretaker as it is. I hear them whisper about me as I weave down the rows weeding or pruning. Of course, when I turn around, no one is saying anything but that doesn't fool me.

Tonight, the tall, slender flowering pea vines dance in twilight breezes looking for all the world like blue moths drifting in and out of Gatsby's party. I hear their silvery laughter on the wind and swear they gossip about the goings on in this growing's social season.

Speaking of parties, indeed, this evening I remember, I had entered the garden to pick vegetables. It was a humid and warm dusk, the preferred light for Fairy solemnities. I became aware of movement; a definite glinting and glowing was going on in the rows of the garden. I had the distinct feeling I had stumbled onto (or been allowed to witness) a very private ceremony. Perhaps it was the angle of the vanishing light, or the refraction from droplets that had rained in a light shower that had just fallen, but the garden shimmered as if it were Oz. Nothing will ever convince me I had not intruded on rites of the fairy tribe. Though my human vision was inadequate, I saw their glimmering presence. They were frolicking up and down with no thought of the rules I impose on my plants in the daylight world.

Who can explain the waning and waxing of this seemingly same garden for thirty years? The more my life changes around it, the more the garden stays constant. I photograph it each year and I can prove what I am saying. Always the brave green flags of spinach wave, the brilliant red globes of beets light the air around them, and green fingers of beans reach for the sky as tall red lamps of Swiss chard nod and wave in summer's breeze.

These citizens rise from the soil each year as the sun finds the seeds, constant companions of mine. There, in the photographs, the identical intent tomato faces look back at me year after year. I am in some of the pictures too and while, over a short period of years, I offered the same face to the lens, I have begun to ripen, and the harvest is not impossible to imagine anymore.

The year will come when this garden rises eagerly, but I will be nowhere in sight.

It snowed for the first time today.

-Cynthia Fraser Graves

November 3, 2015 - Creation And Creators

Dear One,

After your letter from Earth yesterday, it seems appropriate for me to visit with you this morning. I see from here the sun is rising, just now, out of the cooling Atlantic, sending its rosy glow up and over Maine, scarves of light trailing over craggy shores not more than five miles from where you read this. All this beauty is there for you, and may I say by you. If you do not open your door and your eyes to see this display of love in the skies, it does not exist for you.

I trod the unmarked paths of your state in my days on earth, loving all the season's display, the purity of air as it brought the scent of juniper and pine to me on winds from Canada. I loved canoeing in the great rushing rivers as well as the quiet streams of water purified by sun and granite.

All of this is around you as well as are the signs of cruelty and disrespect; it all depends on where you look. There is miscreation all over your earth, carried out by emerging, growing souls who do not understand that the power they seek is nothing but air in the end and will not save them.

There is a little secret I am going to tell you…are you ready?

What you are thinking will take form before you, to show you where you are in your inner landscape. Beware! See the light, not the darkness.

Do not hold onto despair over love. Look to the good around you, the sunrise, the smile of a friend, the delicious taste of food, the hours of your day. Gratitude for these things will bring you more of them at the same time that you create the same for those around you.

I am watching with great interest and encourage you in the Earth school to do your homework. It all starts with you and goes out as a stream of creation, out onto the screen of your life. Be love!

-Henry

November 5, 2015 - Meetings

Dear Henry,

While we walk our snug paths in the worlds we both create, there is another realm nearby both of us, era notwithstanding, where we meet in thin air. You, in Concord, were farther from the sea than I am here in West Kennebunk. Five miles away, give or take, a few roads, once taken, will lead us to the splendid Atlantic, its waves repeating on the beaches and rocky cliffs of Maine's coast. Will you come with me Henry?

November 6, 2015 - Kyrie Eleison

Dear Henry,

We are in the midst of Indian Summer, a spate of warmth coming after a hard, killing frost. We have been touched with a frosty night here and there, but in the garden, kale still grows. Carrots and beets persevere.

In one of your essays, A Winter Walk, I find such beautiful prose! We go with you on a long distant winter morning where you woke to new snow lying looking like cotton. You take us over the sleeping town in a draft of smoke that rises into cold air (makes me think of Dicken' ghosts)… Henry, such masterful images of that long dead world allow us to relive the day on only a page or two of your words.

The experience of your words prompted me to open my door here in West Kennebunk on November 6th, 2015 with the expressed intention to find you and, as you did, to write what was going on in my world. Read of it below:

The burnished leaves of oaks around my house greet me, peer from the foggy cloud settled like smoke to the ground. There is no wind, no movement at all. As I look into the distance, the shape of everything softens, blends together, floats like my yard has lost its mooring. The dark green of pines and firs gleams between burnt leaves as grey air eschews stability. This is only one face of all possibility: a foggy November morning in Maine, 2015. Earth is a cathedral today in which there comes, at the rising of day, the ceremony of awakening. Who walks the earth awake sees the holy nature of all things. In the beginning, on the breeze 'Kyrie Eleison' is heard, simultaneously a petition and a prayer of thanksgiving; an acknowledgment of what God has done, what God is doing, and what God will continue to do through us to bless this day on the precious Earth.

-Cynthia Fraser Graves

Let the beautiful prayer reach as far as you are, Henry. In its chanting we are connected. *"Lord, have mercy"*, and we know that prayer was answered long ago.

Good morning, friend,
Cynthia

November 7, 2015 - Moonrise

Dear Henry,

And I forgot to say that after I reach the road by Potter's barns—or further by Potter's brook—I saw the moon sudden reflected full from a pool—a puddle from which you may see the moon reflected & and the earth dissolved under your feet. The magical moon with attendant stars suddenly looking up with mild luster from a window under your feet.

-Henry David Thoreau, Journal, June 13th

I have it here in your own hand; Henry, we saw/see the same moon. I do search for connections with you in my walks, and I find them! Coming home on a night walk, you see the moon in a puddle and your perspective flips (as does your readers') upside down and I stand beside you.

I will write your 'moon' poem for the world to enjoy. I'll be back to earth tomorrow.

Cynthia

The Moon

*The full-orbed moon with unchanged ray
Mounts up the eastern sky,
Not doomed to these short nights for aye,
But shining steadily.
She does not wane, but my fortune,
Which her rays do not bless,
My wayward path declineth soon,
But she shines not the less.
And if she faintly glimmers here,
And paled is her light,
Yet alway in her proper sphere
She's mistress of the night.*

-Henry David Thoreau

November 9, 2015 - I Love Nature

I love Nature partly because she is not man, but a retreat from him. None of his institutions control or pervade her. There is a different kind of right prevails. In her midst I can be glad about an entire gladness. If this world were all man, I could not stretch myself, I should lose all hope.

-Henry David Thoreau, Journal

Dear Henry,

Henry, you were 35 when you made the above notation in your Journal. I read it here in 2015 and feel the freedom of the words. It encourages me to open doors and walk into the woods and be entirely glad.

And there are troops, by thousands, of others who have experienced the gift of retreat and restoration offered in the cathedral of Nature; there we see that we are interconnected, part of a whole.

When we try to pick out anything by itself, we find it hitched to everything else in the universe.

-John Muir

A conscious walk on the stage of earth restores the senses and offers this gladness you speak of above. There is a release from judgement and fear that levels the path, removes the effects of rigid institutions, leaving us equal and one. It does not escape me that you personify the great soul of Nature as 'she', creation in the guise of the mother.

So, Henry, your writing leads me in ways I would not go without you.

I thank you for your life,
Cynthia

November 10, 2015 - November Litany

Dear Henry,

I am sending you a poem today. I rediscovered it, an old friend, in a journal and thought I would share it with you though I tremble to offer my words to such a one as yourself. It needs no explanation.

Cynthia

November Litany

*The razorbacks of islands surface through
a pewter mirror of morning tide,
November is here, somber month of remembrance.*

*Walking, I count ten by ten, a decade,
stamp a rosary into the hard packed cold sand.
I pray for those whose steps once mirrored mine,
whose hearts warmed the cold air I breathed.*

*Vanishing behind me, my footsteps are
erased by a grey wind off a rising sea.
There will be no trace, no telling
I was ever here.*

*On the horizon, the islands have disappeared
beneath a relentless regularity of tides.*

-Cynthia Fraser Graves

November 11, 2015 - Sky Painting

Dear Henry,

Sunrise and sunset at this time of the year are spectacular. November is now the empty stage of earth in New England, all softness gone, the green and colors of flowers, leaves on trees fled, collapsed back to the ground in the coming of the clement cold of an approaching winter. I know most would say inclement, but Winter is a beautiful gem on the bracelet of the seasons, the white, sparkling stone of rest and renewal in the wheel of growing.

This month's sky is the result of the magic of the sun's rays playing in the clouds. November skies respond in the most dramatic hues and shapes. Along with you, I hear the science of why, but I still see this mystical art as a bit of magic.

I am going to tell you about a cloud event that occurred a few years ago when I was on a walk with a dear friend on an August day. We were walking a path through a field that took us directly above the ocean, with rocks and surf below. Involved in our conversation, we ambled along until something interesting happening in and around the white, fluffy, fair-weather clouds above got our attention.

In one part of the sky a cloud was slowly taking on a pastel shade as if it were being painted, each stroke visible to us. We stopped walking and just stood as some hidden hand painted on and on, the clouds around this one taking color as well. The colors were blue, then pink, then yellow and then green and back again it went, until a good number of clouds were so enhanced. The whole display took a good twenty minutes to complete, the 'painter" slow and graceful with the strokes. All the while, we sat entranced and delighted. We often remember this magical event, still boggled by having been the ones to see it. Like you, I am not afraid to call it magic. It seemed to be for us, although one other person on the path commented on seeing the sky art. He had no idea how it came about either but was just as delighted as were we.

I thought about our experience when I read the quote above. Our attempts at explanations of these wonders can keep us swimming in the awesome sea of the unknown but will never get us to the shore. For that to happen, we must acknowledge the mystery of a loving presence bigger than all we know. Thank goodness this Presence is patient.

Raining here today. The sky is a velvet gray.

Until Tomorrow,
Cynthia

November 12, 2015 - To Seasons In New England

"Now, by 2 p.m., a regular snowstorm has commenced, fine flakes falling steadily, and rapidly whitening all the landscape. In half an hour the russet earth is painted white even to the horizon. Do we know of any other so silent and sudden a change?"

-Myself, Journal, November 28, 1858

Dear One,

I see that you are, as I was, a lover of the seasons. Watching the ebb and flow of your time marked by the stage scenery of Earth is enough to save any life. I cannot tell which I liked better, the newly green shoots daring cold April nights— gaining the air steadily as the sun calls them on—leaves that are golden filigree floating on May's balmy breeze, or the new buds of exquisite flowers. OH! Spring.

And when June arrives and takes her hold, growing explodes in gardens and woods and fields, the heat of Summer calls out maturity to the magnificent design of all growing things. The work of tending and harvesting begins, torpid July's and glorious August's version of earth busily filling our laps with what we need to grow and prosper ourselves.

And golden Fall; the often hot and humid summer air clears. Fully expressed September is seen in kingdoms of green and gold that last for just a moment, perfect, hollering out their loveliness to all, until one October morning by some unheard signal they begin their decline, leaving promise of the next year.

November quietly takes the stage. Leaves burnish, the air itself grays, winds pluck empty branches of trees in the cool song of bereavement and promise, both at once. Mornings come on cold, frost spreads the hint of the white to come... Oh, November, and then, December when all is suffused in white, quiet white. Muffled sounds float in air, punctuated by sharp bird calls as the feathered kingdom searches empty trees for sweet berries and abandoned apples.

January is the test though, the month of isolation, snow and cold so deep on earth as to keep us home by the bright fire; stars in the black sky snapping in the deep freeze. We take the measure of ourselves and our time here during these days; the year turns as well. Next, February brings snow, snow, snow... Then March and her silver darts of frozen rain together with the cry of returning geese high above in the night skies.

And all this loveliness is yours for free. Go forth and see... And remember, you are a living plant of this Earth—the seasons being as true for your life as for any living thing.

I miss the Seasons of Earth still.

Ecclesiastes 3:1-13:

*There is a time for everything,
and a season for every activity under the heavens:*

Henry,
With regards

November 13, 2015 - Gaia

The earth is not a mere fragment of dead history, stratum upon stratum like the leaves of a book, to be studied by geologists and antiquaries chiefly, but living poetry like the leaves of a tree, which precede flowers and fruit—not a fossil earth, but a living earth...

-Henry David Thoreau, Walden

Dear Henry,

Great thanks for your note of yesterday. When you reach back to me, the connection between us flares up and I am encouraged in my daily whispers to you.

Your words on the liveliness of the seasons led me to thinking about a hypothesis that has taken hold here on earth. Put forth by a Mr. James Lovelock among others, it is the belief that the Earth itself is a living organism with self-regulatory functions that maintain a dynamic system with intelligence and awareness, named by human consciousness as Gaia—the Greek goddess of Earth, now revived and applied to this theory. And further, we are reminded that we humans, in our arrogant insistence that we control things, are not cognizant of the awareness of this great sentient Power that allows us our very existence. Respect for the living, breathing Earth is Wisdom in action. Any other treatment of our home here is unconscionable and foolish.

The ancient earth-walkers knew this. We have forgotten it and we violate our trust with Mother Earth daily.

In his brilliant and helpful book, The Seat of The Soul, Gary Zukav makes this lineage very clear. He says that our reality is made of towns and cities, then states and countries, then cultures and nations and that nation is an aspect of the personality of Gaia, the Earth's soul developing its own personality and soul. Our home dynamic of the United States, is a facet of the personality of Gaia.

So, what does the personality of the United States look like to the Earth? As we read newspapers or watch various screens tell of disasters such as the rise of threatening droughts, floods, and ravaging winds, what are we seeing? Are we seeing the compilations of factoids buttressing a scientific theory for agony on earth just now? Even science cannot hide the fact that this mistreatment of our environment has brought on extreme conditions.

Or could we be seeing a living Earth grown tired of the probing, exploding, evaporation, and exploitation that crawls its surface and, in defense of herself, begins to think less kindly of those who misuse her gifts at such breakneck pace? Cinemas of the future show a devastated planet that, in the end, will not support life.

I know, Henry, I am haranguing here. You were good at this. You will forgive me, I hope, for my drift today. I see you walking the pine-scented paths with your guides, the silence of the forest around you, the next river to canoe coming into view ahead. Gaia waits to delight you in her creations, refreshing your very soul. The Gift of Earth is worth fighting for.

Cynthia

November 13, 2015, Again - Walking

But the walking of which I speak has nothing in it akin to taking exercise, as it is called, as the sick take medicine at stated hours—as the Swinging of dumb-bells or chairs; but is itself the enterprise and adventure of the day. If you would get exercise, go in search of the springs of life. Think of a man's swinging dumbbells for his health, when those springs are bubbling up in far-off pastures unsought by him!

-Henry David Thoreau, published posthumously in The Atlantic

Dear Henry,

I am mixing it up a bit tonight. While reading your extravagant, fascinating essay, *Walking,* I find myself spurred on to take your direction, to walk abroad, and to report back to you about my experience. I will not be able to take to the road for the four to five hours you recommend, but I will walk west and walk for as long as possible. I am informed by your words on how to go forth.

So, though this makes the second post in one day, it is an announcement that I will be a bit late posting my letter for November 14. As soon as I return to the house, I will respond.

Good evening, Henry.

Wish me well.

Cynthia

None are so old as those who have outlived enthusiasm.

-Henry David Thoreau

November 14, 2015 - The Walk Taken

Dear Henry,

Cold winds blew out of the north all night, fresh from Canadian mountains and rivers. As I knew I would walk this morning in your footsteps, they seem to say, "Come out, come out. There is much here for you." But I was not about to go out until the sun had risen, so I just snuggled deeper in my bed and let the hours of darkness accomplish themselves.

At last, though, the sun appeared and filled the windows of my house with daylight, time to walk abroad. Dawning clear, the morning wore sharp blue skies above, with strong, cold winds, gusts to 30 mph, temperatures in the middle to low 30 degrees Fahrenheit. I bundled up for my cold stroll.

Leaves in Maine are 95 percent down on earth with only a small population of oak hanging on. Those already down dance across streets in abandon, days like this being few and snow a certainty just ahead.

Here, today we walk on sidewalks and paved roads, through neighborhoods, small villages and out into open fields for a mile or so on Old Thompson Road. A gusty breath barrels across the open fields, picking up power in the lack of barriers of any kind, making a person hold onto themselves in the blast.

Wind is a friend or foe depending on its intensity. Today's wind was a friend, playing resonant chants in the pines, spruce, and cedar of the evergreen woods. It still sings out my window as I write this, wanting me to tell you again about its powerful and beneficial presence. It cleans and clears air, lulls listeners into introspection, rakes leaves either for or against you, and, in this era, Henry, it holds promise for clean energy to run the innovations of this time. A windy day is a gift, if you ask me, and great writing weather.

I walked by an old home set on a small hill and surrounded by towering trees. I thought of The Old Manse in Concord, the house by the river where Nathaniel Hawthorne lived and wrote. The house on my walk was built in the same era, but is falling into decay, the rear of the building now gone. Only the front of the house stands strong in November's daylight. I felt a connection to you when I saw it. I set to wondering about the people who had lived there; how had it come that such a valiant house was left to the elements? There is a story there.

You said somewhere that you *"took a walk in the forest and came out taller than the trees."* Today, I understand that.

Thanks for coming along this morning. The energy and beauty of each day is a clean slate. And yet we sleep.

Cynthia

November 15, 2015 - Seeing Paris 11/13

Could a greater miracle take place than for us to look through each other's eyes for an instant?

-Walden, Henry David Thoreau

Dear Henry,

What is the view from where you are now? Do you look down on the earth from a removed heaven, watching us scurry around in frenzied attempts to keep balance on the material plane, the place where great learning is embedded in shades of pain and joy of the emotional and physical experience? In my conception, you are here in some disembodied way, in the same dimension I walk and breathe within, but you and those who have passed over are energy surrounding us, aware in ways we cannot be. Just behind the veil, you watch and guide when you can, whenever we are quiet enough to hear and feel your mostly silent sympathy and guidance.

The sharpest tool of human perception is judgement, judgement of what one casts as good or bad, different, unlovable, dangerous etc., all of the things that make us count those around us as less than they are, *our brothers and sisters, our family, no matter what their color, race, status, wealth, education, gender*, and on to the end of these artificial descriptors we have created out of our fear.

In our taking on the role of a mean God and executing this judgement—the farthest thing from the Truth of God—each of us dampens the possibility of love for all of us with every judgement we exercise. It is how we are taught.

This fear-filled way of living has come back at us with the vengeance of ideologies. It happened in Paris two days ago; blind rage, accumulated from so much judgement and hate, spouted up in a great wave of destruction and pain.

We must change the way we think about and treat one another. The solution begins with us, each of us. Then, we hope and pray that this love and kindness can calm the prevailing, scorching winds of hate that blow from Syria, from Iraq, from the faceless threat of our own judgements returned to us.

We are in a tough spot, Henry. What would be your advice?

Listening,
Cynthia

November 16, 2015 - Soul Cakes: Small Comforts

Dear Henry,

There is great comfort in small tasks, repeated in our daily lives. I am on the front porch for a few minutes to meet the day. The sky this morning is opal, various pastel hues striated through small milky clouds, the prominent colors being blue and pink, with yellow where the sun has touched the whole.

The fire in the stove must be fed, so out to the woodpile I go to get an armful. While there, I enjoy the fragrance of smoke on the cool air and investigate the woods on our border, then return to the house to lift the lid and feed the glowing embers of the night's fire, dropping wood in, wood that was grown and cut on this land.

Now I make coffee and wind the clocks. It is Monday and that means the old clocks I keep ticking for company (none of them tell the right time) need to be tended. I love hearing them.

These days, my morning appointment is with you. I am to write to you out of the fabric of my days on earth with what I think might be interesting to you and comprise a location between us that we both may inhabit.

Big rewards though. I know, Henry, that you give of yourself every day now as you did then.

Deep love and appreciation,
Cynthia

November 17, 2015 - The Last Manuscript: Wild Apples

To appreciate the wild and sharp flavors of these October fruits, it is necessary that you be breathing the sharp October or November air. The out-door air and exercise which the walker gets give a different tone to his palate, and he craves a fruit which the sedentary would call harsh and crabbed. They must be eaten in the fields, when your system is all aglow with exercise, when the frosty weather nips your fingers, the wind rattles the bare boughs or rustles the few remaining leaves, and the jay is heard screaming around. What is sour in the house a bracing walk makes sweet. Some of these apples might be labeled, "To be eaten in the wind."

-Henry David Thoreau, Wild Apples

Dear Henry,

The temperature is 29 Fahrenheit; a fuzz of frost is on the brown grass which emerged after the raking and blowing for the past few weeks. The air is bracing. That means you feel it when you breathe it. The cold column of life-giving oxygen slides down the passages to your lungs like icy wind. Very energizing!

My text today is apples, wild apples. I wrote of them a month or so ago and hesitate to bring them up again today, but on a drive home after the four o'clock hour, when the sun was setting for the day, I found country roadsides I traveled studded with craggy trees of lost apples, trees from seeds sewn by birds and animal scatter, or, perhaps, from remnants of old farms now melted into thin air, leaving only traces of themselves in trees like these.

This year I've spend with you has been very formative for me. I find myself unconsciously searching everything within my view for its connection to you and your time on earth. Nothing speaks louder of you, my dear friend, than these wild varieties of apples. After your death in 1862, in some set of lucky circumstance, someone had your last manuscript published in The Atlantic magazine. I was reading it before writing this morning and recommend it to anyone who loves wild apples gleaming in thickets we pass—an offering to whomever takes the time to stop.

In this essay, you remind us that the little apple has been seen as precious enough to be the test of man's faithfulness to God within the Adam and Eve tale and was cited in mythology as gifts of the gods and goddesses. We of greatly eroded wisdom take this fruit for granted, wasting its healthful properties in favor of the sugar laden treats of our day. (I had better stop there, I feel a rant coming on.)

Well, last night, November 16th of this very year, these apples by the side of the road in a circle of wind were the polished jewels around a weathered trunk in the now deserted field. Had I stopped, taken time and energy, I could have gone home with bushels of these blessings, apples cured in fall winds, tasting very like the ones you talk of on your walks. We waste a great deal here. At least, because of you, I saw them and remembered your words.

All we need is the will to walk out and gather them.

With affection,
Cynthia

November 18, 2015 - Woodsmoke

Smoke
Light-winged Smoke, Icarian bird,
Melting thy pinions in thy upward flight,
Lark without song, and messenger of dawn
Circling above the hamlets as they nest;
Or else, departing dream, and shadowy form
Of midnight vision, gathering up thy skirts;
By night star-veiling, and by day
Darkening the light and blotting out the sun;
Go thou my incense upward from this hearth,
And ask the gods to pardon this clear flame.

-Henry David Thoreau

Dear Henry,

As I opened the front door this morning, wood smoke wafted in wrapped in very cold air. It is 22 degrees Fahrenheit on the back porch. Within my woodsy neighborhood, columns of smoke rise from chimneys up and down the street seeming to come from nowhere as the houses overall are not visible. For a moment, one thinks of the fires of America's first inhabitants rising, pillars rising from forests and plains.

I fed the flames in the stove before settling to my computer. I wish we still preformed the romantic act of picking up pen, but we use the keyboard to give outward shape to thought. It serves us well as it encrypts thought rapidly. I wonder if we conceive of thoughts more quickly than writers of your years. I would guess we don't think as deeply, the pen and its strokes giving a more generous time lapse to work the thought to its conclusion.

According to your Journal, the first snow in 1852 fell on November 23rd. In November 2015, we are holding our breath to see when the first snowfall will come. It is late this year, giving us all false (probably) hope of a benign winter. This is usually a mistake, as winter will be winter. When the white stuff comes with its silence and surrender, I will let you know. Right now, everything is in waiting.

Your poem about smoke is lovely. When I visited Walden in the fall, I noticed that the last two lines of this poem had been chiseled on your hearth.

Go thou my incense upward from this hearth,
And ask the gods to pardon this clear flame.

I do wonder, Henry, what you were asking pardon for? Had your empathy with the nature, as present in wood, gone so deep that you dismayed using it for heat? Did you somehow know that smoke, even the forest scented smoke of a woodfire, had consequences for human health?

I withdrew yet farther into my shell and endeavored to keep a bright fire both within my house and within my breast.

-Henry David Thoreau, Walden

Tending fires, within and without, and withdrawing to reflect, this puts us to shame here in this time where the whole is dedicated to distraction. Again, thank you for your loneliness and courage on this path that you have cleared for us.

Waiting for snow,
Cynthia

November 20, 2015 - Rangeley, Maine: Height Of Land

I went to the woods because I wished to live deliberately, to front only the essential facts of life, and see if I could not learn what it had to teach, and not, when I came to die, discover that I had not lived.

-Henry David Thoreau, Walden

Dear Henry,

We, (you and I), are going on a trip. I leave tomorrow for a week in the Western mountains of Maine: moose country, ski country, hiking country—all present in a village that time forgot. After a drive of three hours (give or take a few minutes for weather as there is little traffic), the small town of Rangeley on the shores of beautiful Rangeley Lake comes into view. It is a trip back in time.

Temperatures up here in the mountains drop by ten degrees and will be in the 30's during our trip. Most probably, snow will be on the ground even this early in the year. It's a retreat, Henry, a place removed from the mainstream of world events. At this time of the year—non-tourist season—there is one market open, one coffee shop, precious few eating establishments, a good bookstore you will be glad to know, an excellent library, and a few churches. The town is a jewel, a living presence of the natural gifts of lake and mountains.

In 1847, your observations on wildlife, weather, terrain, and the nature of Maine, and of the people you met along the way were shared—loggers, rivermen, Abenaki guides—helped to create Maine as a territory accessible to those who read your books. I will stand on this land, breathe that clean air, see the sun rise and set, meet the people of this place in your stead.

It is this Maine I go to for one precious week, a week I am surrounded by the quiet green candles of trees standing in snow, where roads wind up craggy mountain passes to the top of the Height of Land and an incomparable view breaks upon you, startling, beautiful, no matter the season. You are as likely to see a fox trot across your yard as to have a small herd of deer or a bear show up in close view.

I will write to you of my time there, of our moose hunt (no guns, simply cameras), of weather and, well, who knows what? The delight is in the discovery. I wish to see differently.

Pack your bags, Henry, we are off in the morning to drive into MAINE, the real Maine.

Cynthia

November 21, 2015 - Into The Wild

I wish to speak a word for Nature, for absolute freedom and wildness, as contrasted with a freedom and culture merely civil—to regard man as an inhabitant, or a part and parcel of Nature, rather than a member of society.

-Henry David Thoreau

Dear Henry,

Up we go, winding into the mountains of Maine to the lake, the great tourmaline under gathering winter skies. Rangeley Lake is not yet frozen, only a web of ice stretches its boundaries as waters glisten under the late fall sun.

One can touch the loneliness of the human condition acutely here in this place; winds whistle around our cabin at night stirring the fire on the hearth into glowing embers. Outside, a whole wild world creeps, searching for sustenance. Stars are brighter here because of the absence of artificial light. The whole is made of green, and gray, and black, interspersed with the silence of white snow.

I mean to keep my morning appointment with you each day, who knows where I will see you. You said, *"In Wildness is the preservation of the world."* I am going into the wild to search for the wildness within in a place where the existence of Nature has not yet been erased or controlled but is part and parcel of the whole.

Until tomorrow, from Rangeley…
Cynthia, with great expectations

November 22, 2015 - A Maine Morning

Every creature is better alive than dead, men and moose and pine trees, and he who understands it aright will rather preserve its life than destroy it.

-Henry David Thoreau

I am looking out the cabin window into a seemingly unending stretch of woods. There is a dark gray bloom of clouds overhead. The temperature is 37 degrees Fahrenheit, winds to 17 mph, and snow showers are forecast. Oh joy, what great weather for a walk in the woods.

After living in this part of the world for as long as I have, one can predict things by interpreting little details of what's out the window. This morning, trees are swirling in a subtle circular motion. I know this means a storm is approaching. We are excited. Finding the ground bare when we arrived, a cover of white will improve the view.

We reached Rangeley around three o'clock yesterday. The early November sets even earlier here, sun leaving us by 4:07, a light show drifting over the lake as the sun spins colors hard to name. Let me try; indigo, swirled with soft peach and bright yellow, bordered in gray… All reflected on the mirror of the water, colors which deepen and intensify until they are absorbed by the dark, dark blue land masses—art in a studio of sky.

I will watch this afternoon's new version of sunset. Daytime continues to shorten until December 21st and then it will slowly expand, giving us light to live by.

Until then, we cluster indoors, light the fire on the hearth, and turn to dreaming…

November 23, 2015 - The Surprise Of The Sacred

With all your science can you tell how it is,
and whence it is, that light comes into the soul?

-Henry David Thoreau

Dear Henry,

The weather in Rangeley is a citizen—extolled or damned in response to how it has shown up—and a great topic of conversation in winter when it can turn dangerous on a dime. Today's weather is 30 degrees Fahrenheit and winds of 12 mph with partly cloudy skies. No snow. As this is the snowmobile capital of Maine (or one of them), this "No Snow" is not good news. Along with Saddleback Mountain Ski Area, the business of Rangeley depends on snow for tourists to take the drive up here.

Today's text is the Surprise of the Sacred. We attended the 9 am service in a small white-steepled church perched beside the waters of the great lake in the center of town. The congregants in this church, not dressed for looks, come in warm, rugged clothes: boots, scarves, hats. They live here; love being in this remote, beautiful place.

As we stepped into the small, light-filled church, we were warmly greeted by the priest who would lead the service. He drives many miles on a Sunday to service communities in this mountainous stretch of earth, as far as Oquossoc and the Sugarloaf Mountain region.

The service began with a strong hymn. The lake viewed from the windows of the church was a peaceful context above the words of the familiar ceremony. All around the white space of the church vibrant colors of stained glass shot their message from so many windows. Behind the altar, a series of four rectangular panes depicted earth, wind, water, and fire in symbols. They floated above the head of the priest. A welcoming angel ruled one pane, and a lofty, iconic moose was featured in another. They brightened the gray day outside.

A surprise at the end of the mostly predictable service happened when the elderly priest looked out to his flock with tears in his eyes and, in a voice choked with emotion, told them that this was likely his last mass in Rangeley. Beset with very serious health challenges, he was obliged to see an oncologist and to be near a hospital for long and invasive treatments that would limit his ability to serve.

This man has given his life to bringing light to this far-flung corner of civilization. He will most likely not be able to serve further. I know, Henry, that you were not an advocate of organized religion and did not attend or defend its influence. Yesterday morning, upon hearing of this priest's abrupt departure, the people there assembled wept. A light-bringer was leaving their close circle.

The choir director played The Battle Hymn of The Republic, (why we always picture God in battle is perplexing and wrong), and we all sang. The mass ended, light still streaming through the gorgeous glass, and time turned a page.

I didn't expect this when I walked into the church, but I was grateful to be there and be reminded that love is always going forward everywhere.

Bless him for his service and God Speed.

Cynthia

November 24, 2015 - The Sound Of Water

Nature will bear the closest inspection. She invites us to lay our eye level with her smallest leaf and take an insect view of its plain.

-Henry David Thoreau

Dear Henry,

IT'S COLD! At this hour, the temperature is 20 degrees Fahrenheit with winds of 25 mph in the forecast for today. Clear skies and the glow of sunrise in the woods around the cottage illuminate the ruffles of frost on everything. You can no longer walk out the door without coat, hat, gloves, and scarf.

Rangeley Lake is one of the major headwater lakes of the Androscoggin River drainage. It has many inlets entering from all around the lake. Its outlet, the Rangeley River, flows northwest into nearby Mooselookmeguntic Lake (a lake you loved I think), and from there into the Androscoggin River, Merrymeeting Bay, the lower Kennebec River, the Gulf of Maine, and the Atlantic Ocean. The deep, cool, well-oxygenated water provides good habitat for salmon and brook trout. The lakes' elevation is 1,518 feet (463 m) above sea level and its area is about 10 square miles (26 square km). Depth is shallow near the shore with a central basin averaging about 95 feet (29 m) deep and a maximum at 149 feet (45 m), deeper than Walden Pond, which was 108 feet.

The big lake has islands floating on its clean surface. It provides a natural habitat for a whole world of creatures that live just beyond the border of the woods along most of the roads. The mighty presence of the Lake is powerful, visible from everywhere in the little town of no more than two streets. People who come to live here do so to be in Nature in a very up close and personal way. They build their

101

houses on remote mountain lots, roads running straight up and into the woods. When dark falls, the drive home is on roads that wind into forest, very few landmarks to guide you. Here and there, the lights of a home twinkle off road. You had better know where you are going.

This is your kind of place, Henry. Folks here are unpretentious to the extreme. They *"live deliberately."* All is quiet on these November nights as the whole of the town is closed for a rest before ski and snowmobile season begins.

Cynthia, with affection.

November 25, 2015 - Simplify, Simplify

I find it invariably true, the poorer I am, the richer I am. What you consider my disadvantage, I consider my advantage. While you are pleased to get knowledge and culture in many ways, I am delighted to think that I am getting rid of them. I have never got over my surprise that I should have been born into the most estimable place in all the world, and in the very nick of time, too.

-Henry David Thoreau, Journal, December 5th 1856

Dear Henry,

We are back in West Kennebunk this morning; temperature 22 degrees Fahrenheit, winds 2 mph, a sunny day. Here on the ocean's edge, we have milder temperatures but are susceptible to ocean storms and cold winds off the Atlantic in spring. Weather fronts parade through our skies like dancing girls with gray scarves, covering over the sun for weeks, bringing rains that keep Maine green. With the scarcity of water everywhere on the globe, we should be thankful for this rain, and generally, we are, but the wait for sunlight can get long.

We drove out of Rangeley yesterday, mid-morning, winds howling and temps shivering. The beautiful Lake shimmered in our rear-view mirror as we drove, blue taffeta on green velvet in a bowl of deep purple mountains. Ice glistened at the edge of streams rolling down with us to sea level. The big freeze is on.

I think of your call to *"Simplify, simplify."* That is not as easy a thing to accomplish in life, though you would think it was. In the end, the things we had to do, the ongoing situations of our lives, were too much to hold back, hold away from the space up there in Rangeley. We caved, packed, and left to come home and attend to things. It really doesn't matter what those things are; as we sat in the quiet, with all that beauty around us, albeit in freezing air, we were moved to move along.

The difference between the busy, surface outer life and the silent calm of the inner life takes courage to discern and follow. In your writing life, this was your cause, your theme; your days at Walden shout out that the inner self is lost and submerged rather than complimented by the fabrication of society and culture. The distraction of what we 'must' do to please others is the death knell of who we really are. It is in deep quiet, beyond the mind and its lists and fears, that we find ourselves.

You are a courageous man, Henry, one who blazed and still blazes the trail for all. Even though the quiet gets too deep to wade in, I know the difference.

Tomorrow is Thanksgiving in America.

I am thankful for you.

Cynthia

November 26, 2015 - Thanksgiving 2015

I am grateful for what I am and have. My thanksgiving is perpetual. It is surprising how contented one can be with nothing definite—only a sense of existence. Well, anything for variety. I am ready to try this for the next ten thousand years, and exhaust it... My breath is sweet to me. O how I laugh when I think of my vague indefinite riches. No run on my bank can drain it, for my wealth is not possession but enjoyment.

-Henry David Thoreau

Dear Henry,

Can you hear the (relative) quiet from here? Listen. Most stores are closed (for a while anyway) and people have been given the day off. Many of the homes in this America of ours have a turkey in the oven with stuffing. Cranberry sauce waits in the refrigerator; squash and potatoes, vegetables you would recognize, are in preparation for the gathering. There will be a feast today, a feast in memory of the treacherous first year Colonists spent on the soil of the New World.

Some history:

Throughout that first brutal winter, most of the colonists remained on board the ship, where they suffered exposure, scurvy, and outbreaks of contagious disease. Only half of the Mayflower's original passengers and crew lived to see their first New England spring.

In March, the remaining settlers moved ashore; they received an astonishing visit from an Abenaki man who greeted them in English. Several days later, he returned with another Native American, Squanto, a member of the Pawtuxet tribe who had been kidnapped by an English sea captain, sold into slavery before escaping to London only to return to his homeland on an exploratory expedition. Squanto taught the Pilgrims, weakened by malnutrition and illness, to cultivate corn, extract sap from maple trees, catch fish in the rivers and avoid poisonous plants. He also helped the settlers forge an alliance with the Wampanoag, a local tribe, one that would endure for more than 50 years and tragically remains one of the sole examples of harmony between European colonists and Native Americans.

In November 1621, after the Pilgrims' first corn harvest proved successful, Governor William Bradford organized a celebratory feast and invited a group of the fledgling colony's Native American allies including the Wampanoag chief Massasoit. Now remembered as American's "first Thanksgiving"—although the Pilgrims themselves may not have used the term at the time—the feast lasted for three days. While no record exists of the historic banquet's exact menu, the Pilgrim chronicler Edward Winslow wrote in his journal that Governor Bradford sent four men on a "fowling" mission in preparation for the event, and that the Wampanoag guests arrived bearing five deer. Historians have suggested that many of the dishes were likely prepared using traditional Native American spices and cooking methods. Because the Pilgrims had no oven and the Mayflower's sugar supply had dwindled by the fall of 1621, the meal did not feature pies, desserts that have become a hallmark of contemporary celebrations.

The Pilgrims held their second Thanksgiving celebration in 1623 to mark the end of a long drought threatening the year's harvest and prompting Governor Bradford to call for a religious fast. Days of fasting and thanksgiving on an annual or occasional basis became common practice in other New England settlements as well. During the American Revolution, the Continental Congress designated one or more days of thanksgiving a year, and in 1789 George Washington issued the first Thanksgiving proclamation by the national government of the United States; in it, he called upon Americans to express their gratitude for the happy conclusion to the country's war of independence and the successful ratification of the U.S. Constitution. His successors John Adams and James Madison also designated days of thanks during their presidencies.

1858, on November 25th, you wrote in your Journal:

While most keep close to their parlor fires this cold and blustering Thanksgiving afternoon, and think with compassion of those who are abroad, I find the sunny south side of this swamp as warm as their parlors, and warmer to my spirit. Aye, there is a serenity and warmth here which the parlor does not suggest, enhanced by the sounds of the wind roaring on the northwest side of the swamp a dozen or so rods off. What a wholesome and inspiring warmth is this!

How like you Henry, to be off sauntering as the day was celebrated, to break free of the world of the 'parlor' in deference to the living room of swamp and woods. We see that Thanksgiving was in practice in the year of 1858. Today, it is a national celebration with many facets of thankfulness.

We remember and venerate the suffering and bravery of our forebearers. We take time to be grateful for the staggering luxury of life today with all choices available, food, clothing, education, health care. We are fortunate indeed, and we remember those on whose shoulders we stand.

Cynthia

November 27, 2015 - Everything Waits ....

The finest workers in stone are not copper or steel tools, but the gentle touches of air and water working at their leisure with a liberal allowance of time.

-Henry David Thoreau

Dear Henry,

In New Haven, Connecticut, the fog is thick this morning. A full moon slopes to the horizon in a gauzy mantle. The temperature is 42 degrees Fahrenheit; no wind to speak of. The week ahead will be warm, daytime temps reaching upwards of 50 degrees. Humidity, 100 percent. This is unsettling weather for New Englanders; in the patterns of past years, we should be waking to freezing temperatures at night, low forties, and high thirties by day. We should have snow. As delighted as most of us are by this temperate anomaly, it feels odd. We all know the weather is a changeling and can spin into a storm from gentle winds, encouraging to fierce and dangerous.

I am in the process of editing my novel, Dusk on Route 1. In this tale, the female lead character, Pamela Iverson, drives in despair to the beach seeking a reprise from tragic memories. Not aware of a nor'easter steaming up the coast of Maine, the double punch of snow and gale force winds isolates her between an angry sea and the unknowable landscape of snow. She falls asleep in the warm car, wakes after dark, and is trapped in her car by a dead battery. As the monster waves from a jetty threaten to flood her car and tip her into the roiling sea, she must go out into the storm. It is Christmas Eve, and no one knows where she is…

Pamela opened the door and stepped out, immediately turning her back into wind that raked her clothes, throwing her off balance, then slammed the car door shut leaving her standing on the surface of the moon. There were no recognizable landmarks under the shifting carpet of heavy snow.

One streetlight in the parking lot spread an eerie glow on the featureless terrain.

Her back to the wind, she held onto the car to keep from being blown away. Looking over the hood, she saw the beautifully dangerous waves curling high and tight, racing down huge granite jetty stones as if it were a garden path. Hills of water surged into the parking lot, spilling a threatening pond under her car, pushing her away.

Prisoner of a small circle of vision, Pamela walked, able to see no more than two feet around her. Confused about what direction to go, she relied on the wild sea's pounding, keeping it at her back, to move away from danger.

-Cynthia Fraser Graves, Dusk on Route 1

I read of your struggle to get your work into print. I am about the same thing here on earth these days. That said, I enjoy the process of writing the most. Any help you can muster on my account, my higher dimension-ed friend, I will appreciate in the extreme. The book is available on Amazon... A bookstore in the air.

We are all in a time of waiting. We approach Advent, the season in many Western Christian churches of expectant preparation for the celebration of the birth of Jesus, a person of great influence still today. We wait to achieve the best version of ourselves and our lives; to find and to share our Light. Every thought, every action creates change in our lives and in the collective LIFE on the planet.

Exciting possibilities.

Cynthia

November 29, 2015 - Allowing Loss

Not until we are lost do we begin to understand ourselves.

- Henry David Thoreau

Dear Henry,

Temperature 28 degrees Fahrenheit , wind 2 mph, 0 precipitation. The energy of this time of year, the dregs of fall, waiting for snow, is so different from the green, thriving energy of spring. It's not something we notice overtly, but it is actual. The land is waiting, silent, dormant all around me here in West Kennebunk, hues of bronze, gray, dark green, and black. Gone is the green haze of leaves and the pastels of flowers.

As I continue to fill myself with your thoughts via your writing, you were more comfortable in the silent woods, never mind the season or weather, than in any parlor or assembly hall.

Somehow, you could let go the outer calendars of busy-ness that we cling to and allow the great continent of inner awareness to be the land on which you walked. There are those alive now who chide you for living so close to your mother and family, for your walks toward home for sustenance of food and connection while you were in Walden. Henry, it didn't matter where you went or who you befriended... You were lost in the most essential way; within your every thought and action, you pushed the boundary, discovered the wisdom of the lost.

Allowing loss to happen clears space for new vistas to open. It happens naturally when one loses loved ones; the space once filled by the beloved, already a holy place, is filled with new understanding, new connection to what is beyond life. Loss of a job, of a friend, of possessions, all seen as unfortunate at the time, can be reevaluated as clearing space for new understandings, new people, new visions of what can be to arise in that place.

The difference between the two very different interpretations of loss lies in the courage to sit with what is in peaceful acceptance and see the blessing that was hidden within. To do that, Henry, takes the kind of faith you found in yourself. Living, as you did, outside of society, outside of the staunch Puritan Credo of your day that held on to the perception of the sinfulness of man and his unworthiness, you gave us walking behind you light, hope, and a blueprint for our own personal freedom.

I remember first picking up your Walden. Henry, your words were a fresh wind— a sun's warmth and hope. I saw that effect in the students as well. When we read in Civil Disobedience, they were so affected, they staged a sit-down protest about the lunch service in our school. I was secretly delighted!

The administration, predictably, was not.

You saved my life back then, and many days since.

With Affection,
Cynthia

Winter 2015 - December

And now, the great curtain of white falls. We are invited into the womb of color and sound to reform ourselves in its brilliance... I wonder if that was what you were about in the deep white woods of Walden?

December 1, 2015 - Tree Hugger In A December Wood

Dear Henry,

The term "Tree Hugger" brings to mind your influence and love of trees. I quote:

I love and could embrace the shrub oak with its scanty garment of leaves rising above the snow, lowly whispering to me, akin to winter thoughts, and sunsets, and to all virtue. Covert which the hare and the partridge seek, and I too seek. What

107

cousin of mine is the shrub oak? How can any man suffer long? For a sense of want is a prayer, and all prayers are answered. Rigid as iron, clean as the atmosphere, hardy as virtue, innocent and sweet as a maiden is the shrub oak. In proportion as I know it, I love it, I am natural and sound as a partridge.

-Henry Thoreau, Journal, December 1st 1856

And so, you began the month of December 1856 in your journal, age 39. You are in the woods, in your mind if not actually. It is cold and quiet. As you walk your paths there, or wander off those paths into the thicket, you can see the ubiquitous and humble shrub oak as an entity with consciousness and personality. You stop and consider the tree, receive its affection for you, hear its soft whisper in the wind. Then you want to embrace the tree, if not actually enfold it. (I bet you did.)

In a session during a conference, we went into a wood and were asked to select a tree that "spoke" to us, to sit for a time in meditation nearby and with that tree's energy and then, to embrace the tree and give it thanks. It was an awesome experience. The whole trick is to become quiet enough to let the discomfort of the uniqueness of this encounter disappear until you can "hear" the tree. (Yes, you can hear the tree as it rises out of the landscape, an entity present to the seeker.) There is much comfort here—and much to learn. What it takes is attention and intention! No fee required. And the woods are villages of these presences.

I will hug a tree today! I will begin December by walking into the woods to find a simpatico tree and spend time with its great or small presence. Then—in your name Henry—I will embrace that tree and find out how the partridge feels in its protection. I am encouraged, as ever, by you.

The great star of Bethlehem is rising. Much to speak of this month. Enjoy this day. Into the woods with me.

I frequently tramped eight or ten miles through the deepest snow to keep an appointment with a beech-tree, or a yellow birch, or an old acquaintance among the pines.

-Henry David Thoreau

December 2, 2015 - Acquaintance Among The Pines

Good morning, Henry,

On the road south again. In five hours, we will get into a packed car and begin the drive. In a week we will reach our winter home in Hobe Sound, Florida. I just recently discovered that the inimitable Mary Oliver lived a few streets away from me in Hobe Sound until her death. Had I known that then, I'd have searched her out.

Here, we ride out the deep snow and howling winds of the north, temperatures in the negatives, long dim gray days until March winds and April's rain begin to temper the northeast. Leaving day is always difficult. I very much miss Maine during the months I'm absent from my little village.

I am reading an annotated version of your journal, I To Myself, edited by Jeffrey S. Cramer. On December 3, 1856, you write of your neighbors in terms that compare them to Homer, Christ, and Shakespeare as they work at the task of being themselves as their lives, and yours, move on. Mr. Cramer supplies the names of these neighbors in Concord: *Minot, Rice, Melville, Goodwin, Puffer.* I wonder what they would have said had they known that you—the odd, wandering saunterer of Concord—took their measure, inscribing their names for all of posterity in such a way. They were good men, living lives as my neighbors and friends are here in this time and in this village. I do wonder, Henry, why women were so noticeably absent in your reflections. I'll save that for another day.

For nearly two score years I have known at a distance, these long-suffering men whom I never spoke to, who never spoke to me, and now feel a certain tenderness for them, as if this long probation were but the prelude to an eternal friendship. What a long trial we have withstood...

-Henry Thoreau, Journal

Right on Henry! The cast of characters in our individual dramas, even those not more than walk-ons, all live for us. Gratitude is to be extended to them in smiles, in notice, perhaps in the recognition of a handshake.

I never go to your words to come away empty handed. You always teach me something, give me a gift that brightens my day.

In exchanging conifers and pines of Maine for palm trees, we will explore the southeast coast of Florida together.

On the road for the next week, my letters must reflect where I am. I will get the missive posted each morning. My commitment is sure and steady.

Time to pack more...

Be well. (I suppose that is taken for granted where you are.)

Cynthia

December 3, 2015 - The Yellow Brick Road

Dear Henry,

The note this morning will be brief. Being on the road doesn't lend itself to spacious thinking.

Rummaging for a thought today, I came upon this quote.

All change is a miracle to contemplate; but it is a miracle which is taking place every instant.

-Henry David Thoreau, Walden

The particulars of our lives change day to day. Though we don't understand that we are the Creators, everything gyrates in our perception. *"It's not what you look at that matters, it's what you see"* was the way you put it. Finding the good or the beauty in everyone and every situation is the finest thing we do. A brand-new opportunity to create this miracle is offered each second. This belief was a daily practice in your life. Trooping along behind those of you who left us their light, we are encouraged.

As I go here or there, I am tickled by this or that I come in contact with, as if I touched the wires of a battery.... The age of miracles is each moment thus returned.

-Henry David Thoreau, Journal, December 11th, 1855

With affection,
Cynthia

December 4, 2015 - Looking Behind As You Leave

Dear Cynthia,

I hear the reluctance with which you drive away; leaving the North country behind, seeing the solemn forests evaporate, cities rise around you, the familiar fades slowly, all of this generates a feeling of change, of loss. The familiar elements of each day here at home, by which you measure your life's reach—family, friends, neighbors, the trees, and earth of your land—will remain with you in your mind and heart. They are part of you. You cannot leave them behind.

It is not a question of where you are though, my friend. It is a question of how you are.

As I said in my Journal on January 12, 1852:

"Go not so far out of your way for a truer life; keep strictly onward in that path alone which your genius points out. To live in relations of truth and sincerity with

110

men is to dwell in a frontier country. What a wild and unfrequented wilderness that would be."

Forgive me for quoting myself, no arrogance intended. Cynthia, your happiness is really an inside job, up to you to create. The real frontier is within your own perception.

The seasons bloom and fade in Southern climes. The actors in your life wait for something or someone that they can't quite put their finger on but feel its absence. The sun above will cast your shadow as truly there as in your homeland. There are things to learn in every corner of every day, everywhere appointments made for you by unseen guides.

I think it was the great Wayne Dyer, a brother newly passed on, who said that you cannot drive a boat by watching the wake. Look before you for the gifts of the day.

From my perspective, outside of time, the events and energy of your life are all happening in a millisecond of brightest light; think of each day as part of this flash of brilliance and worry not. Lofty advice it is that I give.

With admiration,
Henry

December 5, 2015 - Crow Season

Dear Henry,

My spirits buoyed in your kind and wise words yesterday. Change—be it seasons, locations, even habits—comes hard, though it is going on around and within us ceaselessly. Thank you!

I have always had a very special relationship with crows. I pay attention to them, watch them, but never count them. They congregate in numbers in my backyard in Maine in what we have named the Crow Congress. In 2007, I wrote a book that uses crows as an internal scaffolding metaphor: Never Count Crow, love and loss in Kennebunk, Maine. I included a rhyme that my Mother-in-law, Marion Johnstone Graves, spoke to me years ago:

"One crow, Sorrow, two crows, Joy, three crows, a Letter, four Crows, a Boy, five crows, Silver, six crows, Gold, seven crows, a story that should never be told."

Not counting crows as they alight before you is wise and almost impossible. They swarm and move and change ceaselessly within minutes.

Crows stand out and show up for me often. When I was writing my memoir and decided to take a break for a walk, they cawed (I take it as a shout) at me all the way down the street until I went back to work. They proved that they recognize different people and follow them at times. They kept me at my purpose. And you at yours…

Thou Dusky Spirit Of The Wood

Thou dusky spirit of the wood,
Bird of ancient brood,
Flitting thy lonely way,
A meteor in the summer's day,
From wood to wood, from hill to hill,
Low over forest, field and rill,
What wouldst thou say?
Why shouldest thou haunt the day?
What makes thy melancholy float?
And bears thee up above the clouds,
Over desponding human crowds,
Which far blow
Lay thy haunts low?

-Henry David Thoreau

I know you saw magic at work that most do not.

Good day,
Cynthia

December 7, 2015 - Hawkeye

Dear Henry,

One more day in the car, one more day of captivity in this steel capsule of travel, and we can alight for a while.

The hen-hawk (red-tailed hawk) and the pine are friends. What we call wildness is a civilization other than our own.

-Henry David Thoreau, Journal, 1859

During these yearly journeys south, I have learned it is better to have some use for the hours that one must sit. I began doing Hawk Counts a few years ago. Hawks perch above me in trees that border I-95, or perhaps they are in flight as we speed by. I count every hawk I am aware of. One year, my total was fifty six.

In 2005, Louis Lefebvre, a Canadian ornithologist, discovered a method of measuring avian "IQ." Based on this scale, hawks were found to be among the most intelligent birds. They perceive not only the visible range of light, but also the ultraviolet part of the spectrum and have always been known to have the sharp vision of able hunters. The female is generally larger than the male, and as they migrate in winter, they are just coming to the end of their migratory season currently, this month of December.

In New Jersey yesterday, as the sun rose into a thick fog, we resumed our journey south. The first hawk sighting was in Maryland at approximately 9 AM, appearing high on a limb over I-95. Its white breast gleamed in the new day's sun. I spotted five hawks this day in Maryland; one beautiful red shouldered hawk and two with red coloration around their throats. All five with the brown hood prominent.

There were four hawks on I-95 in North Carolina and five hawks in South Carolina. We observed countless hawks soaring high over the road during the whole trip. I did not count those for their number would have approached hundreds.

Henry, these birds inspire one. Their attention and patience, evident to me, makes my trip worthwhile. After North Carolina the light changes and weather warms, so we are out of their territory. Today, we travel from Georgia to Florida. I will keep my vigil and report back.

Other sightings were many large hornets' nests in the high crooks of trees (perhaps I spied ten or more), one little deer feeding by the side of the road in Virginia, and eight memorial markers placed at locations where some person had lost their life. Fluttering sun-bleached ribbons and wreaths at these departure points were reminders to the river of cars streaming by: savor the minutes and hours of this day, for tomorrow is not yet assured.

And back into the journey I go,
Cynthia

December 8th, 2015 - The View From (T)here

Dear Henry,

The journey has ended! At approximately 3:30 PM EST, the car stopped! We spilled out after eighteen hours of confinement. The temperature is in the low 70's, a lovely, balmy wind ruffles all the trees and plants into a welcome wave as the sun shines on us. A mile away from where I stand, Atlantic surf crashes on lovely white beaches.

At this moment, I could be Ponce de Leon as I stand at last on dry ground after the long voyage. What I see bears little resemblance to what I left behind. Though

I have made this trip for over ten years, returning from the cold north to this temperate place always feels unexpected.

Now the cleaning and arranging of the homestead for the months of winter ahead begins. This is an act of creation, of re-creation, each time offering the possibility of doing a better job, of making a place for a new and lighter version of myself, of remembering what did not feel right in the years past and to avoid that in this year. You said:

However mean your life is, meet it and live it: do not shun it and call it hard names. It is not so bad as you are. It looks poorest when you are richest. The faultfinder will find faults even in paradise.

-Henry David Thoreau, Walden

My life here is hardly "mean". On the contrary, it is rich with possibility beyond any standard of wealth. The adjustment is how I see and live it. I am a student at the University of This Day, This Moment. May I wisely choose to see as an optimist.

A question, Henry. Why is it that no one is ever seen as or heard of a cockeyed pessimist? In my opinion that is much more the case.

I love nature, I love the landscape, because it is so sincere. It never cheats me. It never jests. It is cheerfully, musically earnest.

-Henry David Thoreau, Journal, November 16th, 1850

I am wondering what the view is from up/in/over there, wherever you are? I don't think my brain, as awesome as it is, can even conceive of your Homeland now. I know you know what I am about here, have even heard from you, but I have no address except the following:

Henry David Thoreau, The Ether

I will be watching as time winds through my days here; I'll get back to you.

With affection,
Cynthia Of the South

December 11, 2015 - One Hundred And Sixty Years Ago Today

Dear Henry,

One hundred and sixty years ago today, you stood in some meadow, or walked some path on your rounds, stood stock still. Perhaps it was snowing, and you tilted your head back to let the flakes of white land softly. It was early morning, as you loved to be out before the population of Concord stirred, loved the sense of intimacy Nature enjoyed and indulged you with when you were alone together, showing you things no one else could see.

There was a wind blowing a dance in the trees and shrubs around delighting you, gusts of cold wind tugged you along. You believed anything could happen, believed that you were the richest and most fortunate of men to be able to put your foot to the blessed ground each day, and walk it, to discover what treasure had been laid just around the bend. Coming upon the squirrel, the hare and partridge, you greeted them as family. These being brothers, you walked on in the company of the Great Society of the Woods.

I see you from here, your rapt attention going from sky to woods, to leaf and back, a skip in your step, alone, but if one could see joy, you are surrounded by it. You need for nothing, Henry, nothing that does not come to you, offering itself freely. Even Winter is the greatest of gifts, its great drama of snow and melody of wind seen as a whole—beautiful—instead of the piecemeal irritation that most see in a storm or the cold or in rain, for that matter. *"Great winter itself looked like a precious gem"* you said.

I am there now with you on that path no matter where I seem to be, no matter what the season, the snow falls. This is your gift to me. Beauty is in the eye of the beholder, and you have taught me well.

In the quiet of those snowy woods,
Gratitude,
Cynthia

P.S.
I will share one of my poems of winter tomorrow.

December 12, 2015 - Tableau, A Dream Poem

Dear Henry,

Today, a departure. Many years ago, I had a dream that became indelible in my mind as I dreamed. The dream was important, sacred. I was walking in a copse of woods, walking with someone who had stepped through the veil in death a short time before. The woods were quiet, soft, hopeful, offering solace as an embrace.

It was a gift to me, and now, to you.

Cynthia

Tableau

we are at the center,
you and I,
within …a grotto,
deep in the woods.
delicate trees bend toward us,
reach over our heads,
stretch fondly
in protection and affection.
and the light…
kind, warm,
rises, foams around us up into
the dusky cup of sky.
warm, snow fills the air
embraces us, makes us as of one.
deer stand a small
way apart, glossy
radiance flowing from their
large eyed interest.
coming close, they offer us
warmth, a cloak.
we are together,
awe in the silent
procession of the coming night.
music from stars
strokes our skin as we look on each other.
we are waiting,
waiting for something to come,
waiting in that holy place.

-Cynthia Fraser Graves

December 14, 2015 - Henry, We Hardly Knew Ye

Love must be as much a light as it is a flame.

-Henry David Thoreau

Dear Friend,

They are talking about you down here, and some, in not so nice a way. Recently, in a long essay in the New Yorker—a widely read weekly magazine—someone said, you were self-obsessed and narcissistic, fanatical, adamant as a human being, requiring nothing beyond yourself in the world. She said you are a hypocrite, and that Walden is a sham piece of writing that commended living in the meanest of terms.

Now, when such a discordant, critical voice erupts over the praise, encouragement and thankfulness that fortress your work, work that is the reflection of your entire life, good days, bad days, lovingly encrypted for those of us who follow, it causes one to stop and look at the source. As if the wisdom, humor, and guidance that flow from your experience at the time you lived and in the personality that you were wearing in that life could possibly be dimmed by a person using a lens of her small perceptions to focus the enormous and beneficent scope of your life. She may cackle all she will, especially one that lifts us traveling behind to new ways of seeing. The faults she finds in you, my friend, she recognizes within herself.

I don't care who did your laundry, Henry. I am for you.

Thankfully, there is another view of the validity of your contribution. Mr. Donovan Hohn, writing in the New Republic (a clearer window for your worth) tells us you were a poor student who once lost a hound, a bay horse, and a turtle dove and spent his whole life searching for them. He calls you a moral philosopher and a patriot, a committed abolitionist, a sufferer of tuberculosis from your youth, as well as a naturalist who studied a pond and found the whole ecosystem and stars reflected inside.

And so it goes, Henry. Those in fear of your conception of a reverse world from their academic dogma quiver and throw darts.

Today, the sky at dawn is the smokey gray of quartz shot through with liquid gold. The Florida birds are calling, playing in the soft breezes... That's what is important. Nothing to sneer at here.

Thank you for your life,
Cynthia

December 16, 2015 - A Powerful Idea Is Born

Dear Henry,

On December 19, 1843, a novella titled A Christmas Carol was published in London. Its author, Charles Dickens, was a contemporary of yours, Henry, but one who lived in a very different world from your bucolic Concord.

Charles Dickens lived as witness to the enslavement of the poor in the impoverished alleys and streets of London—most pitifully and especially children.

The suffering and injustice he witnessed galvanized him to put pen to paper and create a tale that, as his most beloved character, Scrooge, said at the end, *"would hope to do some good."*

Dickens himself lived in the same poverty and child abuse that he set out to affect. At age twelve, his father was imprisoned and Charles was forced to find his own meager lodgings, sell his books, leave school, and find work in Warren's Blacking Factory (which produced boot blacking) on the banks of the Thames where he worked under terrible conditions. Living this meager life, Dickens felt personally the injustice and brutality around him. When his father was released, Dickens had to continue in this work to provide for the family. These experiences created in him sympathy for suffering.

I have always thought of Christmastime, when it has come round...as a good time; a kind, forgiving, charitable, pleasant time; the only time I know of, in the long calendar of the year, when men and women seem by one consent to open their shut-up hearts freely, and to think of people below them as if they really were fellow-passengers to the grave, and not another race of creatures bound on other journeys.

-Charles Dickens

A Christmas Carol today tells of Ebenezer Scrooge (the name being a composite of screw and gouge, two nouns of excoriation), the representative of society and its greed at that time, and his transformation into a gentler, kindlier man after visitations from the ghost of his former business partner Jacob Marley, who tells Scrouge of visits from the ghosts of Christmas Past, Christmas Present, and Christmas Yet to Come. Written at a time when the British were examining and exploring Christmas traditions, this little book changed and softened the heart of the world.

The novella was an instant sellout success. Dickens was not the first author to celebrate the Christmas season in literature, but he refashioned the holiday into the humanitarian one it hopes to be today (minus the unimaginable marketing opportunity made of it since).

In the act of picking up his pen, Henry, writing from his heart—the very nexus of Creation—his tale changed the course of human existence here on planet Earth. We are gentler and kinder because of this story, and we all do KNOW this story though some would rather, again in Scrooge's words, *"leave it alone."*

Cynthia

December 19, 2015 - A Windy Day Here

Dear Henry,

The balm part of balmy has disappeared. At 7 AM, it is 65 degrees Fahrenheit, winds of 16 mph blow promising to increase to 20 mph during the day. There will be rain on and off, a different sort of day, no sun, none tomorrow for that matter. On this day, the Atlantic will be surging to the shore a mile away from me. I hear it from here, thundering onto sand in high, dangerous curls.

This weather invites us to take the day off, to relax. Gray skies invite introspection, rest. People of this most southern state think that it is a cold day. At anything below 70 degrees, coats come out and people bundle up to hurry in and hurry out of stores.

Wind is howling around our small place here, rattling windows, clanging chimes in trees, and singing through screens. It's wonderful. This particular gray reminds me of Maine's moodiness when skies of this color stretch over The Country Of The Pointed Firs, also the name of a novel written by Sarah Orne Jewett in 1896. She lived just up the road from West Kennebunk, in South Berwick, Maine. She wrote with the best of men at a time when women writers were eschewed. She had an inner focus that reminds me of you, Henry. She found interest in everything and everyone. Nothing was too meager for her pen.

There was something about the coast town of Dunnet which made it seem more attractive than other maritime villages of eastern Maine. Perhaps it was the simple fact of acquaintance with that neighborhood which made it so attaching and gave such interest to the rocky shore and dark woods, and the few houses which seemed to be securely wedged and tree-nailed in among the ledges by the Landing. These houses made the most of their seaward view, and there was a gayety and determined floweriness in their bits of garden ground; the small-paned high windows in the peaks of their steep gables were like knowing eyes that watched the harbor and the far sea-line beyond or looked northward all along the shore and its background of spruces and balsam firs. When one really knows a village like this and its surroundings, it is like becoming acquainted with a single person. The process of falling in love at first sight is as final as it is swift in such a case, but the growth of true friendship may be a lifelong affair.

-Sarah Orne Jewett, The Return, The Country of The Pointed Firs

I can't keep on the same path for long with this breeze. Even the great press of the Christmas rush seems to be blowing away. In my research for this letter, I found a weather commentator who gave me the answer for this unhinged state. The wind is coming from NNE 23.3 mph, that would be north northeast. It is a wind from home and I recognize its smell, its sound, its feel. The weatherman called it 'fresh' and that it is, Henry, fresh!

My best to you,
Cynthia

December 22, 2015 - A Moment In Time: Winter Solstice

Dear Henry,

Last night, at 11:49 PM, the sun reached its maximum elevation in the sky and the gears that guide Earth's elliptical orbit ground to a halt. The slow reversal of a gradual lengthening of nights and shortening of days began. The kindly Sun commenced its walk toward a closer alliance with the northern hemisphere.

We must learn to reawaken and keep ourselves awake, not by mechanical aides, but by an infinite expectation of the dawn, which does not forsake us even in our soundest sleep. I know of no more encouraging fact than the unquestionable ability of man to elevate his life by a conscious endeavor. It is something to be able to paint a particular picture, or to carve a statue, and so to make a few objects beautiful; but it is far more glorious to carve.

-Henry David Thoreau

Down on Earth, fires were kindled as labyrinthine dances were danced and wishes were wished. It is a new season in the skies. All things are possible for those who watch and observe the Winter Solstice. It—like its sister on the calendar page, New Year's Eve—makes us pause, celebrate, evaluate and, perhaps, re-form.

It has been thus for almost all known human history. This event, Solstice—even when what was happening in the great cauldron of the skies was not known—held hope for those dark years. Holy-days, festivals and rituals marked it as far back as our Neolithic ancestors. Stonehenge's great and mysterious stone circle was designed in honor of the cyclical movement of the sun, and so were thousands of stone circles in Ireland, Scotland, and England where ancestors gathered on nights like last night.

What I find most interesting about the Solstice or Equinox is that they take more time for the change to begin, a pause, a day or two's hiatus where no movement is perceived; when stasis reigns, it is deeply quiet.

This quiet is going on now over my head, waiting. In this calm, let us see to the height and breadth of possibility. Let us look up to what can be. The seeds of Spring are sown. We will throw them to the fertile soil of tomorrow knowingly, intentionally.

A New Year begins here, Henry. Where you are, Eternity is. Root for us in time, Henry.

I know you do!

Cynthia

Go confidently in the direction of your dreams. Live the life you've imagined.

-Henry David Thoreau

December 24, 2015 - A Magic Night

Christmas Eve, 2015

The way you spend Christmas is far more important than how much.

-Henry David Thoreau

Dear Henry,

Christmas Eve is a night of wonders. Hearts are open all over the world. Though we have heard of the event that inspired this great celebration of peace and goodwill to man, it takes courage these days to say it as it is very banal to believe in God. Still, this whole secular and religious party being thrown is because of the birth of Light in the guise of a baby, a baby of great importance, a baby born in Bethlehem.

In this year, 2015, the earth is in dire need of the message of this baby who, as Jesus (Jeshua ben Joseph), was perhaps the greatest spiritual teacher to have walked the earth. His message was one of love, love for all, everyone, love, and forgiveness—the letting go of perceived wrongs. This is the only path to take us out of the snarls of hate and suspicion in which we are entangled.

I propose that there is real magic in this night, that things that have never been possible before ARE possible tonight. The spell of Christmas Eve tempers anger, cools hatred, erases suspicion, confirms doubt, and is up to quelling war. We are the agents of this magic. Wherever we go, we include our intentions. May our intentions be of Peace and love.

I realize that I am preaching to the choir in writing of this to you, Henry. Now beyond human existence, you have eyes that see within and beyond to what our lives mean.

May we take time to step out of the party for a few minutes, an hour, whatever we can grasp to reflect on our time here on earth. Let the magic of tonight flood in as light, Light, LIGHT kindled within to guide us to a kinder, gentler world created by, for, and with ourselves and our brothers and sisters. It is the only way.

O Holy Night, Henry!!
Cynthia

December 25, 2015 - The Christmas Full Moon

Dear Henry,

I am in an empty living room, Christmas tree in the corner lit and hung with ornaments that have become keepsakes as the years passed. Presents are opened; the children of the household are busily engaging with the new worlds their gifts offer, pretending, playing, the wonderful possibility of imagination wafts through the house like perfume. As well, great gifts of food have been given and taken gratefully. We are sated with the feast, transfixed with abundance and the opportunity to be in each other's lives for these days of Christmas

Soon it will be time to go back to our own homes, to our paths. Here comes January 1st, 2016. Can you believe that time has passed so swiftly? That question probably makes you laugh. Your view of time is like our cinemas, each life a parade of characters across a screen, in the end no more than shadows in events that happen all at once hopefully rendering some new understanding about the nature of being alive to respect and value our lives, to live intentionally, as you encouraged us to do so often.

I am glad of it. Tonight, the Christmas Full Moon will rise over Princeton, New Jersey, as well as the whole of America. In its wavering, filmy light, new things are dreamed of in all our worlds of possibilities. The New Year is ahead.

Can you see the moon from where you are?

This turn of the year offers a chance to reform our existence, to mount the screen as a new, intentional character knowing we are in charge: to lose that weight, to end that fight, to be kinder, better, to be responsible for the life we have in our hands.

Outside, the temperature is 65 degrees at the end of a month that should be nearer to freezing than this balmy, foggy air mass. Across the street, a Magnolia tree approaches its spring bloom stage. Yesterday, on a walk, we saw daffodils with buds set, waiting the few days before they open, yellow cup-like flowers in air that will soon not be friendly. The cold will come; all these premature buds will feel yet the sting of January, and February. What is to happen next?

That is the real mystery... What is to happen next?

I wish you a Merry Christmas for the last time in 2015.

Looking forward to the New Year with you, Henry.

Cynthia

December 26, 2015 - The Twelve Days Of Christmas, Day One: The Kiss Of A Conscious Earth

Dear Friend,

We begin the Twelve Days of Christmas today, the destination of which is the Epiphany on January 26th, also known as Three Kings' Day, a Christian feast day that celebrates the revelation of God within Jesus. In Western Christianity, the feast commemorates the visit of the Magi to the Christ child, Jesus' physical manifestation in time.

Christmas, really, was not always the biggest feast day. It became this way when the yearly journey of Santa Claus replaced a quiet birth under the stars somewhere in Jerusalem. The original feast was the Epiphany, when Jesus—as foretold by prophets of centuries before—was born in all of his humble glory to cut a new path through the forests of time. (Much like yourself, may I say, despite those who think you a hoax. Jesus had that problem as well.)

We, here, are all very familiar with the tune that marks the Twelve Days, they begin...

On the first day of Christmas
My true love gave to me
A partridge in a pear tree

This is the first verse. Henry, just for fun. I will trust that I can find corresponding gifts to the twelve days as we continue from here, the 26th, to the 6th of January, 2016. I will offer them to you, even though their delivery must be of the atmosphere.

On the first day of Christmas
My true love gave to me
A partridge in a pear tree

And so, I give to you one whole, conscious Earth's kiss delivered in the wind, the sun, the rain, the snow... In the glowing life within each molecule that makes up this planet where we all attend Earth school daily, whether we will or no. See above where her kiss comes, Henry, in the visage you saw around you everywhere. She is mother to us all.

Tomorrow, DAY TWO... What will I find? I love a mystery!

Cynthia

Wealth is the ability to fully experience life.

-Henry David Thoreau

December 27, 2015 - The Twelve Days Of Christmas, Day Two - Two Pennies

Dear Henry,

I am speeding along Route 95 South at 8:11 on this day, December 27th, 2015. Needless to say, Henry, it does not engender a reflective mood. However, I have made and will keep my promise of a missive each day for a year.
Today's gift, Day Two of the Twelve Days, is two pennies...

On the second day of Christmas,
My true love gave to me
Two turtle doves and a partridge in a pear tree...

But in my version, it is...

On the second day of Christmas,
My true love gave to me
Two pennies and the kiss of Gaia in a pear tree

Now, pennies denote the smallest denomination within our currency and have been around since before the Roman Empire.
Strangely enough, though, pennies are the conductors of many miracles. Anyone who has had the experience of loss will probably have had pennies show up where they should not, or even could not have been found. Take the movie Ghost, in which Patrick Swazye, as the ghost of the movie, uses the humble penny to communicate with his love through the veil of death. She sees it moving and knows he is near. (If somehow you have not seen this film, Henry, DO!)
I have had my moments with pennies, messages delivered. They galvanize belief as the impossible shows up. I am, as are all of us, rich in what we understand. Pennies in strange places wake us up, allowing us the knowing we are needed.
'Til tomorrow...
I trust that a gift will be given on Day Three.

Cynthia

December 28, 2015 - The Twelve Days Of Christmas, Day Three: Frankincense and Myrrh

Dear Henry,

This little project of mine is more challenging than I thought at first. Of course, some of it is that my writing space this morning is the front seat of a Prius moving down the road at 81 mph while I try to collect my thoughts and form sentences. I enjoy it though and know I will be back at my solid desk wrapped in the quiet of early morning soon. This is the last day on the road. I am glad to be up to the challenge.

Today's stanza of The Twelve Days of Christmas is as follows:

On the third day of Christmas,
My true love gave to me
Three French hens

I watched and waited for what would come to me, and it is the Gift of the Magi: gold, frankincense, and myrrh. We are informed in the Gospel of Matthew that, led by a new star in the heavens, a group of distinguished foreigners visited Jesus after his birth. When a new star appeared in those ancient skies, it was a very big deal, Henry. It signified something new and important happening. These learned men began a journey to discover its message.

And so the story goes. I am sure that in your time, Henry, you knew this tale. I see you out in the winter field at night gazing at the stars and wondering about their portent, even then, in the mid-1800's. We have now let that wonder dull, much to our disadvantage.

The gifts the magi bore the Child King were three:

Gold, to signify kingship. They had no other system with which to honor him, so, the title of King had to suffice. We know the story, so we know the kingdom was not of this world and we know too that Jesus did not want to be king. He, the Brother, was a Way-Shower of great Love and Mercy. That was his Kingdom, a world of love for and between all.

Next was Frankincense, the gift of holiness and righteousness, a mediator between God and Man, a fitting most gift.

And last is Myrrh, the burial ointment foretelling of the most important death to come, of life for all Mankind.

These Gifts are given to us as well.

In the story it is made clear that all that was required of Jesus is required of us. We are the Way Showers of love and mercy as we walk the Earth today. There is no one else to do it but us.

We are the mediators between God and man. In the quiet of our hearts, if we can be still, we hear the Voice of love, always singing. It is an inside job. We leave the Earth for the realm of souls bringing our lives in our hands. May we be happy with our living.

Unwrap the gifts, be glad, and leave no one behind.

On the third day of Christmas,
My true love gave to me
Gifts of the Magi, three

Until tomorrow, for the Fourth Day of Christmas,
Cynthia

Be true to your work, your word, and your friend.

-Henry David Thoreau

December 29, 2015 - The Twelve Days Of Christmas, Day Four: Four Things You Can't Recover

Henry, the Four Calling Birds of today's verse have, in my game of words, become the Four Regrets. I'll wager there is no one who has been or is alive that cannot recognize their own behavior in each of the four categories below. I know I can.

The Thrown Stone, be it an actual stone (in one case a stone that almost caused serious injury) or a plate or a bigger and the most dangerous missile, words meant to hurt. As children, we discover sympathy through this act, whether it is directed at squirrels and birds, or playmates and beyond.

The Word After It Is Said, the greatest tragedy. In the hands of rage and fear, we have all said things that bring us shame when we remember them, things that break hearts and lives, changing relations with loved ones forever. I like to think and hope that years bring a tempered response to this act. Gossip is the lead actor in this play; words said that destroy others in the eyes of the world and poison the speaker as well. Ouch!

The Occasion After It Is Missed, comes in all sizes and varieties. It could be as simple as a student who ignores homework for a class, or, as complex as a decision in world politics that sends events spinning in disastrous directions: global warming, the activities of war, care for those who are less fortunate. I know of a young man who missed a promised visit with a grandparent for no reason at all only to have that grandparent pass on the next day. There is regret there!

The Time After It Is Gone speaks for itself. What was it you said, Henry?

As if you could kill time without injuring eternity.

-Henry David Thoreau

Time is the gift of each day to be reviewed and cherished at the close of each day, the close of the year, the close of the decade, and the close of life.

Cynthia

December 30, 2015 - The Twelve Days Of Christmas, Day Five: Five Golden Rings

Dear Friend,

This morning's search for an image to replace the five golden rings of the fifth stanza...

> *On the fifth day of Christmas*
> *My true love gave to me*
> *Five golden rings*

Was a bit easier. Who can miss the great Golden Ring of the Sun as it rises over the landscape?

Sunrise was sacred to you, Henry. You write of it so often being often the first person in Concord to see it—although farm communities in your landscape had their early risers. The gifts of Sunrise were strewn at your feet.

The morning, which is the most memorable season of the day, is the awakening hour. Then there is least somnolence in us; and for an hour, at least, some part of us awakes which slumbers all the rest of the day and night... All memorable events, I should say, transpire in morning time and in a morning atmosphere.

-Henry David Thoreau

So, on this Fifth Day of Christmas, as we approach the great opportunity of the Epiphany, I leave you with the golden circle of sun rising expectantly into each soul's sky each day.

> *On the fifth day of Christmas*
> *My true love gave to me*

Five golden suns

Good day to you Sir…
Cynthia

December 31, 2015 - The Twelve Days Of Christmas, Day Six: Six Crows a Cackling, The Turn of the Year, 2016

Dear Henry,

We have arrived at the border between a brand spanking new year and the last day of a lived one. It's an imaginary faultline as time really doesn't exist. We on Earth use time like a marker in a book, keeping the stories from running all together and becoming completely unmanageable.

I see this as a chance to transform one's experience, a place from which one looks back on the last 365 days, on the energy which we turn towards the present, at the point of all power as it flows toward the future (which really is the present as it arrives), and imagine change in intentions. The energy of the New Year is fizzing and open, malleable and portentous. My lists for this transformative step forward are shopping lists, but what is listed is usually not material. (I know what you thought of material stuff, Henry.) Although there was a year I intended on a house and found it was being built not long after, this intending is painting, using energy, color, and emotion as your medium; seeing and reaching into your very sentient future.

You said it all when you said,

If one advances confidently in the direction of his dreams, and endeavors to live the life which he has imagined, he will meet with a success unexpected in common hours.

-Henry David Thoreau

Intentions fly on the wings of subtle energies. You must have them before they can work. I fully INTEND to make a juicy list for this coming year, and I watch as my intentions rise into the present. I welcome the *"success unexpected in common hours."*

Now, about the Six Geese a Laying that have become Crows in my version of the 12 Days.

Crows are very intelligent birds. I don't really know about geese. I know they are mighty navigators and that they stick together, but I tend to favor crows over geese.

There is evidence that Crows actually identify and follow certain people. It is certainly the case with me. When I was writing my memoir, Never Count Crow: Love And Loss In Kennebunk, Maine, they were my bedfellows practically, cawing loudly outside my window to get up and write. They fit better into my life's theme than the goose, who—whether flying above or floating on unruffled streams—doesn't seem to have the passion of the crow.

On the sixth day of Christmas
My true love gave to me
Six geese a laying

Becomes

On the sixth day of Christmas
My true love gave to me
Six crows a cackling

In an old crow chant I once heard, Henry, crows are seen as prophets:

One crow, sorrow, two crows, joy, three crows, a letter, four crows, a boy, five crows, silver, six crows, gold, seven crows, a story that should never be told.

That means our Six Crows of today mean gold. I wish us all that. But don't ever Count Crow... As if you could.

Happy New Year, wherever you are Henry.

Cynthia

Winter 2016 - January

January strides brazenly in, wearing her deep blue velvet gown. She fills the night sky as she whirls within ferocious winds wearing diamonds that glitter to form her eyes and throat. Her laugh is hard and shrill; her silence fills all of space. Her days dazzle as the cold sunlight reflects on the ice of her touch everywhere. Her breath freezes ponds, forms icicles, paints frost scrolls on windows. Little birds hide in thickets from her, she frightens them.

January 1, 2016 - The Twelve Days Of Christmas, Day Seven: Happy New Year

But when I have only a rustling oak leaf, or the faint metallic cheep of a tree sparrow for variety in my winter walk, my life becomes continent and sweet as the kernel of a nut.

-Henry David Thoreau, Journal

On the seventh day of Christmas
My true love gave to me
Seven swans a swimming

Dear Henry,

I would have this first day of the new year start slow, the seconds, minutes, hours collecting like snow falling, soft, quiet. The raucous party shouts and fireworks that usher in this untraveled year do it no justice, and as they quiet and fade we are left with a new day.

Come on a winter walk with me this morning. We will see the swans of the Seventh Day of Christmas and receive the gifts of a New Year. It is just your way to begin 2016, slowly, deliberately.

I feel you with me as we begin to step out in this new land together.

January 2, 2016 - The Twelve Days Of Christmas, Day Eight, Day Nine: My Error Revealed

On the ninth day of Christmas
My true love gave to me
Nine ladies dancing

Dear Henry,

I was startled yesterday when someone who knew better than I announced that yesterday, January 1st, was the Eighth Day of Christmas, not the Seventh as I had supposed. I was very disappointed in myself, honestly, to think that I had been out of step with the twelve-day sequence. What I had not done was counted Christmas Day; Christmas Day is day one, the day of the Partridge in The Pear Tree—or, in our case, the Day of Gaia's kiss.

That means we have blown right by Eight Maids a Milking, giving them very short shrift.

Now, for the Nine Ladies Dancing, we will stay in character and watch a Youtube video in which nine ladies dance. They are the Red Thistle Dancers of the San Francisco Bay area. They perform Scottish Country dancing and—if we watch all of the 1 minute, 42 second selection—we can see the next cast of characters arriving, Ten Lords A Leaping.

Their dance is simple and charming, one from another age. I enjoy its grace and movement.

All of this marking of the twelve days of Christmas is in preparation for the great, momentous feast of the Epiphany, which will arrive on January sixth. Only four days away. Then, we can get back to the more personal wanderings of our reflections.

It seems a long process, living through these twelve days of Christmas. The time feels heavy, we have almost had enough.

The Epiphany will cheer us all up.

Til tomorrow,
Cynthia

January 3, 2016 - The Twelve Days Of Christmas, Day Ten: Ten Cows a Jumping for Joy

Dear Henry,

This is the Tenth Day of Christmas, ten lords a leaping, but I couldn't think of much to say about that. I had to go back to the silence of the walk with you on New England's winter fields, to hear your thoughts through your Journal all the way to me, today, in 2016. I miss those walks.

I did find a rare and inspiring video; one I wanted very much to post along with this letter. It is of an actual group of leaping lads and ladies vis a vis a herd of cows that, because of age and infirmity, had been slated for slaughter until a kind man bought them and released them into a pasture after years of being penned.

Henry... Those cows go into that pasture kicking up their heels, gamboling like a group of calves, their joy at being free on view and so contagious. And, Henry, let's not miss the import of this... They KNEW they had been given a day of freedom and they loved it so much.

Take the leap, it is a joyful act.

Cynthia

January 4, 2016 - The Twelve Days Of Christmas, Day Eleven: The End Is In Sight

Dear Henry,

When I hear music, I fear no danger. I am invulnerable. I see no foe. I am related to the earliest times, and to the latest.

-Henry David Thoreau

I am stretching the use of these Twelve Days of Christmas to the maximum. Struggling to find representations of them in this day, this age, that are of interest to you where you are. Tomorrow, we arrive at the station of Day Twelve, twelve drummers drumming, and all will be set for the Epiphany, Alleluia!

After this exercise, I will stand in the holy instant of each moment, one by holy one, and record them. If we are open to seeing what these moments hold, we are never bored. That is what I hear in your excitement within each seemingly insignificant discovery. Everything is of interest to you. Take for instance:

Am pleased again to see the cobweb drapery of the mill. Each fine line hanging in festoons from the timbers overhead and on the sides...

-Henry David Thoreau, October 19, 1858

And

The pincushion galls on young white oaks are now among the most beautiful objects in the woods. coarse wooly white to appearance, spotted with bright red or crimson on the exposed side.

-Henry David Thoreau, June 1, 1853

My count of Days of Christmas is almost complete; after this, we will resume our sauntering through the remaining months until July.

Today, we will confine our thoughts to the performance of eleven pipers piping in a performance in a Scottish cathedral. Not difficult these days to see on YouTube.

For today, enough.

Cynthia

January 5, 2016 - The Twelve Days Of Christmas, Day Twelve: The Lonely Drummer

Dear Henry,

My friend, please let me express my thanks for staying patiently during these long, twelve reflections on the song of the Twelve Days of Christmas. Once I set a task, I find it hard to give it up, and so, I have not. We persevered and have come through.

If a man does not keep pace with his companions, perhaps it is because he hears a different drummer. Let him step to the music which he hears, however measured or far away.

-Henry David Thoreau

In representing the Twelve Drummers, it occurred to me that you, Henry, you are that drummer! Our life and words have affected and lifted the education, culture, and literature of all time since your years on this earth. And you go on doing so. In my research each day, I find you everywhere! Thousands of pages of your drumbeats resound on earth. There are discussions upon discussions about what you meant, about the value of your affect; there are even arguments about who did your laundry and cooked your food. You are the icon of transformation, standing tall for one's original self, uncorrupted by social pressure or the ravage of meaningless wealth, and most importantly, standing against the numbness of separation from Nature. We bask in the clarity of your life, spurred on to simplifying our own. It's what you mean now.

You and your enlightened Essays, Journals, and Walden itself are the parade route to march surely on. Your words have the power of thousands of drummers drumming, growing still all these years later. The message is of self-awareness, compassion, clarity, and encouragement.

Tomorrow, Epiphany at last.

Cynthia

January 6, 2016 - Epiphany Station; All Aboard

Dear Henry,

The train has pulled into the station. We have arrived at the Feast of The Epiphany, the finale of the Christmas season, the great festival in commemoration of the coming of the Magi and the manifestation of the Babe to the Gentiles. There will be religious celebrations today, worldwide, marking and venerating a rising of Christ-light into the darkness of the world.

The experience of this Light, then and now, has become the term for a whole experience.; an epiphany.

noun: Epiphany; noun: epiphany; plural noun: epiphanies

1. A sudden realization or Eureka moment
2. The manifestation of Christ before the Magi
3. A festival on January 6th

Your writing is full of epiphanies of many sizes and magnitudes.

Your wholehearted and intuitive grasp of what was real, true, and holy, is what we honor in you still, and follow like the light it is. Your experience of life is ours for the reading and holding.

Epiphanies happen! They are the right of each person who lives. Who has not stood in amazement when they suddenly saw through the gauzy fabric of events to what was waiting just behind for their good? Some insight that we may have made much or little of was given us. Epiphany deepens when we allow it to touch us in the silent interior of being, to change us into the next lightest version of ourselves: always ascending.

You think that I am impoverishing myself withdrawing from men, but in my solitude, I have woven for myself a silken web or chrysalis.

-Henry David Thoreau

The chrysalis of transformation is solitude, no thought of loneliness, the eye of creation. It is ours with no price but that of attention, intention, and breath.

Tomorrow is queuing up over some hill, unseen. Never mind, get onboard for today.

Cynthia

January 7, 2016 - Venus And Saturn

Dear Henry,

I am up early today and must be out before sunrise. All is dark as I drive away from home on an errand. Foggy roads, humidity gathering on the windshield, temperatures in the low 60s. I am certainly not in the Northeast. The temperature in Maine (and I suspect Concord) is 16 degrees, humidity 61%, as compared to the 95% humidity here.

Today, up in the eastern predawn sky, on this January 7th, the waning crescent moon is visible close to the planets Venus and Saturn the configuration foretelling some prophecy for Earth if it could be read. Venus and Saturn will be closest to earth on the morning of January 9th, their closest conjunction since August 26, 2006 (and the closest of any two planets since March 22, 2013). All of this is going on above us on these, the darkest days of the year.

I found and took an opportunity to go for a predawn walk with you. Keeping to your words, we close the door behind us…

The recent tracks of the fox or otter, in the yard, remind us that each hour of the night is crowded with events, and the primeval nature is still working and making tracks in the snow. Opening the gate, we tread briskly along the lone country road, crunching the dry and crisped snow under our feet, or aroused by the sharp, clear creak of the wood-shed, just starting for the distant market, from the early farmer's door, where it has lain the summer long, dreaming amid the chips and stubble; while far through the drifts and powdered windows we see the farmer's early candle, like a paled star, emitting a lonely beam, as if some severe virtue were at its matins there. And one by one the smokes begin to ascend from the chimneys amid the trees and snows.

-Henry David Thoreau, The Dial

My Friend, you recorded the morning in words that allow me to walk beside you now, here. I see you wrapped in a hat, scarf, coat, boots, ankle deep in the white cold. You never waste a minute.

We don't have the luxury of your simplicity. Car lights pierce the fabric of our dark nights, neon signs glow—things you cannot know about interfere with solitude.

But that is not an excuse for us.

These are jewels strewn in our path.

Cynthia

January 8, 2016 - The Pond In Winter

Dear Henry,

So much living went on around that small pond of yours. The busy lives of the animal kingdom provided you with entertainment for hours. Travel on the Walden Road, the puffing train rumbling within view of your small cabin, was enjoyment.

Also fishing in both summer and winter, ice fishing on the frozen lake; a sort of farming for food.

After a still winter night, I awoke with the impression that some question had been put to me, which I had been endeavoring in vain to answer in my sleep, a what—how—when—where? But, there was dawning Nature, in whom all creatures live, looking in at my broad windows, with serene and satisfied face, and no question on her lips.

-Henry David Thoreau, Walden

I enjoy your version of the humble pickerel of Walden Pond.

They are not green like the pines, nor grey like the stones, nor blue like the sky, but they have to my eyes, if possible, yet rarer colors, like flowers and precious stones, as if they were the pearls, the animalized nuclei or crystals of the Walden water. They, of course are Walden all over and all through, are themselves small Waldens in the animal kingdom, Waldenses.

-Henry David Thoreau, Walden, The Pond In Winter

How do you make a jewel out of what others would conceive of as a homely, unimpressive creatures of Nature, Henry? And, how important it has been to us here in the future that you have.

I am encouraged to go out today and find some little common thing and to discover its miraculous nature.

I won't have to look far. We have lizards running about down here in Florida; each one a marvel of perfect design.

As I woke for my morning letter to you, a dark, puffing monster of a train began its whistling at each crossing as it went down A1A, brandishing warning as it zoomed through the little town in which I reside. I felt connected with you as you listened to the trains passing through the woods so near to where you were. Trains trail thoughts of somewhere else behind them like smoke, making one more aware of where they are.

Nature looks in my window as well, though she doesn't have the room to stretch out here as she did in Walden. I want to stay with this chapter on The Pond in Winter. There is so much love for where you were within it. More tomorrow.

We are connected, Henry.

Cynthia

January 9, 2016 - Waveless Serenity

Dear Henry,

I envy you this morning. Right here from the comfort of a modern home in the 21st Century, I envy you. The tasks of your living brought you into close connection with a realm that offered you purpose. I suppose that is why we in this timewave love to go camping. To have to go out onto a frozen lake to find the water of life, well, even as a metaphor, it will work for you.

Then to my morning work. First, I take an axe and pail and go in search of water if that be not a dream. After a cold and snowy night, it needed a divining-rod to find it. Every winter the liquid, trembling surface of the pond, also sensitive to every breath, and reflected every light and shadow, becomes solid to the depth of a foot or a foot and a half, so that it will support the heaviest teams, and perchance the snow covers it to an equal depth, and it is not to be distinguished from any level field. Like the marmots in the surrounding hills, it closes its eyelids and becomes dormant for three months or more. Standing on the snow-covered plain, as if in a pasture amid the hills, I cut my way first through a foot of snow, and then a foot of ice, and open a window under my feet, where, kneeling to drink, I look down into the quiet parlor of the fishes, pervaded by a softened light as through a window of ground glass, with its bright sanded floor the same as in summer; there a perennial waveless serenity reigns as in the amber twilight sky, corresponding to the cool and even temperament of the inhabitants. Heaven is under our feet as well as over our heads.

-Henry David Thoreau, Walden, The Pond in Winter

As you dedicate yourself to this task, the woods creatures are on you, buoying your spirit out to the clearing of the lake where an early sun offers you small warmth but great light. It is quiet. A net of bird calls, perhaps the sharp squawk of the Blue Jay or the sonar sounds of a hawk wheeling takes your notice. Their calls sift down through cold air like snow between the trees and out you as you strike ice for a perceived depth before cutting. You hear these sounds as companions. When you have arrived at the place as told to you by some third sense, the conversation is complete.

This moment with you would turn any day from despair to delight. Heaven is indeed under our feet as well as over our heads, and as well as in our perception.

May we use this day aright,
Cynthia

January 10, 2016 - Wood Heat At Walden

Dear Henry,

As for what you did during those long, quiet days when you were installed at Walden Pond—the two full years when you came and went out of that small door into your yard of pond and woods—you were seemingly quite busy hauling found wood out of the woods, skating it across the frozen pond in winter, digging out roots of fallen pitch pine trees, splitting bean stalks that had grown food just a season before. And all this done with regard for the growing forest, cutting nothing that was standing strong. The effort of this vital part of your survival paid back in manifold ways. Not only did it provide you with heat in the fetching and burning, but it provided a platform for work and meditation from which you observed the theater of Nature deeply and from very close…

I withdrew yet farther into my shell and endeavored to keep a bright fire both within my house and within my breast. My employment out of doors now was to collect the dead wood in the forest, bringing it in my hands or on my shoulders, or sometimes trailing a dead pine tree under each arm to my shed. An old forest fence which had seen its best days was a great haul for me. I sacrificed it to Vulcan, for it was past serving the god Terminus. How much more interesting an event is that man's supper who has just been forth in the snow to hunt, nay, you might say, steal the fuel to cook it with! His bread and meat are sweet.

-Henry David Thoreau, Walden

Anyone who has the experience of real cold will marvel at how trustingly you faced that challenge. I sometimes left a good fire when I went to take a walk in a winter afternoon; and when I returned, three or four hours afterward, it would still be alive and glowing. My house was not empty though I was gone.

-Henry David Thoreau, Walden

And so, out you went for a three-hour walk in winter's woods, leaving a fire burning on the hearth and never locking a door? How that makes me chuckle here in these days of immediate heat without any of the warmth, and with the fear we have grown since your days.

In the second year at Walden, the wood stove you installed distanced you from the fire itself, denied you the hours of dreaming by its side, seeing "the face in the flames." This was progress? We hardly ever see fire now.

The sun is just rising here; there is no need for fire in Florida. The grace and hypnotic powers are still appreciated, but we are far from that intimate living you tell us of in your kind words. I am thankful to be invited to watch with you through the window of Walden, as the great storms sing and dance around your bright hearth and you reach for another log to feed the flames.

Cynthia

January 11, 2016 - The Great Snows

Dear Henry,

It is January 11 of this new year already. Up in Massachusetts (I am still south from there, in Florida), there is NO SNOW. We, those of us on the planet at this time, are living through an anomaly—one caused by distressingly careless shepherding of the fruits of Earth—but an anomaly all the same.

I weathered some merry snowstorms, and spent some cheerful winter evenings by my fireside, while the snow whirled wildly without, and even the hooting of the owl was hushed. For many weeks I met no one in my walks but those who came occasionally to cut wood and sled it to the village. The elements, however, abetted me in making a path through the deepest snow in the woods, for when I had once gone through the wind blew the oak leaves into my tracks, where they lodged, and by absorbing the rays of the sun melted the snow, and so not only made a bed for my feet, but in the night their dark line was my guide... As I walked over the long causeway made for the railroad through the meadows, I encountered many a blustering and nipping wind, for nowhere has it freer play; and when the frost had smitten me on one cheek, heathen as I was, I turned to it the other also.

-Henry David Thoreau, Walden

Reading of your walks through the shifting drifts of great snow, spending weeks by yourself with little confirmation of the existence of others than the very occasional forager for wood brought me to memories of my own youth in Western Maine. We had snow so deep and long in winter that we played for months in igloos that we made in front of our houses.

You talk of snow in 1717 so great in depth as to cover a house completely, it being found only by its chimney hole by an 'Indian' passing by.

This is all about to change, however, as the wind patterns are shifting as we speak, spilling the—until now—contained cold down across the country including southern states. Cold and snow are on their way. The experience of Winter will be installed.

What has changed irrevocably though is access to the weeks of quiet gifted your intention and the Great Snows. Harder to come by in this age, but not impossible. You keep reminding us of where the center may be found, even in a blinding snowstorm.

From Florida,
Cynthia

January 12, 2016 - Earthing

Dear Friend,

At the outset of Walden, you instruct your readers that the journey of your book is not to be one of great worldly experience. Instead, we will walk the "narrowness" of your path with you, but we will go deep. It is not Concord and its environs we see; it is Nature, the whole of which is in each part, everywhere.

Every morning was a cheerful invitation to make my life of equal simplicity, and I may say innocence, with Nature herself.

-Henry David Thoreau, Walden

I am reading a book that travels brand new territory, although much of it sounds familiar. The book: Health Revelations From Heaven And Earth. What I am keen on sharing with you, though, is one of the Revelations called Grounding or Earthing. Its message is seemingly simple, but one that very few Earth travelers know. It is the discovery that this Earth, the one we walk upon in ordinary contact, is a conduit for a natural, gentle negative charge that silently feeds the human body, and is necessary to health.

As our lives were distanced from the Earth by the barricades of homes, cities, technological whirlpools, the disconnect from the Earth has made us more vulnerable to stress, illness, depression, and on and on. Modern lifestyle has disconnected us from this primordial charge.

And what is this information doing here in a letter to you, you ask? When I read the simple prescriptions that recommend standing on the Earth unshod and in close contact with it for at least five minutes a day or walking in natural settings and renewing the close touch with Nature we were meant to have and to honor, Walden and your experiences of being with these silent charges from the Earth came zooming into mind.

Henry, your work is a vital discovery of what, today, is being rediscovered. Of course, there are those who say it is all bogus... As there were when you moved into the clear-sighted realm of seeing Nature as the Prime Necessary—but who listens to them? You didn't. You were the Scientist in the act of discovering the vital effects of a walk in the woods, barefoot if possible.

Henry, you knew it all along.

Cynthia

January 13, 2016 - The Path To Walden

I am in awe of your innocence and bravery! To live your life outside of the prescription of the rigid rules of your time on Earth, to forge on resolutely, deliberately, swimming in the water of others' disapproval, jumping the waves as it were. That was and is courage in action then and continues being instructive and encouraging still.

This small lake was of most value as a neighbor in the intervals of a gentle rainstorm in August, when, both air and water being perfectly still, but the sky overcast, mid-afternoon had all the serenity of evening, and the wood thrush sang around, and was heard from shore to shore. A lake like this is never smoother than at such a time; and the clear portion of the air above it being shallow and darkened by clouds, the water, full of light and reflections, becomes a lower heaven itself so much the more important.

-Henry David Thoreau, Walden

No one else could have dignified this path as you did, no one could carve this way of living for the generations lost in the prescriptive lives they inherited. And still, Henry, generations read your words, putting the ideas into practice: work with and for integrity within a life not described or inscribed by prescription, but by the individual voice from within, by closeness with the natural world, its space and silence for reflection gifts. These ideas are as light going forward.

Walden—the deep, freshwater pond in Massachusetts and its once *"dark surrounding woods"* sparkling within—are now a portal, as sacred as the Ganges, by a return to innocence and observation for the student of any age who wishes to know and is ready to dispossess themselves of tribe membership, of comfort, of arrogance to walk the road to Walden.

Since my time with you, Henry, I do things differently, and some things I no longer do at all! If the cost of something is time wasted or self-respect lost, I leave it alone. When someone tells me how I should feel or act, I walk the other way. I wish to be original, to reach within myself for the original path that is before me in the moment.

And, still, we come to your door to knock and wait for you to ask us into your lofty cabin of ideas, the fire of passion burning merrily on the hearth. We bring our innocence for the cost of the lesson given. The road to Walden is well trodden and will always be—at least if Earth is under foot.

Outside, all Nature creeps up with perfect safety to peer into your windows, curious about this new type of human who sees and respects all living things, regards them with love and intelligence.

I wonder so, what you were thinking when you were building your cabin in the woods? Did you have any idea what a monumental structure you were putting up?

With admiration,
Cynthia

January 15, 2016 - The Huckleberry Baron

Dear Henry.

It is pouring rain in Florida; great clouds dance above our heads playing a push/pull game, soaking up moisture from the warm Atlantic and watering this very green state profoundly, keeping everyone indoors.

Self-awareness is a gift, one that has us standing outside of the press of details and events in our lives from which we view ourselves, not with judgement, but with clarity of where we are so far in this experience of life, and where our present path will lead.

As you expressed it:

By a conscious effort of the mind, we can stand aloof from actions and their consequences; and all things, good and bad, go by us like a torrent. We are not wholly involved in Nature. I may be either the driftwood in the stream, or Indra in the sky looking down on it... I only know myself as a human entity; the scene, so to speak, of thoughts and affections; and am sensible of a certain doubleness by which I can stand as remote from myself as from another. However intense my experience, I am conscious of the presence and criticism of a part of me, which, as it were, is not a part of me, but spectator, sharing no experience, but taking note of it, and that is no more I than it is you...This doubleness may easily make us poor neighbors and friends sometimes.

-Henry David Thoreau, Walden

The odd young slacker of a boy that you were, albeit brilliant in parsing meaning beneath the surface of the Puritan village of Concord, left you center in the ring of criticism and denial. How fortunate for us that you had already established your home within yourself, and the slings and arrows of Society could not reach you.

We all can take a lesson here: when the arrows fly around us, there is ever present refuge.

Cynthia

January 16, 2016 - Chains

Dear Henry,

We are in the fog this morning; The sun has risen and lit the whole gauzy atmosphere in pink to orange tones. But every morning has its unique presentation. This one demands nothing of us but to wait for the fog to clear.

I am starting on a search for how things, or people, get to be who, what they are. Where do things begin?

He who cuts down woods beyond a certain limit exterminates birds.

Henry David Thoreau

The quote above is from your Journal, and it captures my theme exactly. At what point do we go beyond growth and start pulling creation down—whether the material earth or human beings as a whole people?

Growing up in Rumford, Maine, I recall vividly being taken aback when being educated in the "way things were." One little example that still stands out today is the renaming of rainy weather as 'inclement.' I have spent a lot of time wondering about this obvious error. It was the canary in the coal mine signaling that something had gone very wrong somewhere. Rain, the most clement of all things, inclement?

(Sure, I know there can be too much, but try living without it.)

Then, there is the worth of human beings. If they are of a different color, class, or race than yourself, some feel they are not the same and may be marginalized, used, or even dispensed with without those responsible feeling a great loss. I have gotten into lots of trouble debating this.

Last night, a sequence of aerial photographs on television showed the gouged earth, miles of it, a wound exposed, because of the extraction of coal and oil for energy here on Earth. And what we saw was just the smallest picture of what happens every day. Seeing this great insult to Earth felt unbearable.

So, I return to reading Walden and your Journals, walking the woods quietly with you, looking from leaf to leaf as if they were the jewels that they are. *"A man is rich in proportion to the number of things he can afford to let alone,"* you say.

On my walk just behind you, my energy rises into the neighborhood of hope and, yes, love. I see one who did not 'buy' what was the accepted wisdom and went his own way and discovered a heaven, garnering respect, and thanks for it.

So, there is always hope. Some bell somewhere is ringing a warning. The Earth is awakening. Are we?

Cynthia

January 17, 2016 - "The Day Is Forever Unproved"

And then the rich warble of the blackbird may still occasionally at this season be heard. As I come over the hill, I hear the wood thrush singing his evening lay. This is the only bird whose note affects me like music, affects the flow and tenor of my thoughts, my fancy, my imagination. It is inspiring. It is a medicative draft to my soul. It is an elixir to my eyes and a fountain of youth to all my senses. It changes all hours into an eternal morning. It banishes all trivialness.

-Henry David Thoreau, Journal, June 22, 1853

Henry,

We really walk with you, hear, and see what you are hearing and seeing, through the written word? Are we affected by the same thrush singing to you, then as now? I think so.
You say more about that.

How can the infinite and eternal be contemporary with the finite and temporal? So there is something sweeter and more nutritious, than in the milk which the farmers drink. This thrush's song is a ranz des vaches to me. I long for wildness, a nature which I cannot put my foot through, woods where the wood thrush forever sings, where hours are early morning ones, and there is dew on the grass, and the day is forever unproved…

In Florida this morning, winds are stirring up the predawn dusk, gusts to 35 mph singing through screens, a wild ringing of chimes on porches and in trees, an alarm up and down the empty street. It is warm, 76 degrees, the excitement in the thrashing palms and flowering foliage makes light of the balmy promise of peaceful Caribbean scenes. The rain has just begun, and it will be a force, tropical, abundant, daunting. There is no thrush to sing in the meadow, but the grackles will soon roost here in droves, to the feeder, their sharp complaining talk loud around us, a blanket of sound. In my home, the light is lit, one of the few on the dark street. I am writing to another time, another place, without definition. It is the gift of this particular morning. I will post this moment, now.

From here and now,
Cynthia

The world globes itself in a drop of dew.

-Ralph Waldo Emerson

January 18, 2016 - "Jove Nods To Jove From Behind Each Of Us"

Dear Henry,

Yesterday morning, at Unity of Stuart in Hobe Sound, Florida, the service was launched with a quote from your colleague and friend, Ralph Waldo Emerson...

Place yourself in the middle of the stream of power and wisdom which animates all whom it floats, and you are without effort impelled to truth, to right and a perfect contentment.

-Ralph Waldo Emerson, Spiritual Laws

150 years ago, Mr. Emerson spoke so powerfully that it has been passed down to here and now in a chain of breath from near six generations before. Anyone who has stood in rushing water, clear and bubbling, made of rain or snowmelt from the heights of mountains, knows the freshness that passes from this powerful water into the body with no cost but awareness.

We are refreshed, wrapped in the mantle of the "unity of thought" with nature, and feel hope again. Within the experience:

They all become wiser than they were. It arches over them like a temple, this unity of thought, in which every heart beats with nobler sense of power and duty, and thinks and acts with unusual solemnity. All are conscious of attaining to a higher self-possession. It shines for all.

-Ralph Waldo Emerson, Spiritual Laws

Mr. Emerson also said that *"divine teaching is the incarnation of spirit in a form."* That makes yesterday a very exciting day. Stepping into that "stream of power and wisdom" was my choice to make. The opportunities to enter this temple are present every second. Eternity intersects each second of each life, offering new experiences with hope and purpose, and often, delight, no matter what perception clouded it with previously.

Henry, I see the effect of your friendship with Mr. Emerson working within each of you, clearing the path ahead each for each. We become part of this circle within the practice of what you discovered and spoke out to us.

From 1841 to 2016 within a few words, the gift is given.

Gratefully,
Cynthia

January 19, 2016 - Way Leads On To Way

Dear Friend,

You said somewhere in your Journal that each day's description is important enough to be recorded as it dawns and dusks. There are countless records of weather and conditions, going back in centuries, scribbled by farmers whose lives were measured by weather and its benign or punishing characteristics.

Today, on the East coast of Florida, as I write in my cabin just opposite the great eye of Lake Okeechobee, the temperature at dawn is 49 degrees Fahrenheit. Winds today will be 17 mph, humidity, 57 percent—which is surprisingly the same as the humidity in the northeast. There is 0 percent chance of rain, with clouds and sun intermixed. At the top of the temperature range today, it will be 61 degrees. Cold by Florida standards.

There you have it; January 19th, 2016. So, how to spend the Original energy of this day?

On January 4, 1852, at the age of 34, you penned this advice in your journal,

If thou art a writer, write as if thy time was short, for it is indeed short at the longest. Improve each occasion when thy soul is reached. Drain the cup of inspiration to its last dregs. Fear no intemperance in that, for the years will come when otherwise thou will regret opportunities unimproved. The spring will not last forever.

-Henry David Thoreau, Journal

Then, how to live this day in a new way, forsaking old pathways? How not to walk the direction of yesterday?

...how deep the ruts of tradition and conformity.

-Henry David Thoreau

That is the risk before each of us, to seize the day with optimism and excitement of the artist on the edge of intuitive revelation, the scientist, alive with understanding at last, the teacher, blessed by the transfer of understanding, the human being humbled by seeing themselves in others.

I left the woods for as good a reason as I went there. Perhaps it seemed to me that I had several more lives to live and could not spare anymore time for that one. It is remarkable how easily and insensibly we fall into a particular route and make a beaten track for ourselves.

-Henry David Thoreau, Walden

Each morning, I face the enormity of my pledge, to write to one such as yourself, to say something you might nod your head to and smile knowingly. Some days it's a breeze, literally, and some days it takes a great leap of faith. It is always worth all my effort. I take delight in the creation.
Ahead, daily!

Cynthia

January 20, 2016 - Silence Baying At The Moon

Dear Henry,

Starting today and for a month until February 20, we may step out our early doors to gaze on the planets, Mercury, Venus, Mars, Jupiter, Saturn, in alignment looking south. The crescent Moon will be joining the alignment later in the month.
The planets will appear in the sky one by one, starting Tuesday evening with Jupiter around 9:20 p.m. in New York. Mars will follow as we observe the giant appearing as a reddish dot at approximately 1:11 a.m. E.S.T. Wednesday. Saturn next at around 4 a.m., followed by Venus—the brightest orb—nearly an hour later. Mercury will be last, around 6:17 a.m., lingering until the sunrise comes, about 7:15 a.m. on Wednesday, making it too bright to see the planets.
This display is the first such in a decade and will be visible again in the late summer sky of August, looking north. The great fulcrums of the sky will not so move for many years after as we run about beneath their silent travel.
I loved the comment in your Journal of January 21, 1853, in which you say that because we have named these heavenly bodies, plotted their movements with mathematics, we feel satisfied that we know their function and meaning.

If they appear fixed, it is because that hitherto men have been thus necessitated to see them. I see not merely old but new testaments in the sky.

-Henry David Thoreau

Might we each step out in the morning while this heavenly alignment appears above us and let it affect our subtle selves—changing things like intuition, intention, inspiration, imagination. We are walking under stars in new configurations. Let them work on us, alter us, make us more a part of the cosmos.

But it is the stars as not known to science that I would know, the stars which the lonely traveler knows...I am not to be distracted by the names which they have imposed...As I leave the village, drawing nearer to the woods, I listen from time to time to hear the sounds of silence baying at the Moon... I hear the unspeakable.

-Henry David Thoreau, Journal, 1853

Opportunity is always abroad.

Cynthia

January 21, 2016 - Earth Time, Up In The Eastern Predawn Sky

Good morning, Cynthia,

"It is as hard to see oneself as to look backwards without turning around."

I have been poised to return your letter but have been very busy. It would be hard to explain about that given your grounding in Time; here, we are not locked into sequential anything but can do all things at once. Doesn't that give you a spin?

My words above, I have chosen carefully from the tomes I wrote on Earth. You are all so busy trying to assess who you really are, looking for confirmation in the reflections of yourselves on the mirrors of the many souls around you... Endlessly comparing, judging, and repressing what seems different from the prescribed norms before anyone can notice that you are unique! I would laugh at the contortions you go through if it were not such a waste of Life. I remember the pressures of your precious planet, but I remember too the freshness and opportunity born in each second, and it is of this I wish to write today.

If my presence on the Earth affected anything, it was the sacred nature of an Original soul. The dark thinking of my 'tribe' caused strong repugnance in the dictum to suppress my nature and personality for the sake of conforming to the old, worn patterns of Society, Government, and Religion. I made that quite clear, I think.

The chaos of your time, Cynthia, amplifies by the thousands the impressions and voices that demand and sell conformity as a product. Being unlike others within the tribe is still very risky. But much good is coming from enlightened speakers, writers, and film makers who lead audiences into fresh pastures of freedom and self-worth.

No one sees you but YOU. Your image, if not seen from the inside out, is distorted by fear and guilt. Do not give up your precious worth for the trinkets of being "the same." These baubles have no worth and no shelf life at all.

Hoping not to sound too lofty. Satisfaction and joy in your life and work is an inside job, the gifts of which once won are everlasting.

-Henry David Thoreau

January 22, 2016 - Traces Remain

Dear Henry,

I return thankfulness for your teachings from beyond in yesterday's post. Your optimism is intoxicating; we take things so seriously here we don't allow our improvement without great angst. We don't see or understand that each person's course is constantly being redirected by small events, small details, the whole journey coming into being through these small corrections. This is where Optimism makes the difference. Pessimism is as powerful a choice, but its gifts of fear and anxiety are such heavy burdens. *"Take care of the minutes and the hours will take care of themselves."* Someone said that.

In Walden, you told us that you had many visitors during your stay; lumbermen came as well as nosy housewives to peek into your closet, to compare your sheets. There may well have been a youth that took to your gentle teaching; you spent much of your early years as a teacher with your brother John. Your desk, Henry, the actual desk on which you wrote, is now in the Concord Museum, described as "painted pine, 1838, given as a gift to the Museum in 1886."

Though you are not physically present here on Earth, your teaching goes on. No longer confined to physical presence, you are everywhere at once, speaking to those who can hear you.

I love looking at that lovingly battered old green desk that sat on the hallowed floor of your cabin. This devotion calls forth a rattling gust of criticism from academics, but this noise soon dies out in comparison to the winds of change you unleashed from your square mile of earth.

It is 17 degrees Fahrenheit in Concord, Massachusetts now, with a mix of sun and clouds, winds of 10 mph. Tomorrow there will be snow showers on Walden Pond. If I were closer, I would go for a walk and look for you there.

Cynthia

January 23, 2016 - Come For A Walk, Henry

The sight of a marsh hawk in Concord meadows is worth more to me than the entry of the allies into Paris.... Only that traveling is good which reveals to me the value of home and enables me to enjoy it better. That man is the richest whose pleasures are the cheapest.

-Henry David, Journal

The snug bump of the door behind me releases everything I know. A strong slap of freshness from winds doubling as they blow across the marsh's level surface wakes me up. My footsteps crunch in fallen and frozen snow, counterpoint to a keening melody played through grasses that grew, green and graceful just a season ago. I begin a rhythm: breath, step, wind, breath, step, wind…this will take me around the checkerboard of the marsh.

There is no one here but me. To the east, a brightening edge of light shows beneath the lid of heavy gray clouds. Their grayness is reflected in patches of ice the wind has swept clear. In a sudden sharp awareness that this January morning gifts me, I see everything clearly. The composition of what is before me is perfect, a painting someone shows me; it affects me, changes my balance within, moves me to some feeling I can't quite identify. I let it all work in me as I walk along, puffs of my breath the only outward comment.

Walking steadily around the rim of the marsh, the velvety gray and dark green of the frozen New England woods waits for the signal of warmth, standing firm, backdrop to the dawn-lit stage of the marsh. The cold on the surface of my exposed skin meets the flush of heat from the furnace of my heart that is pumping gladly to allow me to be in this place. I find I am smiling at how easy being here is, how little the cost of such a rare experience.

Halfway around the perimeter of the marsh, my thoughts go back to the world behind the door that I closed half an hour before; they flee like startled birds when I hear the scree of a hawk fall on everything below like a greeting. I stop walking and root myself to look up and find the phantom bird. When I find it, it is nearly absorbed within the coloring of the woods. I am dizzy for a few minutes, turning round and round as I leave the Earth to fly with my companion. The rhythm of pumping wings matches my heartbeat and I feel the tether of connection pulling, one to the other. This hypnotic instant seems to last a while.

Taking up my walk, time—I can't say how much—goes by in this way. I begin a return to my starting place. The feelings of the morning deepen and lift in me on wings, led by joy of all that is around, all that walks with me, as me, to home.

For you, Henry
Cynthia

January 24, 2016 - January's Full Wolf Moon

Dear Henry,

Morning rises with the sun. It's 38 degrees here in Hobe Sound, cold by tropical standards. Even though there will be nothing but sun today, temperatures will only go into the upper 50s. Winds will be 11 mph and humidity 80%. Not the usual.

We are in the influence of a full moon. While I have this year of conversations with you, there will be twelve full moons. By my count, this one is full moon number seven, January's full moon.

Wolf Moons are traditionally associated with the howling of hungry wolves in the deep winter, but they are also sometimes called the Old Moon or the Snow Moon. Confusingly, the next full moon in February is also commonly called the Snow Moon.

Pretending that what is happening in the heavens above us does not concern us does not exempt us of the physical and energetic effects of the changing of the moon's pull of gravity or the influx of photons and energetic particles streaming in from the cosmos. Instead, it deadens us to feeling and receiving these great celestial gifts meant for us. Who has not been enraptured by a beautiful moonrise, or a star field, and gone back to their house with new faith and rekindled hope in the stardust of which we are all made? That is poverty indeed.

Last evening, some friends came for dinner here to our home in Florida. All the while we were at the table, the January Full Wolf Moon rose in the window over the shoulder of one of the guests. I mentioned the fact repeatedly seated as I was directly across from this person and saw the orb rising out of the Atlantic Ocean. The conversation at the table was usual, but the moonrise was extraordinary, and though we had every reason to jump into a vehicle and race to the beach for the show—or even to stand in the street to observe it in the sky—we did nothing. So, we got nothing.

Henry, you would have overturned the table to be in that light. But you would never have been at that table, being as reticent as you were for social situations.

Once, long ago now, I went out for a walk simply to be in the moonlight. I have never forgotten it. The moon will rise tonight and tonight I will walk in it, bathe in its beauty. The price is reasonable, and the benefits are eternal.

The great story of the night is the moon's adventure with the clouds.

-Henry David Thoreau, Journal

Cynthia

January 26, 2016 - Winslow Homer's Journal

Dear Henry,

Writing to you is never settled or done. As one letter is posted, thoughts go to the next day. I watch carefully for situations or ideas that will have interest within them, have light to them. When I commit myself to investigate and share a topic, I find it opening itself to me, connections becoming visible; then I rise and I write. Sometimes the connective tissue of the idea feels flimsy, difficult to work, like lace; sometimes it is strong stuff, leaving me no doubt that it's worthy of illustration. In any case, I persevere.

When you paint, try to put down exactly what you see. Whatever else you have to offer will come out anyway.

-Winslow Homer

This morning, my text concerns Winslow Homer, a man who knew my drift exactly. Born in Boston, Massachusetts, on February 24th, 1836, Winslow Homer moved in later years to Prouts Neck, Maine, into a carriage house perched 75 feet from the wild Maine ocean. Henry, I have stood in his studio there in Scarborough, Maine, have seen the used, crumbled tubes of paint and the spots of color on the floor, old brushes, discarded canvases that were his tools. The dust tracked from his walks out to watch some great storm, or a sparkling clear Maine day under my feet. When I was there, his easel was still set up in the best light of the room. It was a holy place, so full of the light of his creation. I was there with a group of middle-school children on a field trip. How lucky were they to be in this little shrine of creativity?

Homer wanted to get at the meaning of things, the great Sea, the common people. A dawning sky was not to be looked at and forgotten, it was to be used as substance to parse and to create meaning. His subjects, in the last quarter of his life (he died in 1910), were the strong seagoing men and women of New England, peasants he extolled. He saw their natural energy and courage as subjects for his paintings. His greatest inquiry was into the endless images of the Atlantic from the ever-changing seascape from his windows. Homer recognized in them the same love that had you walking the landscape of Concord.

Creating his work in the very years you were composing Walden nearby, Homer paid attention to what was in and around him. His understanding of the sacredness of nature left images that deepen our appreciation in life, especially for those of us who know rugged, light-filled Maine intimately.

Artists both, you conned meaning from the people, the landscape or seascape you viewed. I wonder if you knew of his work. His years in New England were lived after your transition, Henry, but you had much in common. I will leave you with one of his more famous quotations.

What they call talent is nothing but the capacity for doing continuous work in the right way.

-Winslow Homer

Until tomorrow,
Cynthia

January 27, 2016 - Lessons Of A Starling Murmuration

Dear Henry,

It is early here on the wheel of this day, just past 6 AM. It is raining; the streets shine under streetlights. Everything looks so different in these early hours, not at all like the day-lit street.

I found the words for this morning's letter arriving whether I was ready or not. I heard them in my mind, and music as well, a melody I recognize but cannot name. All of this in preparation for today's most special subject: Starling Murmuration, the wild spectacle of a flock of starlings that forms an acrobatic whole, before roosting, swooping, changing directions and then, again and again, flashing across the sky.

As one starling changes direction or speed, each of the other birds responds and does so simultaneously, in synchronous rhythm regardless of the size of the flock. In essence, information moves across the flock as quickly and imperceptibly as the theory of quantum entanglement, exhibiting what is called a "scale-free correlation."

Here's the magic thing, Henry. At the point where the whole is reacting as one, the group cannot be divided into sub parts, the perception range of each of the birds is as large as the entire group and information is transferred immediately making the group respond as one. The whole has become greater than the sum of its parts. As the researchers admit, *"How starlings achieve such a strong correlation remains a mystery to us."*

In a recent talk on this subject, the speaker, John Mundy posited to his audience that we, as a species, have within us the possibility of rising to the promise of our Oneness and treating each one as we wish to be treated. If we could achieve this Oneness, we might do so much more with our lives.

There is no single bird in the great murmuration in the sky, no one bird bearing the burden of striving to be more than the next. They are all one in this experience. His point is well and beautifully exhibited in the holy spectacle of starlings in the

153

"scale free correlation" of joy that rolls above us like a banner being waved. Pay attention!

I know you must have seen this miracle yourself, Henry. It is not a new thing. Still raining, a very clement day.

Cynthia

January 29, 2016 - The Journals

Henry,

It was difficult to pull myself from sleep this morning. The weather has been gray for days now and extremely wet, very clement indeed. There have been no jaunts under clear skies, no sun, no walks, and I am left drowsy. We will have sun today, winds of 16 mph, and cool temperatures. Just now the rising sun has ignited a cloud bank like fire, peach and mauve layer up the dome of morning promising color in this day's aspect. I will be out soon.

Your Journal held over two million words written over twenty-five years, a double entry variety in which you made notes tracking the details and measurements of the day and its events as they progressed, only to—after some time—reflect in the journal entry. I see you working by the flame of a gas lamp, pencil sharpened, the rest of the room in shadows, only your rugged face bent over paper waiting to receive the impressions of your keen observations. Often, you inserted small, simple drawings that gave shape and charm to your thoughts.

I would fain make two reports in my Journal, first the incidents and observations of to-day; and by to-morrow I review the same and record what was omitted before, which will often be the most significant and poetic part. I do not know at first what it is that charms me. The men and things of to-day are wont to lie fairer and truer in tomorrow's memory.

-Henry David Thoreau, Journal, 1857

Henry, you were joyfully bent on uncovering what lay beneath the dream of the day in which you lived with no dissatisfaction in your life or circumstance. As you wrote to Emerson:

From all points of the compass, from earth beneath and the heavens above, have come these inspirations and been entered duly in the order of their arrival in the journal.

My journal is that of me which would else spill over and run to waste.

-Henry David Thoreau

Until tomorrow when I will walk my streets, journal in hand.

Cynthia

January 31, 2016 - The Power Of Now

Dear Henry,

There was never any more inception than there is now,
Nor any more youth or age than there is now;
And will never be any more perfection than there is now,
Nor any more heaven or hell than there is now.

-Walt Whitman

How amazed you must have been when you first read Leaves of Grass, the self-published book of poetry (as was Walden) that split open the fabric of all poetry extant before it. I bet you sat up in attention as all you knew of connection with original energy through your experience so far was before you on the page—deep, clear, real, and powerful.

There is so much power whirling in Whitman's writing, be it poem or prose, it is difficult to try and contain it in words. Here is the electricity of just one paragraph of the Preface he wrote to Leaves of Grass:

This is what you shall do: Love the earth and sun and the animals, despise riches, give alms to everyone that asks, stand up for the stupid and crazy, devote your income and labor to others, hate tyrants, argue not concerning God, have patience and indulgence toward the people, take off your hat to nothing known or unknown or to any man or number of men, go freely with powerful uneducated persons and with the young and with the mothers of families, read these leaves in the open air every season of every year of your life, reexamine all you have been told at school or church or in any book, dismiss whatever insults your own soul, and your very flesh shall be a great poem.

What is one to say in the charged silence after this prayer? These words encourage, enliven, most probably infuriate many who have forgotten the nascent freedom within their being. Whitman took your philosophy and your creed of quiet living, made a song of it, a song that one forgets once heard. These words have the power to transform the Soul on the spot!

Whitman has given us instructions: walk Earth in conscious joy. Imbibe what is given to you within the unique incarnation you are. Despise nothing! Pay attention!

I am reminded of so much wisdom in my preparation for writing to you. This great poet, Whitman, though I have read his words before, sounds new to me this day. I have you, and him, to thank for these gifts.

We will make this enough for one letter.

Have a powerful day, Henry.

Cynthia

Winter 2016 - February

February takes her time. She is an off-again-on-again lover, one moment feigning Spring and when she has you convinced, it's a blizzard for you. Coy, playful, she is the valentine of months. Her voice is the trembling of streams under the snow as they wake from winter sleep. Her laughter is mockery. She leaves a little early each year, teasing us with March.

February 2, 2016 - Reflections

Dear Henry,

Outside the sky is marbled, tints of pink and slate blue all fuzzed together in a morning fog. The humidity is 99%, winds calm, no movement, stillness.

I still get fooled by the seasons here in Florida. After spending my years in the northeast, this is not recognizable as a February day. The February I know is cold, with fields of snow everywhere, just beginning to lose the sting of January's bite. The night skies of February are softer than the sharpened black pencil of January skies where stars glitter like real diamonds.

February is one small step toward Spring, some of the days almost warm with the thickening of buds and the inception of a deepening red flush that announces leafing. Oh, it will still snow, and snow a lot. But it is a kinder snow than January's icy flux. The full moon of February is the Heavy Snow Moon. February breeds hope, hope of love's return to Earth. It is the month of Valentine's Day. Love wins after all.

On February 7th, 1855, you skated on the frozen waterways of Concord. You wrote,

The coldest for a long, long time was last night. Sheets froze stiff about the faces... People dreaded to go to bed. The ground cracked in the night as if a

powder-mill had blown up… Thermometer at about 7:30 A.M. had gone into the bulb, -19 at least.

And on February 21, 1855…

A warmth begins to be reflected from the partially dried ground here and there in the sun in sheltered places, When I perceive this dryness under my feet, I feel as if I had got a new sense, or rather I realize what was incredible to me before, that there is a new life in Nature beginning to awake, that her halls are being swept and prepared for a new occupant. It is whispered through the aisles of the forest that another spring is approaching.

February 4, 2016 - Green Surrender

Cynthia,

Your light is on. The train is rumbling by on tracks very near where you sit conning a new letter for me. My gratitude, more expansive than ever I allowed on Earth, is a sea in which we both swim this day. A beautiful dawn has risen into the pale blue Eastern skies marbling them with iridescent pink clouds. You can see it now out of the windows of your house as I see it here. It is, as are all dawns, an invitation to take up your life.

"A journal is a record of experiences and growth, not a preserve of things well done or said… The charm of the journal must consist in a certain greeness, though of freshness, not maturity. This day as it were a pen or a brush, an instrument of creation."

I said that on January 24, 1856. The words we communicate within are paltry representatives of the real thing. Take, for instance, the four-letter word TREE; now look at a tree, any tree. Even the smallest of them are marvels so far removed from the symbol, and BIRD… What has that word to do with the color, form, song, and charm of the original, and that applies to everything. So, the journal attempts to capture and hold something very big using very small arrangements of symbols on a page. There is no substitute for being in the presence of the real thing, the sunset, the wind, the starry sky, the smile of one person to another, whether received or observed contains energy that uplifts.

Cease all resistance, give yourself up, give yourself away in the moment to what is around you. You do not know what this moment is for. It is for you and none of your day is unworthy of your respect and attention.

If you really mean to start a journal (I have heard you talking of this) then pay attention to the common hours, the common events, the seemingly empty details of your day; when reviewed with introspection, they will yield fruit. You will, as did I, record this flow of mystery with the symbols of words. Others have done this before you. Take heart.

Pay Attention, Cynthia!

February 6, 2016 - A Journal

Dear Henry,

A cool and windy day is dawning after pelting tropical rain during the night. The sun rose behind clouds with light but no color. Later in the day patches of blue showed up but didn't warm the air. Winds were from the north.

Outside my window early, sentinels. Mourning doves chanting into the wind. If I close my eyes, I could be in the many places I have lived before this one, hearing the eternal doves of those past times.

Grackles will arrive soon. They come to our feeder in black clouds squeaking and squawking, much like the voices of children in a play yard. They jostle and push each other off the feeder, fly away at any noise to resettle only a moment later.

Cardinals also come in mated pairs next, the red streak of the male feeding before his tawny mate. Their repeated syllables is a daily prayer here in the south during winter. In the north, the voice of the cardinal means spring.

Trains speed close, adding a rhythm to a part of the morning song. Trains hurtle by in both Maine and Florida; the difference here, in Florida, is that trains are visible speeding on the flat open land and through the hundreds of intersections as they go up the state's long span, and they are very loud. By law, raucous horns sound three times at each road crossing to warn oncoming traffic.

In Maine, the Downeaster (one) train quietly lopes through deep woods behind my house as it skirts very near the coast. Train horns filter through pines, oaks, and maples. This northern sound inspires a more romantic experience.

I spent a good part of my morning doing what I love most, working on some writing in a local coffee shop. Anonymous in that setting, I open my computer (there are things that defy definition, Henry. The computer is one of them), purchase my coffee (I know you were not in favor of that drink), and dissolve all my attention into the lives of my characters living out the events, enhancing inner dialogues as I hear them. It is great fun. I relish rainy, cold days for this. Sun is a bother at these times. I would like to share a page or two of the novel I am preparing to publish. Perhaps in a future letter?

After that, the day went down to details, things to do, straighten, clean, unclutter. When the afternoon had almost passed, I took to the walking path that I most often trod down to the ocean. A nice part of living here is that the ocean is less than a mile away and so the aqua blue Atlantic of Florida is yours for the walk. You are welcome to sit on the beach and watch the waves wave.

It was a fine day, Henry, a unique day, for all its sameness.

Until tomorrow,
Cynthia

February 7, 2016 - A Morning Song

Dear Henry,

We are all a bit spring-starved down here. Up north, the days and weeks of gray clouds and cold pile up. Even here in the south it has been uncharacteristically cool and gray. Of course, the sun blazes forth for intervals of time, but the inhabitants are waiting for the change of seasons and some warmth.

February is a month of waiting; March the month of alchemy, when the frozen grasp of the winter lets go but only after another icy storm or two. What keeps us hoping are signs that the clock is ticking. Crocuses and the red flush of renewal can be found in lucky places up north.

Birds, under their canopy of chatter and song, are part of a musical score that we don't really notice until they migrate and the air falls silent. They return in February, the curtain of sound dropping around us again slowly, and we hear music and realize how we have missed it.

I once had a sparrow alight upon my shoulder for a moment, while I was hoeing in a village garden, and I felt that I was more distinguished by that circumstance that I should have been by any epaulet I could have worn.

-Henry David Thoreau

I think I'm homesick Henry.

Cynthia

February 8, 2016 - The Song Sparrow: Emily Dickinson

Dear Henry,

I never know where my morning letter will take me. I was ready to talk of sparrows—the humble songsters of salt marshes and brushy areas across most of Canada and the United States—when Emily Dickinson came into my mind. She was named The Sparrow because the multitude of her poems were composed of humble, ordinary images. Like you, she could see forever.

She was on this earth while you were, Henry. Born December 10, 1830 in Amherst, Massachusetts—to die there fifty-six years later, on May 15, 1886— Emily wrote nearly 1,800 poems but only a dozen or so of them were published during her lifetime.

Attending Mount Holyoke Female Seminary in 1847-1848, she was one of the few women of her day allowed an education—and even though she was educated, she returned to the 'closet' of the household as was the pattern for women of her day. There she lived doubting her talent and vision, writing in secret, stashing away the gorgeous knowing of her vision, thinking herself unworthy as a writer mainly because of her sex. It was not a kind or open world for a woman.

A literary rebel, she used slant rhyme, unconventional capitalization, and punctuation displaying intellect women were judged incapable of possessing. The vast body of poems were discovered after her death. Luckily, the originals had not been destroyed by overreaching publishers of her day who tried to alter their brilliance. We may still read them as she wrote them.

So, there you were, walking your meadows and woods, writing of the divinity you saw, encouraged by friends and the literary personas of the day while, only sixty miles away, a woman poet was being suppressed by a patriarchy so blind as to ignore her bright and precious talent. I like to think that if you had known of Emily Dickinson and her work you would have rushed to support her.

I'm Nobody, Who Are You

I'm nobody! Who are you?
Are you nobody, too?
Then there's a pair of us – don't tell!
They 'd banish us, you know.
How dreary to be somebody!
How public, like a frog
To tell your name the livelong day
To an admiring bog!

-Emily Dickinson

Until Tomorrow, Henry, when we will talk of you and sparrows.

Cynthia

February 9, 2016 - A Competent Witness

Dear Henry,

The day is rising in the eastern sky. The clouds have all caught fire in the dawn; the brightest of pinks layered with mauve and slate blue rise upwards. In a few minutes, they will go back to being gray again as this will be a mostly cloudy day. We have 21 mph winds prevailing from the northwest, explaining cool temperatures. The winds drag down from the cold air from on high. There is snow in abundance up north.

The first sparrow of spring! The year beginning with younger hope than ever. The first silvery warbling heard over bare dank fields, as if the flakes of winter tinkled as they fell. What, then, are the histories, chronologies, and all written revelations?

-Henry David Thoreau, Journal

The mighty sparrow was your companion through the years of your life. I find sightings everywhere in your writing. What I am saying is that your notice of the sparrow was constant and grateful. The little bird became your metaphor for the human out in the woods. The sparrow asks no opulence; only the day that rises around them—and yet, their song strewed elegance on the earth, enriching everyone who heard.
On February 8, 1857, you wrote:

In the society of men, or in the midst of what is called success, I find my life of no account, and my spirits rapidly fall... But, when I have only a rustling oak leaf, or the faint metallic cheep of a tree sparrow, for variety in my winter walk, my life becomes continent and sweet as the kernel of a nut.

I love these words written over 150 years ago. Today is as vibrant in possibility for us as it was the day you wrote it. Though most of the wild land you walked daily is not wild now, the thought of that sparrow may set us free in our hearts as surely as it did you in your musings. To say, Henry, that your life was of "no account" falls as grossly untrue.
And later that year, 1857:

But suddenly, in some fortunate moment, the voice of eternal wisdom reaches me, even in the strain of the sparrow, and liberates me, whets and clarifies my sense, makes me a competent witness.

The sparrow has mighty restorative powers, even wisdom to offer. But one must listen and hear to free the magic of the sound. That was your point. The bird is singing for you. Close your eyes and listen; you are back on your path through the woods of Concord, walking stick in hand, heaven under foot.

Cynthia

February 14, 2016 - Heart Day

There is no remedy for love but to love more.

-Henry David Thoreau

Dear Henry,

6 AM in Hobe Sound, Florida. The stars are still bright, though the sun approaches the horizon tinting clouds to the west a dusky red. A gentle morning breeze stirs the palms. No one is up but me, if I can trust the dark windows around me. Today will be mostly cloudy, 73 degrees, winds 9 mph.

It is Valentine's Day, Henry. I chose a quote for this day from your earlier years, when you had fallen in love with Ellen Sewell, had even proposed marriage, remember?

Valentine's Day was celebrated in your time. The first mass produced Valentine's card was from Worcester, Massachusetts in 1841. It is an important day here too in 2016; most people take the time to show love in many ways. Of course, it's also big business. That puts a bit of a damper on it. This day will go fast enough. May all enjoy the heart energy while we live. You are now in the land of LOVE.

Now, to Lao Tzu and the letter I lost yesterday. Lao Tzu, a philosopher poet of ancient China, is known as the author of the Tao Te Ching, the founder of philosophical Taoism. He was born in Henan, China, and though we don't know when, we know he died in 531 BC.

His teachings emphasize simplicity, the elimination of desire, the value of peace, and the importance of balance in life and in the universe. He strove to live modestly and, like you, Henry, extolled the goodness and importance of Nature as a teacher for man.

The literary wisdom that you discovered in Lao Tzu was incorporated into your writing and into your life. There are many similarities between Walden and The Book of Tao like mysticism of nature, a love of simple and primitive living, a dislike of convention and government control to name a few.

An existing piece of evidence supporting this speculation lies in the seven paradoxes you isolated on June 26, 1840. They mirror those of Lao Tzu. Revisit them with me, Henry.

(1) The highest condition of art is artlessness.
(2) Truth is always paradoxical.
(3) He will get to the goal first who stands stillest.
(4) There is one let better than any help, and that is—let alone.
(5) By sufferance you may escape suffering.
(6) He who resists not at all will never surrender.
(7) Stand outside the wall, and no harm can reach you. The danger is that you be walled in with it.

It is inspiring to think of you discovering the ideas of Lao Tzu, letting his profound wisdom seep into your thinking and living. It proves your bravery and your willingness to step out of the caste of the usual and move on into a new dimension. We find the ideas of a seer from 2500 years ago put into action in the woods of Walden, Massachusetts, to weave these ancient truths—as well as your own unique discoveries—into our lives going forward in time.

Happy Valentine's Day, Henry.
I appreciate your courage and love.

Cynthia

(Dedicated to Alice)

February 15, 2016 - Monday Meditation

Dear Henry,

It is just before sunrise. The wind has been with us all through the night, buffeting against windows. It is keening as I write this. The temperatures are mild, 67 degrees Fahrenheit, 58 percent humidity, 9 mph winds from the southwest, a partly cloudy day.

Monday, my favorite, has rolled around again in the queue of days. In the New England week—my milieu—there are things to do defined by days, weeks, seasons, and years. These duties are important in a well-oiled household where a family rises and falls on the strength and success of those tasks.

After the sprawl of a weekend—especially one like Valentine's Day, celebrated yesterday—Monday seems more navigable, more familiar, with well-worn routes to walk and things that must be completed. In the generations before these last two or three, the women of the home stayed within to do the necessaries. During the 1970s, I, myself, took the responsibilities of the 'one at home': keeping order, providing the necessary meals, and attending household duties for a family. When there is the time for and attention to this role in life, its particulars can offer a holy experience. My time at home was sacred to me.

As you strolled out, Henry, for your discoveries, a cadre of women were left behind doing the necessary work to support your metaphysical journey. I know you lived within the love of your family and returned it daily, but the work of the household seemed dispensable as to be never mentioned. It was a man's world you lived within. And yet I'm sure in the saying of this I am mistaken. You were a kind man and therefore most likely participated in the day's work.

One of my favorite tasks is the establishment of Monday as laundry day. Hanging out clothes—sheets especially—into the inhale and exhale of any windy day above freezing was a delight; out would go the wash, pinned in neat rows on a line to dance and flirt with wind, the breath of our breath. Whatever else had to be done, the wash stayed out on the edge of the hours of that day until, depending on the dryness of the air, one went out to collect the fresh, clean items, bring them into the house, fold and store them for the next use. All this economy, no other source but the pure air.

Sheets were the most fun; they flapped and floated like sails, sending semaphore messages for the wise to read. I still love hanging sheets, and I do whenever the need and the opportunity coincide. It is a labor of love.

Here in Florida and in other places, hanging laundry has become considered rude and is illegal within some communities. "Unsightly!" they say. Every atom of my being rebels against this proclamation. Here is where Civil Disobedience is required if you ask me. It is a good day for doing laundry.

Until tomorrow.
Cynthia

February 16, 2016 - Shades Of The Biblical

Dear Henry,

I am in the middle of a monumental, all stops out, biblical storm. The rolls of thunder and constant flashes of lightning flicker up in dark windows, threatening. My shoulders are hunched over the keyboard as if I need to run for cover. Rain in Florida can be a deluge. The Ark could sail up and down this street after one of these storms. We still have power, but any time now that could blow out.

Revealed—when these great tongues of white fire jut into the picture—the scene is one of shades of electric blue coming out of the black to appear flickering for a second, then to collapse back into featureless landscape. A roll of thunder almost twenty seconds in length just whizzed directly overhead. And still lightning is careening up and down the street, seeming quite personal.

This is rich stuff for those who enjoy Nature in all her costumes. Great writing weather for sure. One imagines some lost soul out there somewhere, lost at sea or on the moor, even on this street, seeking shelter. As I wrote this last sentence, I thought of the homeless who are with us in this generation. What do they do during this great storm? There is no protection able to keep a person from this rain. Theirs is a hidden world existing within this day. How did the citizens of Concord deal with the poor and displaced? May they find shelter today.

Relative quiet has taken over above, although it still rains. The rumblings have moved further away though lightning continues to explode in the windows; now with a different, ameliorated attitude.

The sun rises somewhere behind clouds and the black sky will light soon. The magic of this state is that, within a few hours, the sun will be out, today's temperatures will reach 82 degrees, the birds will sing, and this storm will be just a memory.

And now the sky is visible, holding distant flashes of lightning like a whip out over the sea. The storm has passed.

As we lay huddled together under the tent, which leaked considerably about the sides, with our baggage at our feet, we listened to some of the grandest thunder which I ever heard—rapid peals, round and plump, bang, bang, bang in succession, like artillery from some fortress in the sky; and the lightning was proportionally brilliant.

-Henry David Thoreau

Cynthia

February 21, 2016 - Dear Cynthia - The Advent Of Spring

Cynthia,

Good morning.
I see from here that you are poised at the vanguard of Spring in North America. According to your calendars it will begin a month from now, but, in truth, it has already begun. Great clouds of birds are stirring in their winter harbors, the songs of familiar places singing in their blood, calling them to their nesting, moving them north.

Beneath the soil, roots thicken, trees bask in the longer sunshine, ice thins, buds swell imperceptibly, all the processes that led to the locking down of Winter loosen, allowing for the new season to take the stage.

It is a circle, no beginning, and no end, a circle. Like day and night, life and death, no beginning, no end. And what makes the difference in this circle that you and everyone on the earth ride? Choice. Your choice of how to see the endlessly strewn coins of the realm, the minutes, and hours of your life, given to each equally. The worth of a moment in time is what you decide it to be. Choose well.

Cynthia, this is a long preface to what I mean to say in this response to your faithfulness to my request for a conversation with you. Your choice of getting up in the dark each morning to come to this place and speak to and with me is your choice in action, in benefit to me, surely, and to you, and to whoever else chooses to read here. There is love in the choice and in the work of the letter and in the appreciation it brings to you from so, so many directions.

Courage! We are with you as you strive. Spring is on the horizon, seeding new energy and new visions for your learning and enjoyment. Choose to see the love in action displayed all around you.

Your friend,

Henry

February 22, 2016 - Early Spring

Dear Henry,

I am ever so grateful for your response of yesterday. Writing in the early hours, one can get the impression one is talking to the wind—which is a delightful experience, but short on response. To hear from you is grounding, encouraging. As the words leave me and are released into the ether, they disappear. Hearing them come back from you is a great gift. Thank you!

There are moments from each of our lives that, for some reason or other, become etched in our memories. They need not be of some grand event, more usually, they are of little moments that hold delight or sadness or some emotion that changed our landscape in some way. Always present, they are in some out of the way 'room' in the cells and can be called forth when we desire.

One such memory for me comes from many April walks on Hermit Island; a small jut of land dedicated to ocean camping on the coast of Maine. We often went there in advance of the summer season to pace out the campsites, looking forward to an upcoming summer. April is the month in Maine when you can expect spring. It still might snow, but, generally, the rise of sap is on.

On this Island, there are many stands of sea grasses. One large stand runs beside one of the main dirt roads of the area. Here, the birds return, the red-winged blackbirds' antics as flocks of them—each jet black with red epaulets—descend to perch on the stalks of grass, swaying in the still cold ocean winds, eating the last seeds of the previous summer provide great delight. Their warbling, clear and sweet, lifts in those sea winds. I have stood, silent and listening, watching many seasons, and there is nothing to compare with this music of spring. It will come early this year with El Nino in charge.

This memory, as real now as it was then, is always there if I let myself go to it. The inner world, sewn with sequined moments like this one, is precious to you as well. Walden is a symphony of those moments, and we do take hope and refuge there.

The day is an epitome of the year. The night is the winter, the morning and evening are the spring and fall, and the noon is the summer.

-Henry David Thoreau, Walden

The sun has achieved the horizon—but not before tinting the whole cloud cast in shades of mauve and rose. Then, the sacred circle of fire slid into view, gold and yellow as it mounted the sky. And this happens every day!

What does this day hold? It is 64 degrees Fahrenheit, no wind, high humidity, with full sun. Keep the song of the red-winged blackbird in mind. It sings just because it must.

Cynthia

February 23, 2016 - Believing Is Seeing

Good morning, Henry,

The bowl of sky over me is bright with woven light from the sunrise, but no direct sunlight yet. Tones today are of apricot, an almost iridescent pink, and slate blue of clouds that sail along on a good breeze. Chimes on the porch softly sound. For a few days, we will be back in the tropical temperatures until a front takes it all backwards on Wednesday.

Candace Pert, PhD, wrote The Molecules of Emotion, a book that revolutionized how we understand life on earth. As a scientist, she proved with concrete experiments (the kind that most prefer) that the cells of the body have "receptors": portals, specifically designed to receive peptides that carry emotional messages like mail in the body.

These emotional signals coordinate interactions between our organs and systems, either promoting health because of their optimism, or suppressing it if they are carrying stress, worry, grief, fear, or anger. In other words, the electrical signals in our brains and bodies affect the way cells interact and function.

The control panel for all these very important signals happens to be the way we see/view the events of our lives. If we choose to look on events with negative or fearful interpretations, the body/mind is listening and will flood the operating system with the appropriate chemical to produce what you "think" you are seeing. It's all in your hands. The bad news is, the more you tune into destructive chemicals, the more our cells moderate to receive these unfriendly messengers.

That's as simply as I can put it. How do you back out of this unfortunate addiction to unkind thinking? Dr. Pert suggests breathing deeply, slowly, the breath holds a great power over fear. Meditation on a regular basis, yoga, monitoring your thoughts for the harmful ones, letting them go as quickly as possible.

Playing, laughter, nature walks, doing what you love... All these paths are as accessible as their opposites. This is the good news.

And so, why write this to you, you ask? I see an echo of your life here. You discovered this in your years in Walden and shared your discovery with the world in your work. This is a reminder for us all that what you offered centuries earlier has been confirmed in the present by the unlikely discoveries of science.

It's worth everything to discover this power within yourself.

Cynthia

February 24, 2016 - Written Word

Dear Henry,

As a fellow writer this was bound to happen. I want to share my writing with you in these most intimate and honest letters.

A written word is the choicest of relics. It is something at once more intimate with us and more universal than any other work of art. It is the work of art nearest to life itself. It may be translated into every language, and not only be read but actually breathed from all human lips; not be represented on canvas or in marble only but be carved out of the breath of life itself.

-Henry David Thoreau, Walden

The novel on my desk now is written. I edit it looking for better expression of this idea or that, reforming sentences, doing what I can before I let it go to the reading world. I am really finished but afraid to release it.

The story took hold of me many years ago and has never left. With one sentence, it began. With one sentence, the characters walked into my life and would not leave until I wrote their story. I will write that sentence in tomorrow's letter.

Set in Maine, the opening sequence is that of a woman who awakens in her car. It is Christmas Eve and a powerful blizzard has trapped her in a whirling white world of snow and wind. The car's battery is dead. She, Pamela Iverson, is five miles from any traveled roads or any help. Behind her, the waves of the rising sea flood into the parking lot, surging under her car. She is too far out for any safe rescue.

I begin the tale with a Prologue, included below. Something like this happened to me once on a beach in Maine on a September day.

I offer you my words... You know the feeling well, Henry.

Cynthia

Dusk On Route 1
Prologue
Drakes Island, September 1988

Stepping out onto the parking lot, she stops to look straight up above her and is momentarily dizzied by the depth of the cloudless autumn sky, a tent of cobalt pitched above her, and on the sea no horizon visible. No one is on the beach; unusual for Drakes Island. Most weekends, even fair winter ones, families tug children, kites, dogs and strollers into the always blowing wind. Today the landscape is eerily empty.

Taking off her jacket and tying it around her waist, she moves into her warm-up, a few lunges and stretches. The contrast of a warm sun on her face in the cool September breeze feels delightful.

Pamela begins her routine, jogs the boardwalk, running shoes slapping softly on weathered wood. Securing her headset, she jumps off the solid footing of wood to the give of sand. A small surge of white ruffles at the water line; pushing the switch, music spills into her ears.

Settling into a medium pace, she sings with them under her breath, comfortable, focused on the easy push of her body. She has run this beach hundreds of times, can visualize herself up by the tidal river that separates Drakes Island from the mainland beach in Kennebunk where surging tides crumble layers of marsh soil, peel it from banks, push it into the wires of inlets on strong rifts.

Twenty minutes into the run her push pays off. Her pulse is up, a sheen of sweat glistening on her temples, breath even and deep. She smiles knowing she can easily make it to the river.

A bloom of color beside her takes her off stride. She turns her head, expecting someone to run past, but there is no one, only empty air.

Off balance now, she slows, turns, runs backward looking for what disturbed her. Again, no one, nothing. Off comes the headset, the abrupt sound of waves and bird cries doubles in the quiet. Bending to breathe, her heart pounds in her ears, the unwelcome decline of runner's high gathering speed. Pamela walks it out in circles until her breath is normal. That's when she sees them, a few feet in front of her, fluttering, unrolling, a scarf of color undulating mid-air, coming up from the surf line.

As they approach, Pamela braces herself, unsure of what is to happen. Monarchs, hundreds of them, roll and lift around her. At first, she gives herself up in delight. These harbingers are a familiar sight during summer months in Maine; their migrations launch from beaches like this one. To be present on the day they depart for their mysterious journey seems the luckiest thing in the world. Delight soon turns to amazement, and then, disbelief as more and more and more travel up the beach to join the undulating cloud around her, so many now that they approach being mystical.

Acrobats floating, leaping, tumbling over and around each other, now a pyramid, now a cloud, now shapeshifting into a spinning column that moves, surrounds the sole observer who, transfixed, holds her breath in wonder.

At the center, within this kaleidoscope, Pamela looks out through the startling color of wings. She hears thoughts traveling here, moving on an intimate shared highway. She understands these thoughts; they are meant for her. Motionless within this adagio, Pamela seems to float, all that is known about her life becomes a memory.

After an eternity in a moment, a new landscape rises, darkens. She is aware of the sound of water, not waves, only the ripple of a strong stream; she sees shadowed banks... Then, the dip of oars in time to a slow, rhythmic chanting, a lament. Where is this? Why is she afraid? Though being held in the ephemeral embrace of these messengers of transformation, she is not at peace.

As plovers flash in air, some signal given, Pamela feels the mantle of monarchs shifting, rising as one, leaving her. The tornado of orange and black on blue rises to spin away. In a matter of minutes, they are down the beach and have embarked on the blue highway that will lead them home.

Pamela doesn't know how to come back from this; she has fallen out of time. She sits by the dunes in fast cooling air, struggles to understand what has happened. Some natural law has not held. Had they come to her, the huge wheels of their cycle pausing on this island to embrace her? Why?

Shadows shift on the sand; thoughts of her children and husband enter her notice at last. Anxiety pushes her; she will be late for the Sunday they have planned. They are waiting for her.

A woman retraces her footsteps to the parking lot, opens the door of her car to return home. She is not the same woman who drove to this beach hours ago. Something new has begun.

-Cynthia Fraser Graves

February 25, 2016 - Where Things Come From

Dear Henry,

After a very stormy night, this morning's sky is vast and luminous, not a cloud to weigh it down, it floats over us like a cathedral ceiling, the holy floor of earth far beneath.

Yesterday, I shared the prologue of my novel with you, Henry. The writing of this story began twelve years ago so quietly and simply that I had no idea what it would mean or demand of me in the years to come. One sentence, one, came into my mind totally capturing my attention, and from that one sentence, a plot, characters, setting, theme, the whole grew as if that one thought held the seed of the now finished story.

The neon rim of the diner clock spun color into the dim, kitchen-warmed dining room; tints of red, blue, and green pooled on plates like gravy.

That was it, Henry, that was the line from which a book of over 69,000 words, thirty-one chapters in length was begun. The imagery of the Maine coast fascinated me at first, but there was much more there. It turned out that the person seeing that clock in that diner on Christmas Eve was a person called Ed LaCasse. He had a friend, Jimmy Casey, a local cop in the town of Wells, a small seaside community in the state of Maine. Little by little, characters stepped out and introduced themselves to me—Pamela, Darnice, Taddy Stevens, the lives of these people were in my hands. If I did not come to sit for my work for a while, they would come into my mind sitting anxiously, a bit perturbed that I was not letting them move on.

I write to music. I'm sure some writers would shake their heads and wonder how that could be beneficial to the one-pointed laser focus needed in the act of writing. I don't know, but my writing seems to flow more smoothly to music—although it can be only a certain type. In my earlier book, Never Count Crow: Love And Loss In Kennebunk, Maine, I used Tim Janis' sweeping seascapes, especially The Rushing Wings of Dawn.

In Dusk on Route 1, Secret Garden is key. The one song that opens the world of this novel to me being Nocturne; I enter a complete world where this story is ongoing, then, I focus. I am in this world for as long as I can take the heightened state of awareness, for it truly is in some other dimension that I see and write. There is a shadow world there. The powerful surge of entering this world cannot be held for too long.

One thing is sure. I will see and hold this book in my hands before long. Its creation is guaranteed.

In this era, Henry, publishing is not quite the caste system it has been in the past. We can publish in many ways, even send our writing out onto the vibrations of the air... As I do with you.

Enough for now.

Until tomorrow,
Cynthia

February 26, 2016 - A Red Song At Dawn

When the first light dawned on the earth, and the birds awoke, and the brave river was heard rippling confidently seaward, and the nimble early rising wind rustled the oak leaves about our tent, all people, having reinforced their bodies and their souls with sleep, and cast aside doubt and fear, were invited to adventures.

-Henry David Thoreau

Dear Henry,

Just when dawn was beginning to think about itself, a cardinal started warbling his song in the backyard. The rich tones of his call carried his color and shape; I could see him in the sound. He began to circle the house, calling first from one side, then the other. He is out there now, sowing music all around.

I say he because in this variety of bird, it is the male that is the songster. The female will only sing before nesting in the spring. Where you see a male, a female is not far behind, her lighter colored coat and orange crest a compliment to her mate.

As this bird does not migrate, but stays through seasons in one area, I wonder if he is a neighbor; if he knew I was less inclined to get up this morning and was calling me out of my slumber. That is what it sounded like. "Don't go back to sleep. The day is about to dawn. You have things to do. The cursor blinks, the page is empty. Rise." This is what we use for a trusty pencil these days, the computer, and it is not so trusty.

We tell children stories about what things are for; birds and bunnies, cats and dogs, rain and snow and wind; we tell children that these entities are aware of them, are here to help them and know them, but as we grow into the arrogance of our adult knowing, we forget what we once believed, swapping the living, loving world for the dull, dead world of substance that science tells us is there. Although the idea that matter is unconscious is being corrected, rapidly now, we are discovering that everything is connected and made of the same energy as ourselves, we do not extend that childlike amazement and interest to the world we wake into each day.

I like to think that red song was meant for me. It will charm my day. Besides, who is to say it was not?

You give me courage to be and say what I know.

Cynthia

The true price of anything you do is the amount of time you exchange for it.

-Henry David Thoreau, Walden

February 27, 2016 - A Walk At The Society Of The Four Arts

Dear Henry,

I recently spent an afternoon at The Society of The Four Arts in Palm Beach, Florida, a non-profit botanical garden sporting tropical plants of south Florida as well as a Chinese Garden, Statuary garden, and Madonna garden.

On the very warm afternoon of that walk, the many fountains and waterfalls of the gardens offered relief in the sound and sight of water splashing up in warm breezes stirring the heavy, dark green tropical foliage. Blooming orchids trailed from trees they were tucked within, luscious blooms lighting the warm air with their color and fragrance. There were many shaded sitting areas where one could simply sit and absorb all this beauty.

In the Chinese Garden, bright Koi flash in the pool. Several strips of silver paper twist in a breeze from tree branches adding light to the inviting meditation space. Chinese sculpture surrounds the courtyard, lending an air of antiquity to the space.

A visit to this garden at 2 Four Arts Plaza, Palm Beach, Florida, is free and conveys such riches to the observer. It's nothing like a garden in Maine. The cool and downright cold temperatures of the north would disassemble all this loveliness quickly.

This I offer to you, Henry. The citizens of this garden would delight you with their color, delicacy, and fragrance, not to mention the fabulous network of visible root structure that often grows above ground, powerful cables like veins for these living things. Much like the roots observed a while ago on Hermit Island supporting Northern trees.

Tomorrow will have to be an off day for me… I will send a placeholder. Be back on Monday. I will miss writing…

Cynthia

February 29, 2016 - A Rare Day; Look About You!

Dear Henry,

Today's hours are of the rare vintage... Leap Day, a day which appears on our calendars only once every four years. The reason for this day is the balancing of the slight discrepancy between the time it takes the earth to complete its orbit about the sun (365 ¼ days) and the length of the solar year (less by about 11 minutes). This formula almost does the trick of synchronizing our calendar with the sun, but not quite. Leap year must be omitted three times every four hundred years. 1700, 1800 and 1900 did not have leap years, but 1600, 2000, and 2400 were/are/will contain leap years. We are talking about formulas so immense in projection that no one living will see them play out. Incoming generations get their instructions from the outgoing generations and proceed as instructed. Interesting.

If you are born in Leap Year, would you get your driver's license on February 28th or March 1st? a question decided by each state. Most states, however, consider March 1st the official day. For instance, the Michigan Vehicle Code writes for their records that people born on February 29th have been born on March 1st. Your chances of being born on a leap day are about 1 in 1,500 hundred and, oddly, if you are born a woman, it's somehow OK for a woman to ask a man to marry her on this day.

On this rare day, we also look over the horizon to the arrival of March, wonderful March, holding the Vernal Equinox in its icy hands. A commonly accepted prescription from folklore, *"March comes in like a lion and goes out like a lamb"*, is based on the position of the constellations of Leo (the lion) at March's beginning and Aries (the ram or lamb) at the end of the month. We have come to think that phrase refers to the weather at either end of the month, stormy weather to begin the month meaning a gentle end and vice versa. These sayings are echoes of a more superstitious past, a continuity. However, they fade in these years with our decline in reading.

So, wheels of change engage above and below the earth. It's a good day to plan, to leap, to roar, to break down a door you've closed. We're connected to past generations within this calendar just as we are free from its prescriptions by discovery going forward. What will you do on Leap Day?

Henry, I will read your thoughts from the March 1st of days of your recorded life. March is a favorite of mine... All that light flooding the earth after the dark winter. This will be a project worthy of a leap.

Great God, I ask thee for no meaner pelf
Than that I may not disappoint myself,
That in my action I may soar as high

As I can now discern with this clear eye.

-Henry David Thoreau

'Til tomorrow, March 1st…

Cynthia

Spring 2016 - March

March is tempestuous. Her icy cold mornings warm to wonderful afternoons of sun. In her voice is the music of wild geese as they fly night pathways lit by a silvery moon. Listen as you lie warm in your bed; she is singing of your new life. Her cleansing winds rattle your windows, sending a chill of delight your way. Her jewelry is the crystal of ponds, lakes, even puddles as they release their battle with winter's cold icy hold, their edges melting. Her gown is the color of earth returning: the purple of crocus, the red of Robin Redbreast, the flush of new life in the trees.

March 1, 2016 - The Beginning

Good morning, Henry,

I like to think of March as the month of crystal. In the land where I grew up, precipitation was as ice in March, temperatures mostly on the knife edge of freezing. I have seen great formations of returning Canadian geese skim in on marshes resting from their long journeys. They land on cold inlets of the sea as a rain of icy pellets rattles down into grasses. I have seen and felt these arrows of ice streak from gray skies finding their target on colorless winds. I consider myself fortunate to have such memories.

The tug of war between spring and winter is enjoined in this month. March winds blow, freezing and refreezing clear water into lacy ice patterns. I spent hours, days, as a child watching puddles write the story of coming spring, frozen in the morning but melting and simmering in the warmer afternoons until cold night winds began the task of refreezing the whole. As you were with snowstorms, I was the inspector of puddles. Each morning's walk to school offered enormous fascination with what I saw.

March was the first month of the earliest Roman calendar, named for Mars, the Roman god of war and guardian of agriculture and was the first month of the calendar as late as 153 BC. Roman mosaics represent the months of the year, often indicating March as the year's beginning—and so it seems the first flush of reawakening trees and seasonal change will rise this month. On a trip recently, spring's unmistakable blush was budding in the rosy trees along the road.

Overhead, skies of birds on the wing go north from their southern winter homes much like we will soon do. The first robin will bob over some frozen lawn bringing a thrill to anyone quick enough to see it; air will thicken with birdsong; night winds of March will moan. I love the idea that March winds sweep the earth clean for the rains of April to soak the soil, bringing the beauty of spring flowers. May it be so.

All in all, March is a marvelous month. I'm sure to sing its praises often in these letters. I just can't help it. Its drama fills our windows with such beauty and hope.

Time to get this out to the mail, I will stop for now.

Cynthia

March 2, 2016 - The Prevailing Winds

The strongest wind cannot stagger a spirit: it is a Spirit's breath.

-Henry David Thoreau

Dear Henry,

I was disappointed in the weather in Florida today. Temperatures mild, 62 degrees at present, no rain and no wind, 5 mph. The ten-day forecast is for mild weather as well.

In Maine, winds will achieve 20 mph by midday, with cold air much more like March than the sun-drenched air of this southern state.

I am a lover of wind, always have been. It is high drama to see trees, clothes on the line, people as they walk along, all wrapped in the strong embrace of wind. I am unimpressed with little breezes. This month, March, is the REAL month of wind.

Looking to the east from my writing table, the dark red blaze of the sun spreads on the horizon, lightning air above raspberry as it rises.

Is there anything so inspiring as the color of the first tint of dawn? Now it has seeped into the clouds over the sea, and they glow with its touch.

But I digress, back to wind—this time in the flow of gasses on the surface of the Earth. There is so much to know about effects of wind in scientific terms: pollinating soil, bringing, or withholding water (causing or recovering droughts), moving massive temperature fronts on a jet stream, powering sailing vessels, providing wind power for electricity, moving insect populations great distances. The work of the wind is survival on earth. And as we all know, wind can also be dangerous in extreme forms, hurricanes, tornadoes, cyclones, and the like.

Henry, years ago I wrote a story that attempted to convey my long-standing love and connection with wind. I would like to share this with you. It is titled Wind People. Here is the first installment.

Wind People

The child lifted her round face from a piece of paper on her desk in the square space of the classroom. The rattle of glass in the long parallelograms of windows up the side of the room was the first sign of a rising tide of wind outside. She smiled slowly, feeling a familiar rush of excitement. All afternoon she had been filling the paper in front of her with scaffolds of lines; diagramming sentences was the day's assigned activity. From behind her desk at the front of the room, Sister Florette's quick surveillance trapped her as she looked from her work. The child dropped her eyes from the windows to her paper, not wishing to attract any attention to her dalliance.

The clock clicked around the allotted time in its rounds, the pitifully slow hours of this day promising an escape in twenty short minutes. Coats waited out of sight in the dark recesses of the cloak room. What there was left of daylight was sinking with the advancing weather front which marched dark clouds before it.

Mercifully released at last from the long attention of the afternoon, the small bodies of the students leap into activity as the first bel set, the varnish-scented air of the classroom swirling out of its sleep; three o'clock exactly, the longed-for hour of freedom.

Sister stood abruptly, rosary beads clicking as they fell along the skirt of her black habit toward the floor. She nodded, allowed words in the empty air; the faces of her young charges broke into expressions of relief. Plans and dreams blossomed in that serious classroom; second bell rang and the children began to move.

Down long, dark corridors and over stairs the lines scurried, buttoning coats and waving papers in mittened hands. Outside doors swung open at the bottom of the dark stairwell as the lines separated into the girls' and the boys'... Small bodies hurried along by the gritty, metallic smell of grim school air and the nun's suspicious looks.

A first splash of cold air brought tears to the eyes of the children popping out of the wooden portals on the authority of the third bell. Though it was March, snow was in the air; it flew and skittered around dizzily before colliding with the cold earth. Sharp thrusts of wind tumbled them along the walkways and down to the street in disarray, lines broken, silence suspended at last.

Deep inside of this one child, a sweet recognition spread as wind-hands pushed her along the lane toward home. She turned back from the gusts of goodbyes in anticipation of what was ahead. A winding path through the canyons of streets to the hill inhabited by the dark, tall, Wind People rose in her mind. Responding to her hope and delight, the wind's roar deepened to encircle her smallness joyfully.

The smile that had come back to her somber face, was now punctuated with a bright laugh. No longer aware of anything but her floating body in this wonderful ocean of air, she swam into the music.

(to be continued)

I'll finish this story tomorrow… The day is advancing now and I must look about.

Take Care, Henry.
Cynthia

March 3, 2016 - Wind People, Part Two

Tonight, the familiar territory has become a green cathedral, snow floored and sparkling with more precious jewels than ever she has seen before; from all around and from within, a symphony is blowing wild and sweet.

-Cynthia Fraser Graves

Dear Henry,

Today's letter will include the second half of Wind People. I attempt to convey the sense of aliveness, of communication and recognition a small child finds in the woods on the way home from a very dry, cold, and dusty day in school. It will not surprise you to know that the child was me or that the experience of the story was very real. This knowing is something we share, you and me.

In Wind People, I give the experience of this knowing form and content with words, my words, the symbols I have for transferring thought and experience. They are inadequate, but it would make me happy if it succeeded in some small way to please you, my friend.

The wind in Florida will be 13 mph at 2 PM today.

Until Tomorrow,
Cynthia

Wind People, Part Two

Down over Kori's Hill, a turn to the right, across Franklin Street, past St. John's Church where the stone saint himself perched on the turret high above watches her ride the wind, arms out, up, then down, in a ceremony all her own. Oblivious to who might be watching, she approaches the colony of pine trees at the very top of the horizon… Where the Old Ones live.

At this ancient, wooded crest, she stops, and with head flung back and eyes lifted, she falls silent and waits. The trees, lifted on straight trunks of rough bark, appear as crowns high off the earth. A light fall of snow blurs their outlines adding glowing auras around them. Touched with this majesty, the small visitor curtsies. Many a night, drifting off to sleep behind the window in her bedroom, they find her and visit…breathe stories one layer outside of human speech into her ears, wind stories that quicken a sense of mystery and enchantment already in her heart, lyrics of much needed love.

Approaching the Old Ones is done with great reverence and gravity, head back, eyes to the zenith of her vision. As she watches in dimming dusk, trees dance and thrash in greetings from high above, recognizing their young friend. She stands, an enthralled audience, shining face pointed to the darkening sky, motionless in the middle of the affectionate exchange. Usual boundaries of life as she knows it are suspended here; time, tightly coiled within her, is never ending.

Streetlamps on the lane below this copse begin to glow kindly. Standing above them and looking down, they are signal fires leading the way to her castle. The little delight of seeing them sparkle and weave their light in-between branches fades as she knows they signal a ticking of time that had stopped for her; time that has begun again. It is getting late, mother is waiting in the house at the end of her journey through the woods, waiting for her safe return.

Leave-taking from the court begins with a few hesitant steps backward, eyes still locked on the faces of the Wind People. She turns away at last and is pushed along by wind-hands, towards home, pushed against being lost to the dark of night.

Stepping on the path and into the heart of the woods she feels her distance from home and begins to run, treasured papers flying into the gale. White squares of schoolwork sail out and up, into trees like decorations. They are too flimsy to endure the dynamism at work here.

In summer, she and her friends play Indians and Cowboys, Space Creatures and Nymphs in these woods, construct hideouts and camps, villages and tree-houses. Tonight, the familiar territory has become a green cathedral, snow floored and sparkling with more precious jewels than ever she has seen and, from all around and from within, a symphony blows wild and sweet high in the trees. Light within the woods has become an emerald shimmer. This girl stops, closes her eyes to feel the thrill of the storm knowing the lessons of this classroom teach magic and harmony. They overshadow any other learning she has clutched this day. Even years later, she will remember nothing of the school, but will never forget the sound of this wind. It is the voice of her own burgeoning wisdom.

At last, into the yard of her neighbor's house and out of the path. Her coat is now open and no papers from her school day remain to bring home to her mother. She is a little shadow in the gathering dark, crossing the great distance between herself and home.

As she climbs the stairs, she stops one last time, as still as death, watching the eddy of leaves and snow whirl into the corners and cracks of her porch. Delight *shivers across her back at the world she has visited. The wind is only a breeze here; she is insulated from its power and feels the shift.*

Before she is ready, the light on the porch explodes into blinding brilliance and the door of home opens. A watchful mother gathers in the little wanderer, lifting her out of the storm and expressing her relief at the child's return. At the fragrance of her warming supper and the familiar faces peering at her with concern she turns with new eyes to greet them, happy to be among her family. It is only later, as she settles into her bed, she hears the whispered voices outside her window singing still, this time a lullaby. She falls asleep knowing the People of the Wind will always be near.

-Cynthia Fraser Graves

March 4, 2016 - Visiting Royalty

Dear Wind Child,

Your story, Wind People, qualifies you, in my humble estimation, as a true transcendentalist (with a small t that is, we never really wanted to nail the idea down into dogma). You might have had a seat at the table on those rousing nights at Emerson's house when we were parsing the shape of the great, freeing idea that people are at their best when truly "self-reliant" and independent, awake to their lives, living in close touch with Nature and one with the Over-soul, the one beating heart of us all. We most usually live beneath this union, thinking ourselves to be separate and alone, but, no, a different experience is awaiting us when we quiet ourselves and allow it. You allowed it, Cynthia.

Your walk home from school in your story was a congress with the divine that is all around you, and, in your innocence, Nature strewed its jewels in front of you as if you were visiting royalty, which, of course, you are, as is everyone.

I am interested in what you say at your arrival home on that day...

"Delight shivers across her back at the world she has visited. But the wind is only a breeze here; she is insulated from its power and feels the shift.

Before she is ready, the light on the porch explodes into blinding brilliance and the door of home opens. A watchful mother gathers in the little wanderer, lifting her out of the storm and expressing her relief at the child's return. At the fragrance of her warming supper and the familiar faces peering at her with concern she turns with new eyes to greet them, happy to be among her family."

As you return home, Cynthia, the shift of energy lessens as your small feet leave the earth for the floor of a house; connection is lost; you are aware of it. As you say, you turn to your family with new eyes. Your ecstatic interlude of communion has changed you, and you knew this even at that tender age. You have new vision. The memory is with you all these years to return in the telling of this story. Wonderful!

I, too, returned to my home after mystic walks with Presence in Nature. I, too, felt the shift of energy when I went behind doors. I, too, found delight revisiting these experiences for myself. My move to Walden Pond was pure invitation for more of this deep living.

We are one in that, Cynthia, and a blessing on all things comes from that. What is it you are to title this book? A Year With Henry. A perfect evocation of what IS.

Earth strews its riches before us on all days. It is the seeing that makes the difference.

"I think that the existence of man in nature is the divinest and most startling of all facts."

Henry

March 5, 2016 - These Fleeting Moments

Dear Henry,

I make it my business to extract from Nature whatever nutriment she can furnish me, though at the risk of endless iteration. I milk the sky and earth.

-Henry David Thoreau

I am emboldened by your kind response of yesterday. Your intimation that I might be one at the table, present for those mighty discussions that charged and changed the whole drift and atmosphere of thought on earth was stunning to hear. I secretly have coveted such a fantasy. To have been at table with you, Hawthorne, Emerson, Alcott, Fuller, and others, would seem to me to be a seminal experience of a lifetime. To rail at the *"unthinking bonds of conformity"* urging each person to search for their kinship with the universe... That was a gift to us. In all I do and have done, this Oneness is my inspiration.

I read somewhere, Henry, that, in the beginning, whether from shyness or lack of invitation, you sat in the entryway of the Emerson's house and listened to table conversation, calling out your thoughts to the assembled guests from there when you felt them relevant?

While I talk of these dry and ancient things, Henry, the sky lights with fire, cresting like the ceiling of a cathedral over earth. The sun has lifted over the altar of horizon for the moment as the Sanctus bells of wind ring.

Now, whirling rays of risen sun stream a Benediction onto all below whether they will receive it or not. The fleeting moment of dawn has come and gone for this day, and morning is walking the land. An Original day to live within.

I will walk into it with you in mind as I do so.

Cynthia

March 6, 2016 - Thoughts Become Things

As a single footstep will not make a path on the earth, so a single thought will not make a pathway in the mind. To make a deep physical path we walk again and again. To make a deep mental path, we must think over and over the kind of thoughts we wish to dominate our lives.

-Henry David Thoreau

Dear Henry,

Stepping out, I am rewarded with the embrace of a fresh, breezy morning. The sky is a shade of pink or apricot hard to describe. No words for that color, you see.

We have two hundred and fifty or more letters between us now. As I woke and took my path out to my computer for the 250th plus time, I am thinking about how well-worn this habit of mine has become, and how rewarding. Our habits define our lives, and this one is good for me. During my day, I cast nets for something I can talk about to one who has passed through life and is somewhere elevated now. This lofty perspective is one that leads to fearless, borderless thinking. I am glad of it! It guides my days into the fields of all possibilities.

The text this morning is: *"What you think, you create."* We know that! Our lives are painted by the thoughts we hold and invest with emotion and passion. Whether they are of blessings or fear is up to us. We are charged to watch our thoughts and to weed out what we don't want to show up in our lives; to practice thinking what we do want because THOUGHTS BECOME THINGS. The circumstances of your life have responded to your thoughts up to this date and will continue to do so from this living minute onward. Any habitual thinking destructive to you or anyone else— fear, low self-esteem, anger, self-doubt, hatred… I dislike even forming these words as they hold a negative cursor on our page and need to be replaced with acts of gratitude, love, and optimism, on a minute-to-minute basis. Appreciation for all the scenes and actors in your own life is the way forward. And with love for yourself… Love for yourself!

The well-worn paths we tread are cut into our experience by our beliefs which may only be left over ideas from the past. To cut a new path, one with more rewarding outcomes takes imagination, emotional zest, and a reversal from stale ideas in the mind and heart. It can only be done by the Walker (that's you). Some will walk beside you, but only you see the way on your own journey.

Helpful ways to adjust to this quest are journaling your thoughts and especially your intentions, reviewing them during your day and especially nights, seeing where you slipped from the path, and rededicating your efforts on the next day.

And, always, prayer, the opening of the heart to this great knowing, the request for the great power of Source energy to join you on this quest. Your thoughts are prayers, and you are always praying... What are you praying for?

The sky is ablaze now, sun rising as I close. These words were more for those still here, Henry, but you walked that path as well, aware of the power of imagination and belief. We are just behind you.

Good morning, Friend.
Cynthia

March 7, 2016 - Falling Through To Silence

Dear Henry,

When I was younger, on an everyday sort of day, something happened that, though it was seemingly nothing spectacular, has never left my memory. I was a few streets away from home, on Holyoke Street in Rumford, Maine. Holyoke was a short street that ended abruptly as it came up against a steep, wooded mountain. I don't know why it was called Holyoke, but that is part of this story.

I was playing with some kids on a Sunday afternoon. The games were most likely King of The Mountain—a favorite—or marbles, Jacks, or some other innocent game of the day. This was back in 1953 or 1954, over sixty plus years ago now. In any event, after we were finished with the afternoon's fun, the kids went home but for some reason, I went up onto the mountain.

I don't have the particulars of that hike; all I remember is that I came upon a small clearing inviting me to stop for a while. Children of my generation played out every day—and when school was not in session, all day. Without the interference of television, phone, or gaming, we were free in the world in very natural ways. We were not afraid to be in the woods or to be alone. That fear is something that is implanted through fantasies in movies and television and all for what? Money?

On this day, it was mid to late afternoon when I stepped into the clearing. The space had charm and invited me to sit on the earth for a while to let the quiet deepen. There were trees around it, I remember, but I perched in the open space.

Now, I wish I knew what happened, but I only know its effects. I didn't fall asleep exactly, but, for quite a long period of time I dropped through the present to somewhere else, waking, as it were, at least an hour later, when the sun had begun its decline and I felt the need to go home.

Here's the difficult part to convey Henry. I felt so different—calm, sweet, new, older—as I walked home in that dusk. Everything I saw had a new sheen. I seemed to know what 'it' was all for... And that evening, in the ordinary events with my family in my home, there was a space around me, a space of calm, of distance, of light; a new regard for everything. I was changed and it felt like gratitude and joy in the common life I lived. I recognized this even as the child I was.

This memory never left me. I don't know how long the spell lasted. Perhaps it was incorporated into me for good on some level and is there still today. Perhaps in that stillness, Henry, I dropped through to a sacred place there on Holy-oak Street. I believe, with you, that communion with the soul of Nature offers these gifts when they are allowed simply by being in Presence. It is a by-invitation only event usually. On this day, it took a child within its embrace.

And that's my story for this day. It has been waiting to be told. Thank you for your listening.

We see the world piece by piece, as the sun, the moon, the animal, the tree; but the whole, of which these are shining parts, is the soul.

-Ralph Waldo Emerson

Love is an attempt to change a piece of a dream-world into reality.

-Henry David Thoreau

Cynthia

P.S. This story, told here in its original draft, becomes the idea that inspired Maude And The Holy Oak; my second children's book. It was an attempt to convey the delight and simplicity of my childhood experiences in the 1950s. It was published in 2022.

March 9, 2016 - With The Power Of The Sea

Dear Henry,

Sunrise breaches the watery horizon of the Atlantic, only minutes away from a fiery glow. The temperature is 69 degrees at present and will reach 79 degrees this afternoon. Winds will be 19 mph mid-day under a mostly cloudy sky. It's a Wednesday, middle of the week, an ordinary day really, if there are such things as ordinary days.

Space, time, society, labor, climate, food, locomotion, the animals, the mechanical forces, give us sincerest lessons day by day, whose meaning is unlimited…. Every property of matter is a school for the understanding.

-Ralph Waldo Emerson

The words above are from your Concord colleague, neighbor and friend, Ralph Waldo Emerson. Because of your friendship with him, you received validation which set you free to voice your convictions, leading all of us to a higher path. You have encouraged and enlightened countless brothers and sisters.

I recently came upon a description of your first meeting with Mr. Emerson. I love the chains of connection being forged linking people together for purpose unawares.

The history of Mr. Emerson's first acquaintance with Mr. Thoreau is this. When the former was delivering a new lecture in Concord, Miss Helen Thoreau said to Mrs. Brown, Mrs. Emerson's sister, "There is a thought almost identical with that in Henry's journal," which she soon after brought to Mrs. Brown. The latter carried it to Mr. Emerson, who was interested, and asked her to bring this youth to see him. She did, and thus began a relation that lasted all their lives of strong respect and even affection, but of a Roman character.

-Edward Waldo Emerson

Emerson's response to his meeting with you was:

I delight much in my young friend who seems to have as free and erect a mind as any I have ever met.

And there you have it; a friendship is struck. A friendship that had within its bonds the power of the sea—endless, beautiful, dangerous at times, but always surging, at work on changing the landscape in its great waves.

In 1852, writing to a friend whom he would induce to come to Concord, Mr. Emerson said:

I am sometimes discontented with my house because it lies on a dusty road and with its sills and cellar almost in the water of the meadow. But when I creep out of it into the night or morning and see what tender and majestic beauties wrap me in their bosom, how near to me is every transcendent secret of Nature's love and religion, I see how different it is where I eat and sleep. This very street of hucksters and taverns the moon will transform into a Palmyra, for she is the apologist of all apologists and will kiss the elm-trees alone and hides every meanness in silver edged darkness. Then the good river-God has taken the form of my valiant Henry Thoreau here, and introduced me to the riches of his shadowy starlit, moonlit stream…

Such praise, Henry, and from such lips.

I, too, bless and thank my friends for their loving gifts in our lives together. You know who you are. (That includes you, Henry.)

Cynthia

March 10, 2016 - A Point In Space

Dear Star Rider,

It's not what you look at that matters, it's what you see.

-Henry David Thoreau

The burning bowl of morning light glows over my head, a stage set for a play. The train only two streets away races and hoots toward Jacksonville carrying sand and stone to replenish the eroding beaches of Florida. It makes the floor shake, reminding me how patient the earth is, taking all this insult so quietly. Soon, thirty plus yellow and red passenger trains will roar up the Atlantic seaboard at over 80 mph on that same track. What will happen to quiet reflection and peace for anyone near the over a thousand plus miles of track then? Hard to imagine, Henry.

The weather feature of this day will be the wind over 20 mph, blowing warm, tropical air up and into the northeast. The temperature in Kennebunk, Maine, is 57 degrees as the sun rises. To have this balmy air crest over the state of Maine in March is unprecedented.

Here in Hobe Sound, there will be great, simmering wind activity all around. Coming out of the southwest off the ocean, the stiff breeze will cool the air temperature of 80 degrees nicely. But it is dry. We need rain.

I read with envy of a rainy day when you were encamped at Walden Pond.

Some of my pleasantest hours were during the long rainstorms in the spring or fall, which confined me to the house for the afternoon as well as the forenoon, soothed by their ceaseless roar and pelting: when an early twilight ushered in a long evening in which many thoughts had time to take root and unfold themselves.

-Henry David Thoreau, Walden

We, in this moment on the earth, have a harder time *"finding a long evening in which many thoughts have time to take root and unfold…"* There is ceaseless talking around us now, Henry. To be in that quiet, contemplative place takes intention and will. And rain is seen as unwelcome. Imagine that the very source of life on earth is unwelcome by most.

Even when it does rain here in Florida, it is a quick thing. Not the encampment of gray skies for days that one is used to in the northeast. I once spent six weeks in brown, dusty, dry Texas during the summer. The temperatures soared over 100 degrees. When I returned to Maine, I flew (in an airplane) into Portland, Maine, only to gasp when I first saw the lush, green carpet beneath me. It brought tears to my eyes. The cost of that sparkling green are the rainy days in that region. I am glad of it.

As I write this letter, I have rocketed back to Maine in my mind under the weighty gray skies of a spring day. On these days, I read all day long, traveling with my books as surely as if I were on a journey.

There will be no rain here today, but it is raining somewhere. Somewhere, there will be rainbows.

Cynthia

March 11, 2016 - The Evolution Angel

The world is but a canvas for our imaginations.

-Henry David Thoreau

Dear Henry,

The red whistle of a waking cardinal flamed out into the very early dark this morning. I was teetering on the edge of going back to sleep but hearing that clear greeting of sound through the balmy air, I knew it was of no use.

This morning's sky is a cauldron of clouds taking the shades of mauve and boiling around a tepid yellow with a light blue backdrop. The temperature is 70 degrees, winds 15 mph.

Imagination was a very dangerous word when I was growing up. Everything was measured by reason and common sense. That put me at odds with many of the people and much of the environment I lived within. I know you relate to that experience, Henry, as you were a misfit of sorts for your time and place. I went underground; I preferred the world of imagination. Especially within my elementary school, imagination was sought out and squelched as an immoral trait.

According to Todd Michael in his book The Evolution Angel (Jeremy P Tarcher-Penguin), Spirit abounds everywhere and we are only aware of its Presence when we tune out distractions. One way to do that is with imagination; opening the doors of our mind to senses beyond sight and hearing.

This could have been said by you, Henry. We are lost in the chaos of lives not truly lived, but only experienced on the surface because of distractions. Imagination is a vitally real and living realm where anything is possible; an astounding discussion between what is visible to our senses and what lies just beyond them. In our time, this place is known as the Imaginal Realm.

Cynthia

March 12, 2016 - The Full Definition Of Joy

Dear Henry,

I think that cardinal has taken it upon himself (it sounds too red to be his mate in brown) to wake me each morning. Again today, he was just outside my window peeping away with all his heart. I am glad of it. Tonight, we will turn the clock ahead an hour and we shall see if he comes for me at 5 AM or at 6 AM. It will be a good test.

The day ahead is a fair one, temperatures will rise to the 80s, no rain, winds at 16 mph around noon, but there will be a breeze all day.

I am inspired by your journal daily, always picking up a pebble of meaning to cast it into the pond of my thoughts. The ripples created spread out on the surface from center to edges. Sometimes when I am not calm and centered, the surface is more like a stream and the thought-pebbles have diminished effect.

The word-pebble for today is JOY, taken from:

A journal, a book that shall contain your joy, your ecstasy.

-Henry David Thoreau

The definition of joy is 'experiencing great pleasure or delight.' Joy is the kingpin emotion, sought after by most, elusive in these days. According to the dictionary, it is achieved by well-being, success, good fortune, or possessing what one desires.

A writer who does not speak out of a full experience uses torpid words, wooden or lifeless words, such words as "humanitary" which have a paralysis in their tails.

-Henry David Thoreau, Journal

Henry, you understood that if you reversed that definition with your living, if you came from joy first, you would realize well-being, success, good fortune, and what you desired. Joy, strewn like pebbles on the ground, is everywhere. It starts in the heart and radiates out from there. It may sound counterintuitive, but to be joyful comes before any reason for it; that is the truth. Joy is plentiful, free. Pick a few pebbles of innocence up in smiles and compassion, cast them to see the joyful effect. Even in dark times, they are at your feet.

Enjoy this day, Henry, wherever you are,
Cynthia

March 14, 2016 - A Walk About Under The Moon With Henry

Dear Henry,

Moon half full. Fields dusky; the evening star and one other bright orb near the moon. It is a cool but still night…. Now I turn down Corner Road. At this quiet hour the evening wind is heard to moan in the hollows, mysterious, spirit-like, conversing with you. It can be heard only now. The whip-poor-will sings. I hear a laborer, going home, coarsely singing to himself. Though he has scarcely had a thought all day, killing weeds, at this hour he sings or talks to himself. His humble, earthly contentment gets expression. It is kindred in its origin with the notes of music of many creatures. A more fit and natural expression of his mood, this humming, than conversation is wont to be. The fireflies appear to be flying. though they may be stationary on the grass stems, for their perch and the nearness of the ground are obscured by the darkness, and now you see one here and then another there, as if it were one motion. Their light is singularly bright and glowing to proceed from a living creature. Nature loves variety in all things, and so she adds glow-worms to fireflies, though I have not noticed any this year. The great story of the night is the moon's adventure with the clouds. What innumerable encounters she has had with them! When I enter on the moonlit causeway, where the light is reflected from the glistening alder leaves, and their deep, dark, liquid shade beneath strictly bounds the firm damp road and narrows it, it seems like autumn. The rows of willows completely fence the way and appear to converge in perspective, as I had not noticed by day…. In Conant's meadow, I hear the gurgling of unwearied water, the trill of a toad, and go through the cool, primordial, liquid air that has settled there. As I sit on the great doorstep, the loose clapboards on the house rattle in the wind weirdly, and I seem to hear some wild mice running about on the floor…. How distant is day and its associations…? No need to climb the Andes or Himalayas, for brows of lowest hills are the highest mountain-tops in cool moonlight nights.

-Henry David Thoreau, Journal

As I read your Journal entry, I was walking beside you and you were talking to me, and though you suspected I was there, you didn't know for sure. I can hear you breathe and feel the tramp of your footsteps on the dirt road. The passage is one of a translator, one in a foreign land, the land of dusk and the coming night, a land we rarely see as we are busy about the small activities of life, coming home from a day away, preparing food for the evening, any of the many pursuits that take us away from the sentient and mysterious landscape in which we live. You show us that going for a walk in the moonlight is an exotic thing, a rare treasure.

As it came to my letter this morning, I walked out with you 164 years ago. I experienced what you left behind just for me in some imaginal way. I will leave it at that, a walk under the moon with Henry.

Amen.

Cynthia

March 16, 2016 - The Full Moons Of March

Dear Henry,

The sky's canopy this morning before six held no clouds, only a teacup of stars. Since the beginning of Daylight Savings, I am up well before the sunrise and before morning songs from birds greet the dawn. All is still, a few lights on up and down the street. No farms here, Henry, that way of life seems to be disappearing. I imagine your view in a similar walk out: the little town of Concord rising, farms in the hinterlands lit by lanterns, their day well started with chores in progress.

The moon this month is known as the Sap or Sugar Moon and will sail the skies on March 23, designating the month for clear watery sap of maple trees collected and boiled into a delicious, sweet amber syrup.

Legend has it that the first maple syrup maker was an Iroquois woman, the wife of Chief Woksis. One late-winter morning, as the story goes, the chief went out on one of his hunts, but not before yanking his tomahawk from the tree where he'd thrown it the night before. On this day the weather turned quite warm, causing the tree's sap to run and fill a container standing near the trunk. The woman spied the vessel and, thinking it was plain water, cooked their evening meal in it. The boiling that ensued turned the sap to syrup, flavoring the chief's meal as never before. And thus began the tradition of making maple syrup.

Sap used to make this syrup is different from that produced by the tree at other times of the year. This sap flows in the late winter and early spring. After the trees start to bud and produce leaves, the quality of the sap dramatically changes and cannot be used to produce syrup. Nights with temperatures in the twenty-degree range and days that warm to about 40 Fahrenheit are the perfect conditions for sap to run.

This year, 2016, has been one for the books. Sugaring started in late January, the earliest date in the 148 year history kept by the Corse Farm in southern Vermont. We are having a heat wave all over the US. Here in Florida, temperatures are well into the 80's—yesterday reaching 90 degrees, summer ranges. How this will play out over the hot months of the calendar summer—as we are technically still in winter—no one can say, but the bet is it will be the hottest yet.

Let this be a testimony to things as they are today. It will be 54 degrees in Kennebunk, Maine, on March 16th. By any standards, we are in uncharted territory.

Good day, Henry.

Cynthia

March 17, 2016 - Knowledge Of Star Songs

Dear Henry,

I was going to write of other things today until I realized that it is St. Patrick's Day. The world will wake up wearing green today, green beer will flow, there will be dancing and singing until all hours, especially in Dublin, Ireland, the home of the feast. This day's commemoration is of the traditional death date of St. Patrick, c. 385-461, and the arrival of Christianity in Ireland. The feast has become blurred and is now one of the heritage and culture of the Irish in general. There will be public parades and festivals, Church services, and the Lenten restrictions on eating and drinking alcohol are lifted for the day.

This theme sent me whirling back to the memory of the month we spent in Donegal last fall, to the clear beauty of that land and the friendliness of its people. I'm sure there will be singing and dancing in the streets of Dungloe; all the pubs are open, and the feast has begun as I write. We of Puritan ancestry do not know how to celebrate as the Irish do. We do not give ourselves over to our feasts, but only look with distrust at that kind of joyful spending of passion. I would like to be there in Dungloe today.

Opal Whiteley, (December 11, 1897—February 16, 1992), an American Naturist and diarist, once wrote about picking up potatoes and listening to their experiences of growing. She said they had star-songs and earth-songs inside of them. Opal's childhood journal was first published in 1920 as The Story of Opal in serialized form in the Atlantic Monthly, then later that same year as a book with the title The Story of Opal: The Journal of an Understanding Heart. I thought you would find her words as true and beautiful as they are to me. And what could be more of a testimony to a people than this poetry of the potato that kept life going, though barely, through all the hardship the Irish lived.

"In Man's heart is a little room.
He has named it
Oblivion.
And things are ranged along its walls
That he does not wish
To think about.
Every time that he pushes something in there,
He closes the door very tightly.

But in hours when he is weary,
In the hours that walk around some midnights,
When high fires have burned
To a low flicker,
Then the little door swings on its hinges
And no thing
Will make it stay closed
All of the time.

When he is near death,
All the velvet-footed wanderers in there
Join the throng around his bed.
"We will not die," they whisper
To one another,
While Beauty waits with drawn lips,
And dry eyes.

But there is heard
The patter of a little sad rain
In her heart's garden,
Where some little flower buds
That were once thinking of the sun
Will never open,
Because Man keeps a little room
Of oblivion in his soul."

-Opal Whiteley

Happy Saint Patrick's Day Henry. May this spirited people be blessed in all ways.

Cynthia

March 18, 2016 - The Concord River Today

Dear Henry,

In photos of your beloved Concord River, you would recognize Old North Bridge which spans the flow of this much-loved river flowing north to the Merrimack River, a gently flowing stream until nearing Lowell, when it becomes a whitewater cascade.

Called the Musketaquid River by Native Americans, it was renamed in 1635 by settlers from England for the town it watered: Concord. In April 1775, the Old North Bridge was the site of the Battle of Concord, which took place the same day that the first shots of the Revolutionary War were fired over in Lexington. The bridge that stands there now, a reproduction, reminds us of that day. I have stood upon it, imagining what took place.

The line of five companies of Minutemen and five of non-Minuteman militia occupied a hill near the bridge with groups of men streaming in totaling 400 against the British light infantry companies from the 4th, 10th, and 43rd Regiments of Foot under Captain Walter Laurie, a force of 90--95 men. The British retreated across the river and the two sides faced each other across that North Bridge.

If you will indulge me in a historical description of the event: a brief exchange of fire ensued which saw the first instance of Americans firing to deadly effect on British regulars, after which the British retreated. Ralph Waldo Emerson posited that world history pivoted at that moment. He called the first shot of this skirmish the "shot heard round the world" in his 1837 poem "Concord Hymn".

Concord Hymn

By the rude bridge that arched the flood,
Their flag to April's breeze unfurled,
Here once the embattled farmers stood,
And fired the shot heard round the world.
The foe long since in silence slept;
Alike the conqueror silent sleeps;
And Time the ruined bridge has swept
Down the dark stream which seaward creeps.
On this green bank, by this soft stream,
We set to-day a votive stone;
That memory may their deed redeem,
When, like our sires, our sons are gone.
Spirit, that made those heroes dare,
To die, and leave their children free,
Bid Time and Nature gently spare

The shaft we raise to them and thee

Living in the Old Manse next door to the bridge at the time of the charge, Ralph Waldo Emerson's ancestors stood in the innocent field behind their home and watched as deadly force was brandished against Tyranny. They ministered to the wounded in that old house. It still stands by the river that seems not to have changed at all since that day.

This river meant freedom to you, Henry, real estate owned by no one, a roadway into the mysteries of unpeopled forests and woods where your earnest exploration of natural beauty could go on unabated. And you kept a record of your generous living within the pages of A Week on The Concord and Merrimack River. Walking over the Old North Bridge, I look down the water's trail to see your boat disappearing around the bend, just barely in sight.

Without being the owner of any land, I find that I have a civil right in the river— that, if I am not a landowner, I am a water-owner. It is fitting, therefore, that I should have a boat, a cart, for this is my farm.

-Henry David Thoreau, Journal

Big thoughts for a Saturday morning.

Cynthia

March 19, 2016 - Blue Curls

Dear Henry,

I am dreaming this morning of a garden in Maine. Safely nestled inside a sturdy wooden fence, many separate garden plots wait for the sun and warmth to pull frost from the ground, to soften the rich brown soil that will support an abounding harvest this year, as in the twelve years since it was formed. Kinua, meaning community, is the name of the organic community garden of Kennebunk—the benefits of which are shared with community food banks as well as the gardener's tables.

One of my favorite moments in my personal year's calendar happens when I am at the garden in May or June busy with seeding a crop or straightening up rows, hoeing between, or watering the seedlings with the crystal flow of clean water and the first flash of blue swoops in over my head as their song bursts out in the quiet. The bluebirds have arrived! Not there for long, they are usually gone by mid to late August, so their presence is to be savored.

There is a fine collection of bird houses around the space on the garden fence that is full of different bird citizens throughout the summer, forming a bird town with sparrows, wrens, finches, even cardinals—but the bluebirds are my favorites. Their presence adds delight to time spent in the quiet meditation of gardening. Something about the color they add...

In your Journal of March 13, 1853, you wrote,

I no sooner step out of the house than I hear the bluebirds in the air, and far and near, everywhere except in the woods, throughout the town you may hear them—the blue curls of their warblings—harbingers of serene and warm weather, little azure rills of melody trickling here and there, from out the air, their short warble trilled in the air reminding me of so many corkscrews assaulting and thawing the torpid mass of winter, assisting the ice and snow to melt and the streams to flow.

Spring in the skies is only a few hours away; Sunday, early morning, the Vernal Equinox will silently take command.

Thank you for reminding me of bluebirds,
Cynthia

As soon as those spring mornings arrive in which the birds sing, I am sure to be an early riser. I am waked by my genius. I wake to inaudible melodies and am surprised to find myself expecting the dawn in so serene and joyful and expectant a mood.

-Henry David Thoreau, Journal

March 20, 2016 - Plant Your Dreams

Dear Henry,

A brand spanking new season with all the possibilities of new activities rising with it. Spring! When I was a child, the arrival of spring meant that the mountains of snow, up to six-foot banking along the streets, would begin to melt, streaming water into the road to freeze at night into glare ice and melt by day into rivulets. The heavy confinement of winter let go and we were set free to play again in woods and yards around our houses. Great games of marbles were the spring thing, each child carrying their bag of clicking orbs as if their own worth was measured by the weight and size of the collection.

It took a while for lawns and trees to respond to spreading warmth, but the day came when leaves and flowers bobbed in the winds again. In Rumford, an organ grinder arrived about this time—a man who walked the still cold streets, his organ strapped to his back, turning the handle, singing his songs as he walked. People, gladdened by his timely return, came out of their houses to give him a coin which made his living. Some invited him in for a meal. Seems like a dream now as I remember this.

For me now, spring means a return from the south to my home in the north. It means seedlings, soil preparation, opening a long-closed house, seeing faces of long absent friends and family, the embrace of familiar landscapes, the sounds of wind in the woods behind my home at night. The games of childhood have changed into the occupations of making a fruitful life, but the energy of spring is always the same; it is the energy of waking up, of hope, of dreams, of preparation for the easy months ahead. Anticipation is in the air.

In Maine, today, they will have snow, a nor'easter. Winds will blow snow back into the just thawed region, but not for long. The corner is turned, temperatures will rise, and snow will all melt soon. In this last gasp of winter, the gardens are blessed with nitrogen and sulfur bound up with snowfall more than with rain.

Time to plant your dreams, Henry, in the garden of your mind, tend them with intention and faith. That is true here on earth, at least. I see by your words that spring set you free as well.

Cynthia

March 21, 2016 - The Open Road

Dear Henry,

I go forth to make new demands on life. I wish to begin this summer well; to do something in it worthy of it and me; to transcend my daily routine and that of my townsmen; to have immortality now, that it be the quality of my daily life; to pay the greatest tax, of any man in Concord, and enjoy the most!

- Henry David Thoreau, Journal

I love what you say here so much, Henry. On this day in 1852, a plain old March Day, you rededicate yourself to rise above the winter doldrums that have taken hold, to transcend (my favorite word) your daily routine and do something worthy of yourself and those around you. To pay the greatest tax and enjoy the most. The tax you speak of is awareness of the great gift of each moment you are alive. We are so busy resisting things we judge as not interesting, profitable, or pleasurable. I bet you went out for a long walk that day, looking into everything you saw with attention.

Tomorrow, I ride the highway myself, leaving the known behind for the unknown, although, really, every time you step out, you are stepping into the unknown. Entering the flow of traffic, whether foot traffic on a sidewalk, air travel, or the flow of traffic as we all speed around in metal capsules called cars, one's progress becomes part of the progress of all, open to chance meetings of all sorts.

I look forward to the spectacle of it all, trusting that I will arrive where I propose to arrive: New Haven, Connecticut. That will mean that the regularity of my missives to you might be a bit harder to pull off. Nevertheless, I will be telling you of what I see as I go—reporting back. Coming out of the warm south into the cool northeast, I will have to bundle up. Luckily this isn't the travel day. They are having snow right now. The spring birds are caught out in the storm.

So, I make new demands on life as did you. The past will turn into the present under my feet as I go forth. We are connected wherever we go.

Cynthia

March 22, 2016 - To Sing You On Your Way

Dear Cynthia,

I received your note telling me of your trip north…I wish you well. You will be very near my beloved Concord, in the same wind field almost. Oh, to see Spring walk abroad. I never will forget the passion of that time in my life.

"May I dare as I have never done! May I persevere as I have never done! May I purify myself anew as with fire and water, soul, and body! May my melody not be wanting to the season! May I gird myself to be a hunter of the beautiful that naught escape me! May I attain to a youth never attained! I am eager to report the glory of the universe; may I be worthy to do it."

-My Journal, March 1852

This entry above I reissue to you and all who read these letters. In this, the dawn of Spring, let nothing hold your hope hostage.
Find a song for your farewell embedded in the air about you.
Be safe my friend. Be brave! Be quick to come home.

Henry

March 24, 2016 - Fire Rainbows

Dear Henry,

Thank you for the encouraging note of yesterday. It was a difficult day on earth as hate and fear struck out against the innocent again, this time in Brussels. Whenever we feel the effects of this fear, we all are involved.

A few years ago, a friend and I were out on a walk by the Atlantic on a perfectly perfect August afternoon. We were talking of this and that, enjoying all the elements of that path by the sea when we were stopped in our tracks when we saw the wispy clouds above us begin to take on color as if they were being painted by some unseen brush. We stood in awe for what seemed a long time to watch the progression of colors take over these clouds one by one. I believe I have referred to this occurrence in a previous letter. Well, yesterday, I came upon a description of how this happened.

Fire rainbows occur only when the sun is very high in the sky (more than 58° above the horizon). What's more, the hexagonal ice crystals that make up cirrus clouds must be shaped like thick plates with their faces parallel to the ground.

When light enters through a vertical side face of such an ice crystal and leaves from the bottom face, it refracts, or bends, in the same way that light passes through a prism. If a cirrus cloud's crystals are aligned just right, the whole section lights up in a spectrum of colors.

The position of the observer is key. These horizontal arcs cannot be seen in locations north of 55 degrees N, and south of 55 degrees S. Also, there are only certain times of the year when they occur. Deep summer is one of those times.

So, as we stood awestruck watching this fire rainbow emerge, we had converged with many happenings of the natural world to be present at that very moment. We have talked about it for years. It seemed to happen just for us, and I still believe it did.

Nature provides exceptions to every rule.

-Margaret Fuller

It still seems a magical thing to me even when the facts are known.
Something I thought you would like to know…
With love,

Cynthia

March 24, 2016 - Quiznos, Concourse C, and Nick's Tomato Pie

Music is perpetual and only the hearing is intermittent.

-Henry David Thoreau

Dear Henry,

You often said that you allowed a pause between the experience and the response regarding your Journal. Said it was better to let some time pass before reflecting.

And so, this morning, I follow your advice in speaking about an occurrence that took place on March 22nd, two days ago, the morning I traveled up to Maine. I arrived early for my flight, bought a coffee, and sat in a section of the airport to open my computer to work on my letter to you.

The atmosphere on that concourse was one of sorrow, the eyes of passersby downcast; television screens around the area replicated images of an attack of an angry, fearful few on the innocent many. This happens so often in this time on earth.

I had my earbuds in (there are myriads of things that my generation have use of that yours couldn't even imagine. I must trust you understand what I mean by earbuds and airports. Forgive me), and was listening to a British acapella group—Angelis—singing Somewhere Over the Rainbow. The pure tones poured into my ears, an antidote to grim faces and little squares on TV along the passageway.

Then everything suddenly altered. Crowds of people walking the concourse slowed down to what was seemed a crawl, stuttered steps falling noiselessly as they regarded each other with solemn faces, but with hope. The words of the song filled the air, heard only by me, but affecting everything.

I was sitting just across from Quiznos (a sandwich shop), and Nick's Tomato Pies on Concourse C, but those shops *now* disappeared, and we, all of us, fused into one heart, suspended in space. Just for this moment, in this place, we united, hearts on a sojourn on planet Earth.

I wondered if they could hear what I was hearing?

God himself culminates in the present moment and will never be more divine in the lapse of all the ages.

-Henry David Thoreau

Cynthia

March 26, 2016 - Holy Saturday Of The Triduum

Dear Henry,

Early morning light in Princeton reveals awakening flowers and green fizz on trees, all swaying in spring's cool air. A brook wandering away from me at the edge of my view is purling over rocks bordered in forsythia. In this old growth area, ancient trees tower over the landscape, interlaced with small pines that sprout under their protection. Birds swoop in under the sentinels of trees to the brook for water.

Princeton is the city of magnolias. Everywhere you look, explosions of bloom reach up like pink balloons. Walking any street in this city is magical. Beauty is everywhere.

This Holy Saturday we wait for the explosion of Light that is Easter; the altar of the earth has been made ready, flowered, watered, warmed. All we need do is let Light in and know that it was created for us, for this moment, forever.

I stand at the crossing of past and future, in an eternal breath, on the cornerstone of Now. Easter is possible every second of ticking time. Tomorrow morning, Easter joy will take the sky at dawn.

What will we do to greet this great invitation to live deeply?

I know you rose into each day, newly conceived, Henry, and blazed the path to innocent wonder and joy in one way or another ever since.

With gratitude,
Cynthia

March 27, 2016 - Easter Vision

The people that walked in darkness have seen a great light: and they that dwell in the land of the shadow of death, upon them hath the light shined.

-Isaiah 9:2

Dear Henry,

In the Easter mornings behind me, one particular moment emerges as a distinct and unique event. It took place somewhere in the year of 1958 or 1959. I was a teenager at the time. This was the era when Easter service at the local Catholic Church meant a new set of clothes all the way from underwear out to new shoes, new hat, and gloves for the new spiritual year that began at dawn on Easter. Church on that day was the whole show. The Easter bunny took a back seat to the Resurrection.

On that morning, I was in my new suit with matching shoes, hat, and gloves, wearing peach-colored nylons (very exciting for a teenager) just to spice the beige mix up. It was a wildly windy, cold morning and I was walking to church by myself. The dust of all winter's road debris was blowing up in boiling, stinging clouds around me as.

Standing alone at the intersection of roads leading up to the church, and holding my hat in the fierce spring winds, I saw myself standing there, on that corner waiting to cross the road as if I were outside of myself. I recognized I had been here before. In a mix of Deja vu—the phenomenon of a strong sensation that what I was experiencing had already been lived in the past—I was flooded with a tender love for that little girl so intent on being present and good, waiting for someone to see and bless her striving. The gift of seeing that day is still with me.

These many years later, Henry, I am still on that street corner in many ways, waiting to cross the street. I have much to be grateful for, many meetings with Spirit. On Easter mornings, I look back to that one, that first encounter, knowing that whatever came after it in the Mass that day, Easter had already arrived in my heart.

A Blessed Easter to everyone,
Cynthia

March 28, 2016 - A Plain Monday

Dear Henry,

So, we are back to plain old Monday, the Monday after Easter, a day when celebrations cease and the tread of feet heard in this part of the world is to work or a school day; Monday, the first day of the week.

If you have built castles in the air, your work need not be lost; that is where they should be. Now put the foundations under them.

-Henry David Thoreau

I see the latent power within this plain day, see the clear path to possibility simmering within the intentions we hold as we work. *How* we do is as important as *what* we do. In everything we do we are laying up the treasure of our appreciation for ourselves, the result of the day. Whether there is an employer, or you are your own employer, what will the fruits of this day be?

Henry, you resolved to learn every day, whether in the forest and fields, the pencil factory, or the writing room. Your constant quest for enlightenment drew you along the path in good and difficult times, joyful in pursuit. Your reflection at the end of the day crystallized what you had learned into gems for all of us.

I need to get this day, this Monday, started for myself, so I will end here. My work calls to me from just beyond here.

Good morning, Mr. Thoreau,

Cynthia.

March 29, 2016 - Ecosystems Plus One

Time is but the stream I go a-fishing in. I drink at it; but while I drink I see the sandy bottom and detect how shallow it is. Its thin current slides away, but eternity remains.

-Henry David Thoreau

Dear Henry,

A brook borders the land I see out of my window. Children playing in the new spring don rubber boots and walk up and down its glistening road, their reedy voices rising into the trees on strong winds. Their play never ends; games from inside their imagination arrive like bubbles from a pipe and disappear as fast.

When I look upon this ribbon of water, I see light reflected to me, affecting me with calm hope. The usually tranquil flow of water ambles along at the border of my view from the north to south, swelling with rain into a small torrent, a miniature of the great rivers of earth. It is busily, silently, cutting a chasm, three or four feet already achieved. Who knows what a thousand years will make of it, if we as a species have that long on Earth?

Small fish, water bugs, algae and many other unobservable living organisms are in the miniature ecosystem. Birds swoop to feed on the life going on there and for water. The old growth trees overhead, populated with many colorful species of feathered friends, stand sentinel. Chief among the inhabitants of these trees is the familiar cardinal, its red arrow of a body stitching in clear air. It seems to have followed me from Florida. And robins, a carpet of robins after worm castings, look like flowers themselves endowed with flight.

Last night, all night, the lullaby of winds howled from the northwest in digits of over 20 mph, temperatures falling into the 20 degree range. The stars glistened in clear, cold skies. Somewhere, the birds found warmth as they are now out swooping and singing on the still fresh morning winds. I stand out early to listen.

These are the gifts of the environment, complex systems with emergent properties blending effortlessly before your eyes, the whole becoming greater than the sum of its parts, everything connected within me to evoke the wonder of it all.

It is a good day, Henry. I have the coin of the realm in my hand.

Cynthia

I cannot but feel compassion when I hear some trig, compact-looking man, seemingly free, all girded and ready, speak of his 'furniture,' as whether it is insured or not. 'But what shall I do with my furniture?'...It would surpass the powers of a well man nowadays to take up his bed and walk, and I should certainly advise a sick one to lay down his bed and run.

-Henry David Thoreau

March 30, 2016 - John Farmer

Cynthia, about work, beware the attractiveness of "being busy". It seems to prosper you, but, in all but life supporting details, it is a distraction from what is real. I addressed that in a tale I told in Walden. I was often castigated for not being "busy", or, at least, "productive" in a way my townsmen understood productive. Once, hearing a bull frog commence with a story, I stood transfixed for hours listening, much to the verbal disapproval of my family. In this attention to life, I was true.

Here is John Farmer, an Everyman of my day...

"John Farmer sat at his door one September evening, after a hard day's work his mind still running on his labor more or less. Having bathed, he sat down to re-create his intellectual man. It was a rather cool evening, and some of his neighbors were apprehending a frost. He had not attended to the train of his thoughts long before he heard someone playing a flute, and that sound harmonized with his mood. Still, he thought of his work; but, the burden of his thought was, that though this kept running in his head, and he found himself planning and contriving it against his will, it concerned him very little. It was no more than the scurf of his skin, which was constantly shuffled off. But the notes of the flute came home to his ears out of a different sphere from that he worked in, and suggested work for certain faculties that slumbered in him. They gently did away with the street. and the village, and the state in which he lived. A voice said to him 'Why do you stay here and live this mean moiling life, when a glorious existence is possible for you? Those same stars twinkle over other fields than these.' But, how to come out this condition and actually migrate thither?"

The flutes are playing, Cynthia, always, music is in the air above you. Though you row against the tide, the river will be yours when you achieve surrender to it. Be not intimidated by the roar of disapproval and doubt you raise. You will learn that this noise disappears behind you quickly.

Your humble friend,
Henry

March 31, 2016 - Robins And Poetry

Dear Henry,

The last few days, strong winds are about, but a good sun warmed them some and brought blossoms out on every bush and tree in sight. Pink is the color of spring; pink blossoms and blooms bob in winds, all tints and shapes lit with the yellow of daffodils on every lawn. Taking a walk is truly a spectator sport.

The town is just alive with robins. They are everywhere, collecting material for their nests, looking for worms, signaling the onset of spring. Their cheery songs, different for morning and evening, are part of the sound backdrop that we live within without noticing much.

This is the last day of windy March; tomorrow will begin the rainy month of April, National Poetry Month. As a child, I was told that March winds swept the earth clean and April rains watered it to bring forth the flowers and leaves. That would make this new month the right time for Poetry—the flowering of a language.

Cynthia

Spring 2016 - April

April is sweet, shy, generous, and loving. Her rains sing the melody of life coaxing Spring's green haze to rise from bare brown limbs. April's voice is the symphony of rebirth. Peepers sing their rhapsodies deep into Spring nights accompanied by a fugue of birdsong in the first light of dawn. The voices of Earth's children have part in this hymn. Out of confinement at last, they sing in innocent rhythms of jump rope and Ollie Ollie Infree, and love songs punctuated with the cold click of marbles in the backyards of town. Over it all rises the gentle melody of new leaves swelling.

April 1, 2016 - Julia Cameron

Dear Henry,

It's here! April has stepped upon the stage of months and years to beguile us with showers and flowers and it's raining here. Perfect!

It's National Poetry Month, and, as promised, I am offering poems this month, poems I love.

Today's offering is Jerusalem Is Walking In This World, written by Julia Cameron.

Now, because of copyright issues I am only allowed to give you a few lines...I will comply, but, if you are inclined, I will bet the whole poem is available where you are...

Jerusalem Is Walking In This World

This is a great happiness.
The air is silk.
There is milk in the looks
That come from strangers.
I could not be happier
If I were bread and you could eat me.
Joy is dangerous.
It fills me with secrets...

-Julia Cameron

In this poem, Henry, we see beneath the surface of particularity to Union... Lovely! This sounds like your delicious evening in Walden woods...

April 2, 2016 - Amy Lowell

Dear Henry,

Selecting one poem a day from the poetry of my life is more daunting than I expected. Amy Lowell is the poet for today. Born in Brookline, MA, on February 12th, 1874, she won the Pulitzer Prize for poetry posthumously. She died May 12th, 1925. She was a few generations ahead of you, Henry, but her themes would have interested you... "Patterns" explores the aftermath of war experienced by many women during the War of Spanish Succession, when this poem was written, and in World War I. Below find the opening two stanzas of this brilliant work. I encourage you to find the whole.

Patterns

I walk down the garden paths,
And all the daffodils
Are blowing, and the bright blue squills.
I walk down the patterned garden paths
In my stiff, brocaded gown.
With my powdered hair and jewelled fan,
I too am a rare

Pattern. As I wander down
The garden paths.
My dress is richly figured,
And the train
Makes a pink and silver stain
On the gravel, and the thrift
Of the borders.
Just a plate of current fashion,
Tripping by in high-heeled, ribboned shoes.
Not a softness anywhere about me,
Only whale-bone and brocade.
And I sink on a seat in the shade
Of a lime tree. For my passion
Wars against the stiff brocade.

-Amy Lowell

April 3, 2016 - Walt Whitman

Dear Henry,

One can hardly imagine a gathering of poets without the brawny, audacious presence of Walt (addressed as Walter by his mother) Whitman. In my research on this Chanticleer 0f the mid-1800's, I came upon the tale of your visit to him in Brooklyn, NY, with Bronson Alcott on November 9, 1856. It seems you purloined a hot biscuit from his mother's oven (fascinating what details survive centuries) and—coming back the next day as Walt wasn't home for your first try—you and Walt, two of the most emblematic and brave writers of your era, observed each other cautiously.

Both of your books—Leaves of Grass published in 1855, two years later than Walden, 1854—simmered with a variety of truth that opened the doors of fresh possibility for what had become *"lives of desperation"* as you phrased it, Henry. When Whitman announced that his poems spoke for America you crankily responded that you didn't think much of America or, most especially, politics. And let's be brave and say it, the sensuality of his verse did not meet with approval from you. Still, you parted on friendly terms, praising (in private must I say) the works of each other.

I offer a few lines of his Credo... A Song of Myself. They are in the public domain, Thanks Be.

A Song Of Myself

I Celebrate myself, and sing myself,
And what I assume you shall assume,
For every atom belonging to me as good belongs to you.
I loafe and invite my soul,
I lean and loafe at my ease observing a spear of summer grass.
My tongue, every atom of my blood, form'd from this soil, this air,
Born here of parents born here from parents the same, and their parents the
same,
I, now thirty-seven years old in perfect health begin,
Hoping to cease not till death.
Creeds and schools in abeyance,
Retiring back a while sufficed at what they are, but never forgotten,
I harbor for good or bad, I permit to speak at every hazard,
Nature without check with original energy.
Oh, the sound of that peon…

-Walt Whitman

April 4, 2016 - Sue R Morin

Dear Henry,

I'd like to introduce you to a poet friend, Sue R. Morin of Ogunquit, Maine. In her powerful poem, Winter Lake, we skate the sharp ice of loneliness to find the gifts offered. I am privileged to meet in a group with Sue at the Seed and Bean coffee shop. On select mornings, we—there are four of us—parse the experience of being women writers, of being women, and of being. We are much, I expect, like your cadre of friends. We come up with gratitude most days—and maybe some meaning that sends us home satisfied for the hours.

Sue's stunning imagery is a map of the topography of human emotion. It brings us to the heart of hearing music in everyday lives, the gift.

I know that you were a skater in the long, white winters, Henry, and that you skated miles on the frozen crystal of Concord's waters. I know that you knew loneliness well and wrote reams of letters to distant friends. Though you are not physically present for this poem, it will land on your shores as familiar text. Poetry is universal, paying no heed to place. It is in the air waiting to be heard.

Yours in Poetry,
Cynthia

Winter Lake

I am alone there, skating near shore on the white lake.
In the distance men are fishing, their weighty trucks
drawn up beside small huts. Suddenly, an iceboat, whizzing,
snaps a happy couple past, and off they go, sail flapping.

I think about my weight on ice,
only half a couple,
when suddenly I hear
a thunderous lake-crack coming,
sharking by under the snow-ringed surface,
splitting an icy seam
right under my blades, drawing me down.

I'm shaken imagining you upside down
in the darkling water, our skate-blades meeting
like magnets.
Well, you and I, we have our ways to meet.
We are so far apart. We write and send.
So groaning, so intense our intercourse goes
over land, through tunnels under mountains.
Brilliant are our letters frozen
feelings crystallized in type,
splitting quick an envelope of gelid time
gone by, five days, before you tear me open,
read me page by page to get your ahhhh.

Alone, at night we slip between white sheets
sweet feelings, sharply folded, lily-sweet
white soup-smooth paper, wine our ink.
We crack the shell of distance,
skate upside down on opened seams in cyberspace,
slide, gently merged and flattened,
soup-hot breathing, send it out,
into that measurable wine-dark space
between the water and the ice.

Sue R. Morin

April 6, 2016 - William Wordsworth

Dear Henry,

A night wind still blows around the house. Early dawn is an hour away, but I see Wordsworth's daffodils dancing as I sit to write. A lyric poem, it presents the deep feelings and emotions of a poet rather than telling a story. The inward eye, his memory, offers him (and us) the experience of the daffodils when most needed.

As I have just returned from a trip up to the northeast, I have seen the fields and gardens filled with bright daffodils and their spring cousins of all colors and shapes. It is very likely you might have heard this poem, Henry, as it was first published in 1804, albeit, in England. Luckily, Dorothy, Wordsworth's sister accompanied him on a walk on April 15, of 1802 when the two discovered the scene, and wrote of the particulars in her journal:

The wind was furious… the Lake was rough… When we were in the woods beyond Gowbarrow park we saw a few daffodils close to the water side, we fancied that the lake had floated the seeds ashore & that the little colony had so sprung up—but as we went along there were more & yet more & at last under the boughs of the trees, we saw that there was a long belt of them along the shore, about the breadth of a country turnpike road. I never saw daffodils so beautiful they grew among the mossy stones about & about them, some rested their heads upon these stones as on a pillow for weariness & the rest tossed & reeled & danced & seemed as if they verily laughed with the wind that blew upon them over the Lake, they looked so gay ever glancing ever changing.

This poem is not Wordsworth's most transformative. Intimations of Immortality has that honor—but it is most well read and still taught in every English class I ever knew, brought out in spring to embody the light-hearted mood of the new season. It never seems old.

For you, Henry.
Cynthia, in poetry.

P.S.
The cardinal began his morning song at 6:40 A.M. today.

I Wandered Lonely as a Cloud

I wandered lonely as a cloud
That floats on high o'er vales and hills,
When all at once I saw a crowd,
A host, of golden daffodils.
Beside the lake, beneath the trees,
Fluttering and dancing in the breeze.
Continuous as the stars that shine
And twinkle on the milky way,

They stretched in never-ending line
Along the margin of a bay:
Ten thousand saw I at a glance,
Tossing their heads in sprightly dance.
The waves beside them danced; but they
Out-did the sparkling waves in glee:
A poet could not but be gay,
In such a jocund company:
I gazed—and gazed—but little thought
What wealth the show to me had brought:
For oft, when on my couch I lie
In vacant or in pensive mood,
They flash upon that inward eye
Which is the bliss of solitude;
And then my heart with pleasure fills,
And dances with the daffodils.

-William Wordsworth

April 7, 2016 - Stephen Spender

Dear Henry,

Years ago, I attended the reading of a guest poet at my college in New Hampshire. That would have been 1964 or 1965. The poet was Stephen Spender, Sir Stephen Harold Spender that is, later to be the appointed Poet Laureate Consultant in Poetry to the United States Library of Congress.

I had little idea who the refined English gentleman standing before us was—or what important connection to my life, only to be understood later, was taking place. We were a rather giddy, distracted bunch of college kids that night, dismaying Sir Spender as he took to the podium, his blazing poetry in his heart.

When he began to speak, we quieted within the loveliness of his voice and verse. His poems inspired awe and true discovery in his listeners. I have never forgotten that night; have held one of his poems in my heart ever since.

In this poem, Henry, I find you mentioned, although not by name. I would bet that he knew of your life and writing and read Walden. A poet and a novelist and essayist who concentrated on themes of social injustice and class struggle, you had much in common. And Whitman as well is in this poem, the waving wisdom of his green grass.

I wish I could hear again the poet read his beloved poem. That night, we were rendered speechless with the obvious devotion to his art that this man carried at his center.

The poem is so moving, but I Think Continually of Those Who Were Truly Great is not in the public domain, so I cannot quote it. However, if you look onto YouTube, this is his address: https://youtu.be/_iT3SqlWM-E

P.S.
The resident cardinal started his morning song at 6:15 AM today. Someday, I will ask him why he varies the time to launch his music.

April 8, 2016 - Bob Dylan

Dear Henry,

I would miss writing to you about the day, the sunrise, the wind. Though days change with conditions each morning, they are always the frame for early thoughts and hold a freshness no other topics can offer. Today here in Florida, the weather is to be clear and very warm, with no wind. I am waiting for the cardinal's call. The sound of that bird seems to bring the sun.

Today's poet, Bob Dylan, is a singer-songwriter and artist. Much of his most celebrated work dates from the 1960s when his songs chronicled social unrest, introducing the vision of civil disobedience (you know about that, Henry) and becoming a spokesperson for the anti-war movement as well as a return to conscientious living.

I picture a meeting between you and Mr. Dylan. His rather ragged conversational style and your erudite vocabulary would make it difficult for you to hear each other, but the same love and respect for freedom and egalitarian qualities inherent in all men would pull you through. He achieved great popularity and fame while also attracting denunciation and criticism from those the spotlight of his lyrics revealed.

A whole new generation rose in response to Bob Dylan and other folk artists, eschewing how things were for how they could be.

I offer you another YouTube vision. March, 1963. Bob Dylan will sing for you Henry… I have to trust you have YouTube where you are…

https://youtu.be/vWwgrjjlMXA

The red song of the cardinal in the air, and I offer Bob Dylan and his transformative Blowin' In The Wind, which changed the heart of the world with its immense questions. It is as haunting a song today as it was when written, asking why we have conflict and injustice. The answers are still in the wind.

Cynthia,
In poetry

April 9, 2016 - Rumi

Dear Henry,

The poems of Rumi are channels of blessing. Born in 13th century Persia, he was a poet, jurist, Islamic scholar, theologian, and Sufi mystic. His poems have been translated into many of the world's languages. He is known as one of the best-selling and most popular poets in the United States even centuries after his death.

Rumi's theme is the intense joy of the search for the Divine through music, poetry, and dance—all pathways for reaching God. In his journey, the seeker symbolically turns towards the truth, grows through love, abandons ego, arrives at Perfect Joy. Then the seeker returns from this journey with greater maturity, to love and to be of service to the whole of creation without discrimination—with no regard to beliefs, races, classes, and nations.

"A *moment of happiness, you and I sitting on the verandah, apparently two, but one in soul, you and I. We feel the flowing water of life here, you and I, with the garden's beauty and the birds singing. The stars will be watching us, and we will show them what it is to be a thin crescent moon. You and I unselfed, will be together, indifferent to idle speculation, you and I. The parrots of heaven will be cracking sugar as we laugh together, you and I. In one form upon this earth, and in another form in a timeless sweet land.*"

Rumi is not an easy man to talk of. I am speechless, really.

The cardinal first sang at 6:40 AM today, his sweet song echoing in the still dark morning.

Cynthia,
In poetry

April 10, 2016 - Robert Frost

After Apple-Picking

My long two-pointed ladder's sticking through a tree
Toward heaven still,
And there's a barrel that I didn't fill
Beside it, and there may be two or three
Apples I didn't pick upon some bough.
But I am done with apple-picking now.

Essence of winter sleep is on the night,
The scent of apples: I am drowsing off.
I cannot rub the strangeness from my sight
I got from looking through a pane of glass
I skimmed this morning from the drinking trough
And held against the world of hoary grass.
It melted, and I let it fall and break.
But I was well
Upon my way to sleep before it fell,
And I could tell
What form my dreaming was about to take.
Magnified apples appear and disappear,
Stem end and blossom end,
And every fleck of russet showing clear.
My instep arch not only keeps the ache,
It keeps the pressure of a ladder-round.
I feel the ladder sway as the boughs bend.
And I keep hearing from the cellar bin
The rumbling sound
Of load on load of apples coming in.
For I have had too much
Of apple-picking: I am overtired
Of the great harvest I myself desired.
There were ten thousand thousand fruit to touch,
Cherish in hand, lift down, and not let fall.
For all
That struck the earth,
No matter if not bruised or spiked with stubble,
Went surely to the cider-apple heap
As of no worth.
One can see what will trouble
This sleep of mine, whatever sleep it is.
Were he not gone,
The woodchuck could say whether it's like his
Long sleep, as I describe its coming on,
Or just some human sleep.

-Robert Frost

Dear Henry,

This is the wrong season for this poem. It ought to be fall to speak of apples and harvest. No matter, poetry needs no season: it creates its own in the spell it casts upon the reader. Though spring winds are blowing, warming the waiting earth, I can look into the apple tree (as I have done many times) with sounds from the first line of this poem.

We have our own apple tree in the front yard in Maine. This year it rewarded us, and we worked canning, gifting, and consuming the harvest. The sight of apples began to dismay us.

Of course, Henry, Frost's metaphor of a harvest is more of the retrospection of a man looking on a life towards its end—or is it? A poem can lead one down many paths, as Mr. Frost said himself. You are free to take any wisdom from the work, or to take it on its face. This poem is for you.

That quirky cardinal sang at 6:04 AM this morning. He must be flying in the dark. The eastern edge of the sky is lifting in light, rising out of the dark to its daily promise just now with a fading moon, a Waxing Crescent, illumination of 13% on the horizon. A New Moon passed silently over us on April 7th. The poem of today is on the lips of its creator.

May I live it consciously.

Cynthia
In poetry

April 12, 2016 - Carl Sandburg

Dear Henry,

Sometime they'll give a war and nobody will come.

-Carl Sandburg

The problem with Carl Sandburg, if there is any, is choosing what poems to send to you in this letter. A prolific writer, born in 1878 in Galesburg, Illinois, he extolled both Walt Whitman and Ralph Waldo Emerson. Whitman lent him a philosophy to live by as he entered the world of the working man: shining shoes, a hobo, a deliverer of milk, there was no job he would not do and love. He was a man of boundless energy.

Sandburg won three Pulitzer Prizes in his lifetime, two for his poetry and one for the great tome of a biography of Abraham Lincoln, his lifelong hero. There is a lot of hunger in his poems—sometimes literal hunger from the experience of The Great Depression—and a lot of hope and love from his poet's heart. At his death in 1967, President Lyndon B. Johnson said of him, "Carl Sandburg was more than the voice of America, more than the poet of its strength and genius. He was America."

Grass

Pile the bodies high at Austerlitz and Waterloo.
Shovel them under and let me work—
I am the grass; I cover all.

And pile them high at Gettysburg
And pile them high at Ypres and Verdun.
Shovel them under and let me work.
Two years, ten years, and passengers ask the conductor:
What place is this?
Where are we now?

I am the grass.
Let me work.

-Carl Sandberg

The good thing about the present methods of communicating is that everything is available to everyone at any time. It only takes intention and a little button pushing. I have included a moving poem, Grass... I expect Walt Whitman would have loved this one.

The sky is a bright cap of yellow with a few lilac clouds on the Eastern horizon. It will be warm and calm today, no rain possible. The cardinal was true to his duties this morning, beginning around 6:20 AM. I can hear him now to the left of where I am, my resident bird.

The day has begun. I wish you well in it.

Cynthia
In poetry

April 13, 2016 - Edgar Lee Masters

Dear Henry,

I am simply covered in bird song. My resident cardinal perched in the backyard at his usual waking hour (6:20 AM) and sang his heart out. He woke me and kept me enthralled with a leaping, diving aria that filled the whole of my waking as well as that of the neighborhood. He must have tired himself out because he is gone now, or at least he is quiet. It is 6:41.

The poet of the day, Edgar Lee Masters, was born in Garnett, Kansas in 1868, only six years after your death. His most famous work is Spoon River Anthology, published in 1915, a collection of short free-form poems that recreate the town of Spoon River through the epitaphs of deceased residents. Done as a dramatic piece, Henry, you would never forget it. Each of the 212 deceased members comes forward from their graves to speak their truth from transformative moments of their lives, sharing their history, making deep observations of life in Spoon River meant to complain as well as to extoll secret loves. As they are now beyond blame and have no reason to lie or fear, the truth overtakes the moment and in so doing constructs a picture of the town as interconnected, living whole. Gripping theater and unforgettable poetry.

2015 was its centennial, and it was produced and celebrated all over the country.

The challenge is, if you had only the space on your tombstone to sum up and reflect your life, what would you say? Edgar Lee Masters' brilliant and poignant anthology shows us how it is done.

Enough for today. Probably too much. The whole text is readily available online, find below the epitaph of George Gray.

Cynthia,
In poetry

64. George Gray

I HAVE studied many times
The marble which was chiseled for me—
A boat with a furled sail at rest in a harbor.
In truth it pictures not my destination
But my life.
For love was offered me and I shrank from its disillusionment;
Sorrow knocked at my door, but I was afraid;
Ambition called to me, but I dreaded the chances.
Yet all the while I hungered for meaning in my life.
And now I know that we must lift the sail
And catch the winds of destiny
Wherever they drive the boat.
To put meaning in one's life may end in madness,
But life without meaning is the torture
Of restlessness and vague desire—
It is a boat longing for the sea and yet afraid.
And...

-Edgar Lee Masters

April 14, 2016 - Wendell Berry

April 14, 2016

Dear Henry,

I am over the moon within the words of this poet. I could read them forever. I honestly don't know when to quit, and minutes stretch to hours in his presence. His tracings of meaning rise from the natural world reminding you of things you have forgotten but hear again with delight. And he looks like my dear Uncle Ed, which makes the experience of reading his heart more affecting. Born in 1934, a Kentuckian, he is a novelist, poet, environmental activist, cultural critic, and farmer. He has written many novels, short stories, poems, and essays.

A man after your own heart, Henry, he is a dissenter of violence of any kind—personal or governmental—and puts himself in the center of civil disobedience in service to the truth he sees.

Wendell Berry's world is that of the working farm transformed into the eternal. He finds his instructions for daily life there. I cannot say enough about the beauty and love in this man's poems.

He reads The Peace of Wild Things in this video...

https://www.facebook.com/watch/?v=2579764222237654

Cynthia,
In poetry

P.S.

My cardinal is flitting about outside. He first sang at 6:34 AM, a little late. But he is making up for it now.

April 15, 2016 - Edna St. Vincent Millay

God's World

O WORLD, I cannot hold thee close enough!
Thy winds, thy wide grey skies!
Thy mists, that roll and rise!
Thy woods, this autumn day, that ache and sag
And all but cry with colour! That gaunt crag
To crush! To lift the lean of that black bluff!
World, World, I cannot get thee close enough!
Long have I known a glory in it all,

But never knew I this;
Here such a passion is
As stretcheth me apart—Lord, I do fear
Thou'st made the world too beautiful this year;
My soul is all but out of me—let fall
No burning leaf; prithee, let no bird call.

-Edna St.Vincent Millay

Dear Henry,

I have loved this poet for many years. A fellow Mainer, she was born in Rockland and spent her formative years in this state. Her poem, Renascence—a 200-line lyric poem written in first person—was published in 1912 when she was nineteen-year-old, beginning her fame.

In the poem, the narrator—in a moment of contemplation of nature—is overwhelmed and sympathetically experiences her death pressed into a grave but is brought back by friendly rain to a new life of joy; the rebirth or "renascence" of the title. It is a transformative poem, Henry. I remember being stopped cold upon reading it, the experience of the poem becoming part of myself and my personal view of life since. The title, Renascence, is a variation of Renaissance, and means renewal or rebirth.

Edna St. Vincent Millay was a woman of great beauty and deep sadness. Late in her life, bitterness colored her verse, but, even from that April grief, she spoke the truth of her experience. She died in 1950, within my lifetime.

I am not able to post the whole poem, it is simply too long, but review it if you haven't already. So moving.

Renascence

All I could see from where I stood
Was three long mountains and a wood;
I turned and looked another way,
And saw three islands in a bay.
So with my eyes I traced the line
Of the horizon, thin and fine,
Straight around till I was come
Back to where I'd started from;
And all I saw from where I stood
Was three long mountains and a wood.

Over these things I could not see;
These were the things that bounded me;

And I could touch them with my hand,
Almost, I thought, from where I stand.
And all at once things seemed so small
My breath came short, and scarce at all.

-Edna St. Vincent Millay

Cynthia,
In poetry

P.S.
Our cardinal woke me at 6:16 AM today. I don't need an alarm, I have my red bird watching to see that I wake.

April 16, 2013 - Mary Oliver

Dear Henry,

This poet, Mary Oliver, would be one after your own heart. Born on September 10, 1935 in Ohio, she began writing poetry at the age of 14. She spent much of her writing life in your state, Henry: Massachusetts. Provincetown to be precise. And just as one thinks there are no surprises, I discovered that she spent the final few years of her life right down the street where I winter in Hobe Sound, Florida. I could have driven to her front porch in a matter of minutes. Of course, I have too much respect to have taken up residence outside her house, but I would have wanted to, had I known. I found this out only after her death, January 12, 2019.
In this video, she reads Geese:

https://youtu.be/zsr3ZZzH-MA

April 20, 2016 - Tomorrow

My life has been the poem
I would have writ,
But I could not both live
and utter it.

-Henry David Thoreau

Dear Henry,

I must tell you about the sky this morning. It glows apricot-pink with islands of mauve clouds. Simmering color seeps out around these islets of lilac, all visible for those awake. It will not last long as the sun is on the rise and the blinding light of the present will give way to the dimness of the past. I am glad I saw it.

And here is the cardinal, 6:41 AM, chirping his heart out. What a faithful companion.

Just these few minutes I have been away from my task, the apricot-pink backdrop has gone to soft pink, the clouds to slate blue. The effect of the whole is now subtle and mild, not the thrill of my first view.

Today, my friend, is your day as Poet of The Day. Your poetry weaves observation with rhyme and meter, displaying your deep love and attention to the simple living of your life. Any occurrence could be made a poem. The reading and savoring of your verse cause me to wish so much that we could have had an afternoons' free-floating talk, just we two. There is so much to savor and ask after.

Back to that morning sky. I was incorrect to assume the show was over. Now, the subtle pink has gone to glowing again, this time it is an opalescence I cannot confine to description.

Be thou ready for tomorrow: poems in your pocket! What poems would you choose, Henry? What fun that is to speculate about that.

Tomorrow is my day to be a resident poet.

Cynthia,
In poetry

Light-Winged Smoke

Light-winged smoke, Icarian bird,
Melting thy pinions in thy upward flight,
Lark without song, and the messenger of dawn,
Circling above the hamlets as thy nest;
Or else, departing dream, and shadowy form
Of midnight vision, gathering up thy skirts;
By night star-veiling, and by day
Darkening the light and blotting out the sun;
Go thou my incense upward from this hearth,
And ask the gods to pardon this clear flame.

-Henry David Thoreau

April 21, 2016 - Poem in Your Pocket Day

Dear Henry,

It is Poem in Your Pocket Day! Everywhere on Earth, poems will be read spontaneously, changing the usual into the extraordinary. I intend to read one poem somewhere unsafe, somewhere no one expects such a flowering of language, somewhere risky. I'll tell you about it tomorrow.

I'm relieved that this is the last day of my Poetry quest. I need to walk an earthlier path with you, Henry; return to our meetings within your prose.

Today's sky is a reprint of yesterday. Mauve islet clouds simmer in a sea of apricot and pink, wind is up, and there has been singing in the backyard all night. Our cardinal is on duty. There are only seven mornings in Florida left; the car will speed north on the Atlantic seaboard toward Maine and home to rest in West Kennebunk, my Concord. When I get out of the car, I will stand beneath my Sister Trees for a time—poplars that border the property—to hear the constant conversation leaves have with air; they are never still. The frogs' song will rise in the dusk all around me. Spring will be walking in the woods as we pass somewhere on the road home.

Today, I offer my own poetry to you, Henry, and beg an exception to our rules of conversation.

Poems that Pass You By

By the time you remember that poem,
the one you dreamt,
the one spoken in tongues in the shower,
words that would not rinse off
with water, so ready, so fast, no punctuation is possible.

By the time it arrives, it is already beyond you,
has made love to you only to tip-toe out of the bedroom
before you awaken, leave a note on the dresser,
bought a new house, moved out…
had coffee in your kitchen staring into the woods,
then left,
the door unlocked, cutting
deep footprints in brown earth carefully weeded yesterday,
proving
it was here, but now,
is flower breath
on the breeze of this day.

-Cynthia Fraser Graves

Cynthia,

In poetry

P.S.
A small postscript.
Today's poem was not written in 2016.
As I consign this letter to the page, it is actually September 17th, 2021… yes, it's years later.
I met you where writers meet, in the Imaginal Realm and that place has no time limit, or time really. This latest poem was written in the summer of 2021, and such a gift that I cannot help but include it in this book of ours. I know you will applaud my doing so.

April 22, 2016 - Earth Day

Dear Henry,

The cardinal landed as I typed your name: 6:31 AM, Earth Day. He doesn't know it's Earth Day, of course. Each day of his short, beautiful life is spent doing what his species has done since the red flash took to time. He is not one who ruins or takes advantage of the trees he sits in or the sky he soars. He is not unfaithful to his life in any way. His decisions to fly left or right, to sing here or there, have as origins and results, music, and beauty.

Earth Day has been celebrated on April 22nd since 1970—the height of our indifference to the environment. Events will be held today to encourage and demonstrate an environmental vision for the protection of our precious planet. More than 193 countries celebrate Earth Day currently.

In the mid-1800's, no one would have been able to imagine that such a day would arrive. Henry, the water you drank and bathed in, the soil your beans sprang from, are in danger of being fouled. Could you imagine a day when Walden Woods was but a small green fringe between burgeoning cities, the air you so happily breathed tainted? It is so.

On March 26th, 1857, your journal tells us:

A very pleasant day. Spent a part of it in the garden preparing to set out fruit trees. It is agreeable once more to put a spade into the warm mould. The victory is ours at last, for we remain in possession of the field.

May we treasure this *"possession of the land"* and get out of doors to plant something in the *"warm mould"* of today's earth, sink a spade somewhere, plant a flower, a tree, or help those who are doing so.

Until tomorrow,

Cynthia

April 23, 2016 - The Time Is Now

The trouble with this human experience of ours is that we are slow to see that everything is beautiful and worthy of our notice and appreciation. All that is, is for us some part of the mystery of our lives to prosper through, even the very difficult.

The air is as deep as our natures. Is the drawing in of this vital air attended with no more glorious results than I witness? The air is a velvet cushion against which I press my ear. I go forth to make new demands on life. I wish to begin this summer well; to do something in it worthy of it and of me; to transcend my daily routine and that of my townsmen; to have my immortality now, that it be in the quality of my daily life; to pay the greatest price, the greatest tax, of any man in Concord, and enjoy the most!! I will give all I am for my nobility. I will pay all my days for my success. I pray that the life of this spring and summer may lie fair in my memory. May I dare as I have never done! May I persevere as I have never done! May I purify myself anew as with fire and water, soul and body! May my melody not be wanting to the season! May I gird myself to be a hunter of the beautiful, that naught escape me! May I attain to a youth never attained! I am eager to report the glory of the universe; may I be worthy to do it; to have got through with regarding human values, so as not to be distracted from regarding divine values. It is reasonable that a man should be something worthier at the end of the year than he was at the beginning.

-Henry David Thoreau, Journal, March 15, 1852

Dear Henry,

I am late catching the wave of this day. The sun has risen and is plodding its path toward the sunset. I take inspiration from you in your journal entry quoted above. *"May I be a hunter of the beautiful that naught escape me."*

I love the enthusiasm in these words. They are so powerful, so real… They lift me up on their sound even as they flow from 164 years ago into my world, a river of clear, cold, life-giving water. I will copy these words out and carry them with me through the hours of this day, let them simmer in some pocket or purse, let them ruffle the events of this day for me and for those I meet. I may even read them out a few times, to friends or acquaintances. I trust the opportunity to arise.

I will send them out in this letter now.

"May I dare as never I have done."

-Henry David Thoreau

Until tomorrow,
Cynthia

April 24, 2016 - The Pink Full Moon

Dear Henry,

Today, I must be brief. Our red cardinal is singing out in the dark blue air of early morning. It is 6:34. Dark outlines of what will be the familiar street are standing backlit by a brightening sky. Today is begun.

On our way home last night, the gorgeous full moon of April rose in the dark velvet sky, just out of the sea. With no obstruction, it fully displayed all its glory. It is the Pink Full Moon, and as I discovered it carries a very powerful energetic signature—one I have been feeling in the last few days, wondering what was going on. Last night, I saw and understood.

Though the pink was subtle, it was powerful. It was the pink of ground phlox, of the earliest flowers of spring, of pearls of pink tints, of barely blushing pink roses. And, though it was a mini moon—as far from us as it can get in its playground of the Earth's gravity—it was stunning.

As I looked up from my letter, the slate blue sky of a moment ago is now stained the richest of pinks, glowing, slinging its color up and over this small desk of mine. Even as I try to convey this to you, it changes into lilac with gold at the edges, moving toward the blue we are more familiar with. The gift of this celestial art was only for those who were awake now.

Brief it is, but there is tomorrow.

Cynthia

April 25, 2016 - A Knocking Mood

Dear Henry,

We are moving. If you could see into this house right now, that would be plain. Everything is out of closets, off shelves, culled from cabinets, put into boxes, in bags, piles, and stacks. Chaos seems to reign as we dismantle the space where we have lived.

I am writing this letter more for me than to you. I need to remind myself that all this uprooting will not be for nothing. We will settle in the new place, put things away, rearrange, refresh, replenish; peace and beauty will reign, allowing us to live again in the moment. Right now, attention has been conscripted by the shepherding of what is amassed. It is a good time to chant your mantra, *"Simplify, simplify."*

Our cardinal sang for a good half hour this morning. He must know we are not going to be here soon. I chose the quote below as it speaks to perseverance, tells that what you seek is just a few steps away. I trust that.

When you think that your walk is profitless and a failure, and you can hardly persuade yourself not to return, it is on the point of being a success, for then you are in that subdued and knocking mood to which Nature never fails to open.

-Henry David Thoreau, Journal, January 27, 1860

We need all the encouragement we can gather right now as we step carefully between the stacks. Forgive my distractions... I trust the grass is sprouting in my next yard, and that there are cardinals in new trees.

Until tomorrow,
Cynthia

Look into my eyes and hear what I'm not saying, for my eyes speak louder than my voice ever will.

-Author Unknown

April 26, 2016 - Dark Nights, Bright Dawns

Dear Henry,

Everything is unglued, falling out of its usual place. Not only are things floating free—landscapes and people are as well. I am in the process of moving from one home to another at the same moment that I am saying goodbye to my southern companions in Florida, readying myself to get in the car to drive north to Maine where it will be snowing today in contrast to the 82 degrees of sunny warmth here. That's a lot of change to have for breakfast. It tends to leave one losing sight of who that person is looking back at you from a mirror!

As I prepare and move through the hours of the last two days, everything and everyone seems precious in a way that is not present when the conditions of this change are packed away with my belongings. When I hear our cardinal (this morning it was at 6:18 AM), I am affected with a sense of loss... Of being absent already from a place I once was.

Izak Dinesen, in her lovely book, Out of Africa, gives words to my feelings. As she leaves her adopted country of Africa for the last time, she writes about how she feels a connection to Africa, but isn't certain Africa feels anything for her.

Dramatic and affecting her words are, and big. All leave-takings are momentous. We do not know the future, and returning to the past is not only impossible, but not to be desired from the seat of the present. In returning, I will not be the same person who left, and the place I return to will look somewhat the same but will not be truly.

"If I know a song of Africa,-I thought-, of the giraffe and the African new moon lying on her back, of the ploughs in the fields and the sweaty faces of the coffee-pickers, does Africa know a song of me? Would the air over the plain quiver with a color that I have had on, or the children invent a game in which my name was, or the full moon throw a shadow over the gravel of the drive that was like me, or would the eagles of Ngong look out for me?"

— Karen Blixen, Out of Africa

Who said *"you cannot step into the same river twice"*? It is a true thing. Time and tides will flow before I return.

I will look into the eyes of my friends today with great attention, holding that affection close, trusting that the bond will hold us close when apart. I am blessed in their returning gaze.

Rather sadly,
Cynthia

In any weather, at any hour of the day or night, I have been anxious to improve the nick of time, and notch it on my stick too; to stand on the meeting of two eternities, the past and future, which is precisely the present moment; to toe that line.

-Henry David Thoreau, Walden

April 27, 2016 - The Nick Of Time

To the traveler, Cynthia,

You have pulled down the castle walls, turned out all those hiding there. A bonfire burns in the courtyard and the past is in flames. You are moving on, dear one, out of one set of windows and doors aiming for another where new dreams may be spun, new mornings to awaken. Between times, you are free, ungrounded, not the old self recognized by the keys to a front door. Enjoy the energy of this change, let it invade you, releasing you from any agreements you made with the past. Moving is not about the place you go to; it is more about the spirit that carries you forward, the new agreement you make to change things.

I do not underestimate the labor and strangeness of this period between what was and what is to be. In my journey to Walden, I suffered the slings and arrows of public opinion (oh, but that was a constant) that I would not be able to sustain myself in those great quiet woods, of the self-doubt that is a human thing. What drew me on, you might ask? What drew me on was the glowing promise of release from a world that had gone dull in repetition and sameness and the ticket of entry into a living sacramental conversation between the animate neighborhood of Walden Pond, of Nature, and the heart of one Henry David Thoreau. It brought great joy and zest to my life.

I see you moving on the great face of Earth, and I see all the course corrections that are skewing around you in bright new possibilities, like a monstrance. Be Brave, do the work, simplify, your efforts are being met with approval and delight by the Navigators of Destiny. Stand resolutely in the nick of time, let the present fill your intentions with its power.

I will look forward to your letters from Maine. It was a favorite place of mine.

Henry,
with applause and blessing

April 28, 2016 - The Road Home: Day One

Dear Henry,

The road home opens, and I will take it. My craggy-coasted home state waits at the other end of the journey.

Road trips can be many things: fun, difficult, one never knows. Everything seems to be in the air, which is as good a place as any to be. As I go, I'll drop a note or two your way.

Travel today is from Florida to North Carolina or Virginia. Farewell to my beloveds in this place; you know who you are.

With best regards,
Cynthia

April 29, 2016 - The Road Home: Day Two

From North Carolina to New Jersey
No time to chat. On the road again.

Til tomorrow,
Cynthia

April 30, 2016 - The Road Home: Day Three

Dear Henry,

We were trapped in the car for 8 hours. Of the hundreds of miles we drove, I remember events lifted out of the hum of traffic. One was the sight of a white SUV with a Christmas tree from last Christmas still tied onto the roof. It made me want to know why it was still there, but, at 70 something miles an hour, the opportunity to ask was not present.

Another moment of note was a short conversation with the man at the desk in the motel where we stayed. He had been up all-night hand-feeding an abandoned calf. This man was valiant to me, present at his day job after giving up his night's sleep. He was cheerful and very ready to tell us the tale of this calf.

The third remarkable thing was watching spring go backward from the car windows as we sped along. The lush greens of Georgia, South Carolina, and North Carolina quieted down into just barely budding trees with only a filigree of new growth showing by the time we got here to Princeton. The scenery put me in mind of Frost's great poem, "Nothing Gold Can Stay". The trees of this area's trees are arrayed in that golden hue that hovers in sight for only a day or two.

Nothing Gold Can Stay

Nature's first green is gold
Her hardest hue to hold.
Her early leaf's a flower;
But only so an hour.
Then leaf subsides to leaf.
So Eden sank to grief,
So dawn goes down to day.
Nothing gold can stay.

-Robert Frost

Tomorrow: Kennebunk, Maine.

Until then,
Cynthia

Spring 2016 - May

How many things can you go away from? They see the comet from the northwest coast just as plainly as we do, and the same stars through its tail. Take the shortest way round and stay at home. A man dwells in his native valley like a corolla in its calyx, like an acorn in its cup. Here, of course, is all that you love, all that you expect, all that you are. Here is your bride elect, as close to you as she can be got. Here is all the best and all the worst you can imagine. What more do you want? Bear hereaway then! Foolish people imagine that what they imagine is somewhere else. That stuff is not made in any factory but your own.

-Henry David Thoreau, Journal

May 1, 2016 - Arrival In Kennebunk Just Ahead

Dear Henry,

In the car for one more leg of the journey. Kennebunk waits six hours up route 95. Spring is leaping ahead of us. Afternoon light will be dying in the trees around the house we are bound for all along.

The road disappears beneath us; rain on the windshield, a 46-degree world. It's all good!

And sometimes the question rises: what is happening back in the little town of the everyday? Will I return? Who will be waiting?

For now, however, I am happy to be here, only perhaps an imagined mile or so out of that town, it's true, but emphatically elsewhere.

-Henry David Thoreau, Journal

Until tomorrow,
Cynthia

May 2, 2016 - The Trees Are All The Right Height: Home

Dear Henry,

Famously, in a campaign speech a few years ago, a contender for the presidency said as regards the state he was in at the time, "The trees are all the right height." He got into a lot of trouble for saying it, but I thought it apt when I heard it.

Here, in West K, the trees ARE all the right height. The gray of morning is just the right shade of gray, and the peeping of the birds out my window (not our cardinal) is also just right for here and now. It looks and feels like home. The view from the front porch entices one to put down whatever is taking your notice away from the inside of the present where real possibility lies. It calls to come and sit awhile, to watch whatever spectacle is proceeding—be it the spring, as it is now, or summer waiting somewhere south, or fall, or winter.

The rooms of my house have been silent and empty for so long, but now seem full of possibility. I reacquaint myself with them, each holding a pastiche of memory but willingly awaiting redefinition in the moments of this season.

Your advice, Henry, to *"go confidently in the direction of your dreams"* is a refrain the wind blows down from the north, true north, the prime direction by which all other directions are calibrated. It is fresh here, fresh, and cool and full of promise and close to the source somehow.

Off the road at last, I am released to the woods of my neighborhood, my state, my town, released to recreate myself in this iteration of the present. I am much informed and encouraged by your walk in Concord. A town, by the way, just down the road.

I must get to the day. I will go walking.

Cynthia

May 4, 2016 - A Gray Wood

Dear Henry,

The cardinals are back! Or I am back. In any event, on a walk yesterday—a gray day—through a barely sprouting spring woods there they were, calling and cavorting overhead like residents here and I the visitor. These would be northern cardinals, almost identical to their southern cousins that populate my Florida neighborhood. They made my walk home delightful as they chatted around me, playing hide and seek overhead.

He is the richest who has most use for nature as raw material of tropes and symbols with which to describe his life. If these gates of golden willows affect me, they correspond to the beauty and promise of some experience on which I am entering. If I am overflowing with life, am rich in experience for which I lack expression, then nature will be my language full of poetry, - all nature will fable, and every natural phenomenon be a myth. The man of science, who is not seeking for expression but for a fact to be expressed merely, studies nature as a dead language. I pray for such inward experience as will make nature significant.

-Henry David Thoreau, Journal

I particularly like what you say here in your Journal of May 10, 1853. It offers us perspective and suggests how to *"read"* landscape and use it to magnify a simple walk outside. I think, along with you, that we do not see the whole, but only part. When I am walking through woods, I become part of the woods, the conscious part, the being who can commune and interpret what I see. I can, of course, just walk to my purpose and see nothing. Or I can restrict my view to see only certain things, or things in a certain way, but that is not the whole of what is offered me.

On my walk yesterday, I played tag with the redbirds, marveling at velvet gray of skies and rocks around and the delicacy of emerging parasols of green leaves stretching out into invigorating air, air so clean from days of rain and the cleansing breath of evergreens standing guard around in this blessed state. Bouquets of skunk cabbage burgeoned from brown leafy margins near clear water. By the time I reached home, I found I was rewarded for setting out on foot. Exhilarated would describe my mood. All of what I saw were gifts.

And you, my dear friend, are mixed up in the whole, in the experience. Henry. Your left behind words, your legacy, spurring us to look for this inward experience of Nature. Thank you, Henry—as well as the source of this animate landscape. As I leave you today, I want to share a poem about this skunk cabbage, conned on a walk in the neighborhood...

Walk On Old Thompson Road

bright green swirls of skunk cabbage push up,
the silver brook flows, crystal water singing.

you call me, rising jade green
speaking pointed spears from satin spinning
brown earth
covered with curled foolscap
of letters from years past.

it is you! your voice. you are here,

love, etched deep blue silk in eternal air
reaches for me,
ruddy lanterns, nascent leaves open,
droop their tassels, sway,
fill aching space with filigree in light

and shade. frothy blossoms, cherry, apple, giggle in trees,
blush in the potent pulse of your ardor.
unabashed love is rising in the
bronze hands of unfurling ferns.

you are all around me, as me.

a moment walks on
wearing this coat of new silence
though my heart stays behind to
answer you
in a nod and this poem.

Until tomorrow,
Cynthia

May 5, 2016 - To Stand Up Through It All

Dear Henry,

If one takes the metaphor of a walk to be the journey of life, it is an apt one. There are good weather days, and days when the winds blow and rain pelts, snow comes underfoot, and then, flowers and sweet breezes. We become tired from the walk, but after rest and refreshment we are ready to set out again.

I was going to say that the landscape for the walk mattered not, but I don't believe that is true. There is more help, more encouragement available in natural settings. If one is walking a city where traffic and distractions abound, it is a different walk. Still, the sky is always above, and we are in company with fellow walkers wherever we are—unless we wish to be on a solitary, hidden path.

A walk is best judged at its completion, not as one travels. There is no telling what is around the next corner; though new discoveries in physics tell us that we see and experience what we expect. To cower in fear from our own creations exhausts the delight in the travel.

Taking good care of the walker is important. It is a long walk, life. Attention must be paid to sustenance, rest, walking-mates; what we carry must be little, or else we are weighed down and heavy on our feet. Lightness is the best attribute, lightness in all ways.

There are different walkers for the different seasons. The child runs the path with excitement and joy. The youth, with strong expectation and strength. As we grow, the adult walks steadily, carrying care for others. In age, the walker is determined, focused, wise, with a glance behind to see how the others are progressing.

I mentioned, Henry, that I rarely come to this writing table knowing my direction. That is so true of today. Your Journal entry was the seed of these thoughts. They are here because of you. Make what you will of it.

You must walk so gently as to hear the finest sounds, the faculties being in repose. Your mind must not perspire. True, out of doors my thought is commonly drowned, as it were, and shrunken, pressed down by stupendous piles of light ethereal influences, for the pressure of the atmosphere is still fifteen pounds to a square inch. I can do little more than preserve the equilibrium and resist the pressure of the atmosphere. I can only nod like the rye-heads in the breeze.... here, outdoors is the place to store up influences.... The mind is subject to moods, as the shadows of clouds pass over the earth. Pay not too much heed to them. Let not the traveler stop for them.

-Henry David Thoreau, Journal

Until tomorrow,
Cynthia

Now I sit on the Cliffs and look abroad over the river and Conantum hills. I live so much in my habitual thoughts, a routine of thought, that I forget there is any outside to the globe, and am surprised when I behold it as now—yonder hills and river in the moonlight, the monsters. Yet it is salutary to deal with the surface of things. What are these rivers and hills, these hieroglyphics which my eyes behold? There is something invigorating in this air, which I am peculiarly sensible is a real wind, blowing from over the surface of a planet. I look out at my eyes, I come to my window, and I feel and breathe the fresh air. It is a fact equally glorious with the most inward experience. Why have we ever slandered the outward? The perception of surfaces will always have the effect of miracle to a sane sense.

-Henry David Thoreau, Journal

May 6, 2016 - Dear Cynthia, Perspective And Lilacs

Dear One,

There is always the inside and the outside of things. And to be mortal means to flit between the two, to be taken up by the blindness of one's affairs, the return of affections, the material state of one's living, until you become lost and know that this way leads to a maze of roads in a thicket that obscures the path and leaves one unable to move, caught.

I will use the tracery of my own human thought for this letter. On this night, August 23, 1852, I had gone for a solitary walk late in the afternoon to arrive on the cliffs and watch twilight turn to night. I was pondering a sadness, holding it this way and that within my heart, looking for an answer to the question, "Why?" Why was I so misperceived by those I loved, so mistrusted though my devotion was constant and with no boundaries. Yet, the third party of judgement was always present.

Once I achieved my perch on Emerson's Cliffs, I came to the windows of my eyes, felt the wind, walked home in quiet moonlight having been returned to sanity by the medicine that rises from the very crust of the earth. Can you doubt that it does so with the explosion of green power all around you in this cold but burgeoning Spring? Outside your window is the cure for anything that seems amiss within, hieroglyphs for those who will read them. And, in just a few days, the lilacs will bloom, their sweetness so intense, it colors the air around them.

You are a fortunate one, you are. I miss much of the Earth.

Henry

May 7, 2016 - A Bell, Struck

Dear Henry,

I am grateful for your words of yesterday. I agree that perspective is everything. In fact, I am writing to tell you of someone, Annie Dillard, who wrote a book in homage to you, Henry.

In A Pilgrim at Tinker Creek, she attempts to convey the mystical, the indescribable: nature, God, awe. Spurred by the joyful immersion you lived in and by everything happening in the natural world, minute or awesome, she walked her neighborhood in your footsteps and found a brand new shining world.

With as little of a plot as Walden, Annie Dillard takes us with her, wandering between scientific observation and mystical visions. She asks if the point of reading and writing isn't to find and detail the most important truths of the universe.

For me, the book's most electric moment was when Annie went on a simple, meditative walk and was struck by the brightness and color of the world.

Pilgrim At Tinker Creek was written in 1974, one hundred twenty years after Walden. She has been proclaimed your true heir, Henry. Just one of the ripples you caused here in time and continue to cause after leaving.

Full to the brim with revelations about consciousness and creation, Pilgrim at Tinker Creek is one of those books that causes us to experience the world differently for the rest of your life. All for the price of reading. Why would you not?

I have more to say about this writer and her subject, but today's duties call. I'll continue tomorrow

Cynthia,
With affection

May 8, 2016 - Being In Good Company

Good morning, Henry,

As the end of my year with you approaches, I find I come to my desk each morning with a sense of gratitude and deepening reverence for your work. Instead of being anxious that I will have nothing to talk of (which has not happened yet), I feel free to trust this connection as valid and strong, supporting my efforts to reach you. I am in good company! The army of human beings who walk behind you on your saunters, quoting your wisdom as guide, is awesome and growing each day.

The book I am currently reading, The Spiritual Journal of Henry David Thoreau by Malcolm Clemens Young, reflects on your journal and study of nature—as well as your devotion to walking as spiritual practice, within which you forego marriage and connection to foster this holiness. Malcolm Clemens Young sees, as do we, that you are forever waiting for Nature, the great stand-in actor, to portray God, to reveal its great Source of power—but only in limited peeks that these bodies can withstand. To live thus is to transform a life consumed in petty detail to one that is forever on the edge of mystery and the delight of discovery.

Each day now, in response to my year with you, I am watching for a trace of recognition from what most consider mute things and places, a thicket I walk by, the sound of wind, a cloud formation, the landscape's effect on my mood, a running stream. And, yes, one must be ready for the disbelief and taunting that come with such a project. I even enjoy not talking about it, just having it active within me is a gift. Devotees of your *"sauntering forays"* into the woods of their lives have become friends of mine as well. The gifts of this project are too numerous to count.

I must be willing to show up though, to get up early, to keep my focus through the day, to sit and wait for the words to come tumbling, and they do. Thank God for that. I do not create the letter as much as direct its flow.

It's being/been a great adventure.

Cynthia, with affection and thanks.

Beatitude is a possession of all things held to be good, from which nothing is absent that a good desire may want. Perhaps the meaning of beatitude may become clear to us if it is compared with its opposite, misery.
Misery means being afflicted unwillingly with painful sufferings.

-Attributed to St. Gregory of Nyssa around 340 AD

May 9, 2016 - All Things Held To Be Good

Dear Henry,

Though you never darkened a church door in your adult life, you certainly have heard the Beatitudes of the New Testament and have included them into your practice.

In the first of the eight Beatitudes, *"Blessed are the poor in spirit: for theirs is the kingdom of heaven",* a telltale paradox emerges as your truth. The poor in spirit are seen as the plain folk, rewarded with the favors and blessings of revelatory grace, humble, devoid of pride, open like a cup to receiving the Word through the interactive template of the world around all of us.

That would be you, Henry. Your span of years was spent as a disavowal of pride and arrogance, then offered to others through your words and actions. Walden is the perfect text for illustrating the first beatitude; you were the soul who left comfort, position, and approval behind to build a home within humility and poverty, leaving you open to hearing and seeing the kingdom of heaven laid on the earth.

I went to the woods because I wished to live deliberately, to front only the essential facts of life, and see if I could not learn what it had to teach, and not, when I came to die, discover that I had not lived. I did not wish to live what was not life, living is so dear; nor did I wish to practice resignation, unless it was quite necessary. I wanted to live deep and suck out all the marrow of life, to live so sturdily and Spartan-like as to put to rout all that was not life, to cut a broad swath and shave close, to drive life into a corner, and reduce it to its lowest terms.

-Henry David Thoreau, Walden

If you and I were to have a vocal interactive chat, you would object at this point, saying that the reasons for your Walden sojourn were not religious at all, and I would agree. But the effects of your two years so lived, and the rest of your life as it has expanded in time and still echoes today, are pointed nonetheless toward humility, simplicity, and the conviction that he who so humbles himself is richly rewarded with the coin of the realm, happiness.

Just a last thought, Henry. The word beatitude comes from Latin: beātitūdō, noun. It means happiness. Seems like an easy choice.

Until tomorrow when I am back on the road for a while. I will just post a little note as I will be mid-air by morning.

Cynthia,

With eternal thanks

May 10, 2016 - Short Shrift

Dear Henry,

As you read this, I will be on my way south for a few days.
Will be in touch as I go. Florida and our cardinal are straight ahead of us as the crow flies.

Cynthia

May 11, 2016 - In Florida Again

Dear Henry,

I am back in Florida for a few days. We are moving to a new neighborhood with all of the possibility that offers. New views, new sounds, new coordinates on the face of the earth, new neighbors, and new perspectives.

One thing I am aware of as time moves on: the past simply disappears behind us. The differences it has made within us are woven in our persons; opinions, beliefs, things learned from where we have been even when that *where* has totally dissolved into memories.

Engaged in the strenuous act of carrying everything from one house to another, my energies are being somewhat absorbed by hard work. I relish it anyway and am grateful to be able to undertake it with optimism. Therefore, my letters will not delve too much within as I am engaged without.

The resident Florida cardinal found me and began his chant at 6:06 AM this morning from a tree very nearby.

The difference between a Maine cardinal and this one is perspective. In Maine, the song of the cardinal comes from branches of old growth oak and pine, from high above, on cool winds. Here in Florida, he is looking in the window. I will have to think about what that means.

Until tomorrow,
Cynthia

May 12, 2016 - In Memory

Dear Henry,

Apologies abounding this morning. I had been planning for weeks to honor the date of your physical passing from the earth with a memorial letter to you. In some dislocation of my attention, I got it wrong. You did not die on May 12th but on May 6th. I apologize for the mistake. And though I missed the actual day, I don't think it makes too much of a difference on this morning, May 12, 2016.

We are ever dying to one world and being born into another.

-Henry David Thoreau

155 years ago, you breathed your last breath; the life you so carefully tended closed. I have visited your grave in Sleepy Hollow Cemetery, have stood in the silent company of Emerson, Hawthorne, Alcott, so many of your friends. It's beautiful there; filtered sunlight falls through very old growth trees lending everything soft, shadowed light. Your grave is a shrine, Henry. There is a steady line of pilgrims climbing up the winding, uneven path, a testimony to your priceless presence in the world.

If it is true that to save one life in any way is a holy act, then you are a Saint. You have saved so many lives with your words and example it is not possible to calculate the number anymore. My devotion to you in the form of these letters is a small gift returned to you. It is all I can do.

I came upon the image of a man in his canoe on the still waters of a pond. It brought you to mind, you in your boat on Walden Pond, fishing, whether it be day or night—sun or moon's light. It was there you were happiest. I wish to remember you in this way.

I include the obituary written by Ralph Waldo Emerson in honor of your untarnished, beautiful life. I leave you with my great gratitude singing to you.

Cynthia

Boston Daily Advertiser, 9 May 1861

Died at Concord, on Tuesday, 6 May, Henry D. Thoreau, aged 44 years

The premature death of Mr. Thoreau is a bitter disappointment to many friends who had set no limit to their confidence in his power and future performance. He is known to the public as the author of two remarkable books, "A Week on the Concord and Merrimack Rivers," published in 1849, and "Walden, or Life in the Woods," published in 1854. These books have never had a wide circulation, but are well known to the best readers, and have exerted a powerful influence on an important class of earnest and contemplative persons.

But his study as a naturalist, which went on increasing, and had no vacations, was less remarkable than the power of his mind and the strength of his character.

He was a man of stoic temperament, highly intellectual, of a perfect probity, full of practical skill, an expert woodsman and boatman, acquainted with the use of tools, a good planter and cultivator, when he saw fit to plant, but without any taste for luxury, without the least ambition to be rich, or to be popular, and almost without sympathy in any of the common motives of men around him. He led the life of a philosopher, subordinating all other pursuits and so-called duties to his pursuit of knowledge and to his own estimate of duty. He was a man of firm mind and direct dealing, never disconcerted, and not to be bent by any inducement from his own course. He had a penetrating insight into men with whom he conversed and was not to be deceived or used by any party and did not conceal his disgust at any duplicity. As he was incapable of any the least dishonesty or untruth, he had nothing to hide, and kept his haughty independence to the end. And when we now look back at the solitude of this erect and spotless person, we lament that he did not live long enough for all men to know him.

-Ralph Waldo Emerson

As you simplify your life, the laws of the universe will be simpler;
Solitude will not be solitude;
Poverty will not be poverty;
Nor weakness, weakness.

-Henry David Thoreau

May 13, 2016 - Better To Keep It Simple

Dear Henry,

The first rays of the sun have reached into my writing room. The tree beside the front porch is shaking from our cardinal. He is about breakfast at the feeder. He must know this is the last morning for us in this house and wants us to see him clearly as he says goodbye.

We are in the midst of change—not the subtle, ever moving change of seconds, but dramatic change. We will not be here again tonight, or tomorrow morning, or ever. All the coordinates embedded within our minds and bodies, ones we used to tell us where home was are overwritten with new codes. We will wake up in a new world.

Thusly, everything we leave seems precious; people for sure, landscape, sounds, the direction of the sunrise—even the raucous train that causes such vexation often, hooting at each crossing.

I must keep this note simple and short. There is still much to do. In this movement, I am reminded of the small world you traversed but made seem universal. It is really all in seeing. I will have a new world to tell you of tomorrow. It is not far away from here, but there is a new view waiting.

May I move always toward the simpler life,
Cynthia

MAY 15, 2016 - Heading North...Polaris

The truth is …
Henry, I am in a car speeding north on Route 95. I will let that truth speak for me. At 80 mph, my estimated time of arrival in Maine is Monday around 5 PM.
I will keep notes on the road, and a hawk count will keep me focused.

Rather than love, than money, than fame, give me truth.

-Henry David Thoreau

Until later, everything seems relative at this speed.
I dare send you a poem in place of a letter… Polaris, the North Star.
Cynthia

Polaris

He says the words
North Star…
all eyes in the room swing like
compass needles, quivering
his way.

Outside, in dusk, the star climbs
to the centrifugal couch,
holds court, bathed in the ardent
regard of those looking up.

Around it, Aurora Borealis dances its veils,
spins in the breath
of someone big enough to be above it.

The Night longs for this dependable star,
Deer stand beneath, wide eyed in the powerful glow
as it strokes their innocent pelts.

Picture this:
whirling skirts of earth,
white of snow,
woven rivers frozen silver,
onyx stakes of tree trunks holding
mountains down, keeping earth itself from rising
up
to kiss this star.

Red fox, beaver, bear, owl, hawk, rabbit,
all look up,
eyes shining in such clean light.

I am there as well, have left off writing,
I lift into humming air,
breath clouding in cold
atmosphere thinning… up I go,
fusing, fading,
lighter than
light.

May 16, 2016 - Road Trip Continues

Dear Henry,

Well, our journey home has developed a detour. The plan was to scoot up the Atlantic seaboard in two days and arrive at home. And the plan usually works, but not this time.

Yesterday, around 6:00 PM, as we were slowing down for a dinner stop, strange noises started seeping from under the hood; a gear or something or other is in the process of malfunctioning (read: dying). That leaves us stranded a bit, in need of Plan B which we are about to create.

We take so much for granted! That things will always work the way we say they will, that our plan is going to be foolproof. Not this time. The important thing now is to have no fear, no annoyance allowed. This IS part of the journey and there are things to be gained, learned, experienced in this detour as well. Getting home will be all the sweeter. We make a mistake when we think that the only goal is perfection.

It's all good.

Now, to the nearest UHAUL.

Keep you posted, Henry.

Cynthia,
(in Wilson, North Carolina)

May 18, 2016 - Newton's Third Law

Dear Henry,

The air outside my windows is embossed with jewels of flowering trees: magnolias, apple, plum, and pear. The brilliant spring sun is flooding these bedecked limbs with warmth; I expect the leaves and flowers to respond quickly. Being on the road for the last few weeks, I passed summer and spring twice, once coming north on 95 only to arrive in Maine where the great show has begun again. I never tire of it.

For every action, there is an equal and opposite reaction. Newton's Third Law of Motion is in play. He didn't invent the law, he observed it. (This has always been the path of discovery.) The force of this law is felt in small controllable ways: someone smiles at you, you smile back (or don't), you fall and the ground comes up at you with the very force of your fall, you hit a car and the car hits you back with the same speed you exerted, you offer kindness to a person and that flows back to you—although it may take some time. I'm sure you were fully aware of this Law in your life, Henry.

However, there are more subtle fields of affect than matter to matter. When one extends oneself at a terrific speed, pushing breadth and intensity into their outward endeavors and neglecting the inward moments of renewal and rest, then, the undefendable web of activity will spring a trap at some point, and a reset is probable.

I bear witness to that, Henry. A virtual crash occurred that left me on the road somewhere under a heap of circumstances that included a broken-down car, a U haul truck, three days in and out of motels with no proper food or sleep, financial consequences, and a general darkening of good spirits.

Now that I am back in my home territory with the love and support of friends, my home, and my back yard, I see what it was. I was moving too fast, too far and too far away from myself and the watcher within to sustain such speed.

I am about putting your advice into serious practice. *"Simplify, simplify, simplify!"* I only wish I had you here to tell me how, exactly, but I will make a start today, you can count on it.

In gratitude,
Cynthia

May 19, 2016 - Wool Gathering

Dear Henry,

I am a bit late at my keyboard this morning. I have been searching for a way to tell you what happened yesterday. As you know, the last few days have been a serious challenge to me, physically, mentally, and emotionally. I found that I was exhausted, felt compromised physically, and worst of all, had lost my natural tendency to enjoy things, be it cleaning house, a conversation with friends, planning for a future I want, or just being. Not a good thing.

Yesterday afternoon, the sun was bright, there was a nice little breeze, and I had the time, so, I decided I would take a walk. I took my phone, (Henry, I'm sure you know what the device is by now) and my earbuds, searched for something I could enjoy listening to, plugged in, picked up my weights, and went out the door.

The program I chose was Spontaneous Evolution with Bruce Lipton, PhD. As I walked along the loop of streets out into the very green fields and hills of West Kennebunk, Bruce Lipton was telling me vital and exciting news. I have heard it before but, as is the case with so much we hear, it had dulled and dimmed with time.

What Dr. Lipton said was that my body, the one I was walking within on these sidewalks, is a receptor at best, receiving stimuli from the environment. What I make of those impressions makes all the difference. That, rather than being at the mercy of the genes I have been told are responsible for running me, I have the potential to decide for myself; my body is listening constantly to my thoughts and obeys my commands. In the clearest terms, I become what I think about and, more importantly, at any given moment, I may change a mood, a situation, a condition. We spend 5 percent of our day living in the creative zone where wishes and desires are acted upon and become, and 95 percent in the zone of programs that have already been taught. Amazing news! These programs limit our possible selves.

It made for a marvelously mind-altering walk. When I returned home, I had lilacs and lilies of the valley in my hand, a smile on my face and a spring in my step—in other words, I had entered the zone of the 5 percent of creative living and left the heaviness of my recent trauma behind.

It's a lot for a letter, but I had to share it with you, Henry. Dr. Lipton, my walking companion, is to be thanked. I think you already guessed the truth, Henry.

This world is but a canvas to our imagination.

Henry David Thoreau
Cynthia

May 20, 2016 - The Commonest Sense

Dear Henry,

We have a commonality, you and I. That is a compliment to me for sure. The trait we share is that we have no common sense. We don't know enough to come in out of the rain—in fact, we love the rain, the sound and sense of it. We can see the big hand of Mother Earth pushing the gray heavy clouds in place for a good soaking. Yes, it does get out of hand at times, rain, and floods. Earth offers much but charges the fee of duality—there are always two sides to everything here on the material plain—although this does not dull the beauty of a rainstorm. And we did sign on for the earthly experience.

For much of my life, I have been accused of having no common sense at all. So, I happily initiate myself into your Society, Henry. I include an episode of your wool gathering for my readers:

One day ... we children saw Mr. Thoreau standing right down there across the road near the Assabet. He stood very still, and we knew he was watching something in the water. But we knew we must not disturb him, and so we stayed up here in the dooryard. At noontime he was still there, watching something in the water. And he stayed there all afternoon.

At last, though, along about supper time, he came up here to the house. And then we children knew that we'd learn what it was he'd been watching. He'd found a duck that had just hatched out a nest of eggs. She had brought the little ducks down to the water. And Mr. Thoreau had watched all day to see her teach those little ducks about the river.

And while we ate our suppers there in the kitchen, he told us the most wonderful stories you ever heard about those ducks.

-Abby Hosmer

We in this century are just catching up with you, Henry, learning that we create our reality with our thoughts and that, to be free, we must cut the strings of old programs that we were taught was common sense. These ideas have led to conflict, self-hatred, fear, and dislocation on this beautiful planet. The important things are the quiet, free, sensuous things: a walk taken, cloud watching, encouraging the milk of human kindness and acceptance, all of which sounds cliche, but is possible.

We experience what we put out into the energy field. Just as a guitar string tuned to a certain note will inspire other strings of the same note to vibrate when the first string is struck, our perceptions strike strings in the environment and people around us and that is what we receive. You, or we, are in control. It's an inside job! Vibrate for joy!

Love to you Henry on this lovely spring morning in Maine.

Cynthia

May 21, 2016 - Dear Cynthia, The Eternal Society Of Woolgatherers

To My Dear Cynthia,

When I tapped you for this experience all those days ago in Princeton, it was because I saw deep within the vortex of who you are: a fellow woolgatherer, a daydreamer, adept in the noble art of absent-mindedness, the state in which all things are learned. The collected consciousness of regulated society has tried to beat it out of you, but you have persevered, suffered the blows of judgement, condemnation, mockery, and all that comes with being one who believes in what they know intuitively in the face of what is taught as truth out of fear.

And now, you stand in all your years, still able to touch the center of all existence, to hear the wind speak, to see the light in your fellow travelers no matter what uniform they wear, to walk the earth aware, to gather in the gifts of your life and offer them back again.

The term "woolgatherer" connotes one who gathers tufts of wool shed by sheep and caught on bushes. It is an ancient habit; you no longer live in a world where sheep's wool is a necessity; more is the pity. The metaphor is eternally whole though. What is of value is found caught up in the natural world I so loved like tufts of ivory wool, in full sight, waving in the breeze, to be picked and treasured as the prize of the walk.

This day, I welcome you into The Eternal Society of Woolgatherers. There are many here who stand and huzzah for your induction. There are those on earth who will know of what I speak in this letter; their numbers are great and gaining.

They are those who are in love with the earth and her great cycle of caring called the seasons, who walk and commune in the crystal air, who gently reject the idea that we are anything but Earth walking, all of us, none more elevated than the next. No politics, gender, or race distinguishes any more than another; it is the quality of brotherhood that is the sheen on the day.

I salute you!

Henry

May 22, 2016 - Lilac Dusk

Dear Henry,

I rejoice in my new assignment as fellow-woolgatherer and consider it an honor to be included in this society of eminent souls. May I prove true to the high standards set by yourself and the many others who have served as observers and translators, and may I seriously commit a good portion of my time to observation in order to pierce the outer for the inner.

This letter will be posted at a different hour of the day. Dusk is approaching; dusk, the hour light falls to the horizon and the brightness of day softens, blurs, fades. In this magic time, trees leach new spring green into open air, the bouquets of leaves smudge into flowers. Clouds above go mauve and pinkish, releasing the bright light blue of day, transforming.

The lilac is scented at every house.

-Henry David Thoreau, Journal, May 22, 1853

Still grows the vivacious lilac a generation after the door and lintel and the sill are gone, unfolding its sweet-scented flowers each spring, to be plucked by the musing traveler; planted and tended once by children's hands, in front-yard plots— now standing by wall-sides in retired pastures, and giving place to new-rising forests—the last of that stirp, sole survivor of that family. Little did the dusky children think that the puny slip with its two eyes only, which they stuck in the ground in the shadow of the house and daily watered, would root itself so, and outlive them, and the house itself in the rear that shaded it, and grown man's garden and orchard, and tell their story faintly to the lone wanderer a half-century after they had grown up and died—blossoming as fair, and smelling as sweet, as in that first spring. I mark its still tender, civil, cheerful, lilac colors.

-*Henry David Thoreau*

Lilac season has arrived in Maine. Hills and the fields are alive with amethyst blooms in thick borders for miles and miles. They wave beside roads, sprout in backyards, take to the air poignantly in the melancholy acres of cemeteries and churchyards. In other words, they are just about everywhere. We in Maine, one of the coldest climates allows for their cool temperature needs and the last of the United States to behold the miracle of lilacs. It brings me back to childhood days when I would run from bush to bush picking armfuls of them too big for a little girl to carry home and so would leave a trail of blossoms behind me.

I recently walked my street to find lovely clusters along its margins. In the dusk they seeped lilac scent into the air, an invitation to come close, to bury your nose within. And I did, for I would not let you down for anything, Henry. This is joy for free. Some walk by them all day, not seeming to notice the riches within easy reach. What is it you say, Henry? *"It's not what you look at that matters, it's what you see?"* I wonder what they are seeing, Henry. With such beauty at hand, and for such a short time, waste not a moment.

It's a topic worthy of a Woolgatherer.

Until tomorrow,
Cynthia

May 23, 2016 - Spring Seeding

Dear Henry,

It's Monday; chores to be done. Household tasks must be completed today, as well as the first spring plantings. This is to be a warm week, temperatures of 70 degrees and higher, the balmy gift of coming summer. Thursday and Friday we expect blessed rain, so getting seeds and seedlings tucked into their beds before this propitious watering is important.

I will start today with spinach, the dark green vegetable which is a great New England crop as it enjoys the intermittent cool (sometimes cold) spring temperatures. Once the heat is on (July usually), spinach bolts and must be taken out until fall when temperatures begin to cool again.

In Kennebunk's community garden named Kiuna ("community" in a Native American language), forty six fellow gardeners will plant in individual plots. Bird houses around the outer fence of the garden encourage swooping troupes of bluebirds, robins, and swallows to trapeze over our heads as we work. Beehives, set out in a field to promote pollination, allow their worker bees into the garden when the flowering crops begins.

Old New England thrift is present here today. When I read of your bean field, Henry, I recognized your industry in myself and in many of my New England neighbors. We grow and put food stores aside in response to something sewn deep in us by our predecessors who lived through many decades of deep winters. Working the soft spring soil, sowing the seeds, blessing them, and covering them to start the magic of growth is joyful.

The full moon of May, the Flower Moon, illumined our skies on May 21st. That should mean we are not vulnerable to frost now—but that law has been broken before. With today's temperatures predicted at 72, we'll risk it and plant. It will be a good day, Henry. I will think of you in your solitary bean field as I hoe.

We can make liquor to sweeten our lips, of pumpkins and parsnips and walnut tree chips.

-Henry David Thoreau, Walden

With affection,
Cynthia

May 24, 2016 - The Wind Writes A Note

Good morning, Henry,

One of my favorite things to do here in West Kennebunk is to go on a windy day to a place where the wind stirs meadow grasses into patterns and waves and watch. Just as quickly, the wind erases messages you read to write another. There are many fields around my home open and large enough for the wind to inscribe its grand thoughts in tall summer grasses. Particularly enchanting when a field of delicate summer flowers ripples in this emotion of the wind. Nostalgia is still to be found in these large tracts of old country land stretched under the open summer sky. Often, an old, deserted house or ancient cellar hole tells the tale of the inhabitants, now surely not on the earth. Trees grow up from the indentation, cemetery stones remark on the sorrow of years ago.

By the sea, in the marshes endless span, dune grasses flourish. On a windy day, they dance to the great Piper's tune. Ocean waves nearby dance in the wind as well, lifting over barriers that are usually respected.

... all else is but as a journal of the winds that blew while we were here.

-Henry David Thoreau, Letters

One must know where to find these places; the search for them is authentic wool-gathering stuff. In gales, I feel the breath of the Cosmos buffet and play with me as well as the clean, pure oxygen of air infuses freedom within me. I return home refreshed and renewed.

It is almost a better thing when the clouds are gray and the winds cold, stinging a little. I have stood so in pelting rain as well. These are the things that add to us, enlarge us in wordless understanding. I wait for wind; a companion sending me a note about when next it will come to play.

Today it will be gray and rainy, winds under 10 mph—a waiting day. And the whole week is wind-still, but I will be watching.

Cynthia

May 26, 2015 - Now You See It — The Powers Of Heaven And Earth

Dear Henry,

I have been off hobnobbing this morning with the likes of Carl Sagan and Allan Watts—exalted company for a Thursday. It is a regular day here in Maine. We—and in that I include most people—rise and get to the agenda we have set. Feeling the accomplishment of the list of things we must do is why it seems we are here.

Henry, Mr. Watts would like to disabuse us of that notion, and (though he is not in physical form) he encourage us to put the list down, stop thinking, and sit in the center of our experience quietly observing the hide and seek of life from there.

As for Mr. Sagan, he would dislocate us from thinking we are the center of the universe, confident we are not alone in the Cosmos, telling us that there is intelligent life on the stars we watch at night. There is so much we don't understand and so many in power who would suppress knowledge for fear of having to change.

And, while I was off walking with you, I heard you when you said:

How vast and profound is the influence of the subtle powers of Heaven and Earth! We are indeed "the subjects of an experiment."

-Henry David Thoreau

…and how this day will proceed after such lofty beginnings, I cannot imagine!

Nearest to all things is that power that fashions their being. Next to us the grandest laws are continually being executed. Next to us is not the workman we have hired, with whom we love so well to talk, but the workman whose work we are.

-Henry David Thoreau, Walden

Now you see it, now you don't… I will be aware and watching in any event.

Cynthia

May 27, 2016 - Two Crows, Joy

Dear Henry,

I woke this morning aware of a rattling sound coming from outside my open window. Temperatures have warmed enough that we may open windows at night, a blessing. In so doing, what is going on in the woods around the house becomes our business. Right now, a morning breeze stirs the chimes on the back porch—although when I went to find the breeze, I couldn't see it in the trees.

Back to that rattling. It was crows. The rattling kept up until it reminded me of something that happened a few days ago.

Crows live here, in the woods around our house, by the hundreds. There is what we call a Crow Council meeting on the back lawn most mornings; the Council plans their days' excursions at this time. Beautiful to watch, the sleek, black birds—large and proprietorial—take up the whole window. I am aware of them on many levels. In the readings I have done about crows, I have discovered that, in scientific experiments, they can recognize faces, display emotions, use tools, and have dialects in different regions. They are very interactive, intelligent birds.

Crows have played a considerable part in my writing life. Never Count Crow; love and loss in Kennebunk, Maine is the first of my published books, and it weaves crows into the tale as a governing symbol. While I was writing this first book, crows cawed and flew around the house incessantly, seemingly task masters keeping me at the writing. I will include a verse from the story here:

One Crow, Sorrow, Two Crows, Joy, Three Crows, a letter, Four Crows, a boy, Five Crows silver, Six Crows, Gold, Seven Crows, a story that must be told.

I heard this first from my Mother-in-law.

I have just completed a second book, Henry, titled Dusk on Route 1, which will be in the world as a story soon. The other day, the very day I finished the twelve year long writing session of this book, I stepped out the front door to revel in the finale just as two very large crows flew into the clearing and for a matter of ten minutes played tag with each other all around the house, cawing and laughing in some game. I knew it was not a game though. Two crows, Joy, from the verse above. It was joyful. Joy at the completion of the book.

I find, Henry, that since my year with you these small things always make meaning in the day.

Til Tomorrow,
Cynthia

May 28, 2016 - Kiuna Opens Today

Dear Henry,

The garden is officially open today—that would be Kiuna Community Garden here in Kennebunk. Even as I write, gardeners are packing their cars with garden tools, boots, seed packets and seedlings, as well as hope—hope for a good growing season. There are many garden plots, and we are all happy to get together in this great adventure. It's a social event, I can tell you, with many conversations over hoe handles; it makes the long winter here seem like a puff of smoke. Well, not really, but it helps.

The weather today is tailor made for warming the soil those little seeds are about to be tucked into. Temperatures will reach 86 degrees under sunny skies, with no rain or wind to bother the intense work under way. A glance at the week for rain tells us it will be on again, off again—in other words perfect. The seed beds will be warmed and watered naturally.

I was trying to decide if I thought you would have liked the planting today, and I don't think you would. Your senses much preferred the solitary hoe of your bean field where Nature itself stood beside you in silence. In an event like today's, one is distracted by all that is inherent in sociability—opinions, judgements, personality, and the rest—but it is all in good fun and friendship. For myself, I love it. And when one is in the garden alone on the odd afternoon with the energy of all that goodness around you, you are nourished by the glow of it all right through your skin. I always go home singing.

When the last car leaves this afternoon, that garden will be a city of new life, seeds waking up and stretching, seedlings putting roots down in the gloriously rich soil, the green promise of a summer nation here, together, just beginning. The birds live in the over forty bird houses perched on the fence and will swoop above the whole magic show while the bees (I mentioned that we have our own beehives) will be buzzing, waiting for prized blooms to appear.

The garden plays an important part in my summer as I get to be in the company of beets, spinach, carrots, lettuce, kale, tomatoes, and the many other inhabitants that live here. I get to see them in every stage of their lives. The garden also provides fresh vegetables to the food pantries in Kennebunk. On a banner growing season, as much as 4,000 pounds have been harvested and brought to the tables of those without. We are proud of that, for sure.

So, enough talk, Henry. I have a full day ahead. I'll report back tomorrow. No wondering what today is for; I have an appointment with Earth herself.

Cynthia

May 29, 2016 - The Qualities Of Innocence

Every morning was an invitation to make my life of equal simplicity, and I may say innocence, with Nature herself.

-Henry David Thoreau

Dear Henry,

INNOCENT: noun

1. A lack of culpability, sin, or villainy

2. Naive or without guild
3. Chaste or harmless
4. Simple, without forethought or malice

This is an innocent morning. While I revved up my writing engine, a small bird landed on a bush by the window. The innocent breeze played a melody in chimes on the porch. A girl came walking up the path beside the house going into the woods behind only to walk back out a few minutes later. The old growth trees flutter in the wind, gaining strength. Sunlight is occluded. The magnolia is in full bloom, no aspect of wrong within it. None of these events hold any ill intent, guile, or cunning, they are all innocent.

I began this letter in response to something you said in your journal of May 28th of 1854:

It would be worth the while to ask ourselves weekly, Is our life innocent enough? Do we live inhumanely, toward man or beast, in thought or act? To be serene and successful we must be at one with the universe. The least conscious and needless injury inflicted on any creature is to its extent a suicide. What peace—or life—can a murderer have?

I fear you have us there, Henry. There is much embedded in contemporary life that is not innocent, beginning with television programs that broadcast threat, danger, and darkness, and glorify wrongdoing and social mores that create exclusion... Well, I better stop there.

We are all innocent...We are born innocent,
I see myself in the other, the other in myself.
Today dawned innocently; on your advice, Henry, I will tend innocence.
I will see harmlessness and be harmless in all I think and do.
It will be a gift to myself and beyond. And such a relief!

-Cynthia Fraser Graves

May 30, 2016 - Earth Time

Dear Cynthia.

I am ever so touched with your letter of yesterday in which innocence, that truest and most dependable of attributes, was explored. Innocence is the virtue mankind shares with angels. It keeps one connected to the realm outside of duality. Innocence is found, jewellike, at the heart of all natural things. I have extolled the great list of them: night, wind, the wood, a pond... All these simple things hold at heart a balm for suffering.

Innocence is the vision a child is endowed with, a gift when the great experiment of a life begins. What happens to that clear flame is the story of how the knife of fear cuts. The snarls of human emotions can block the flame of that light but can never blow it out. As innocence looks out into the world it sees blamelessness and thus brings blamelessness to all interactions, deflating intentions that would harm and hurt.

You do not live in a perfect world; I hear your laugh at the obvious truth of that, but your insistence on innocence can bring peace of some measure around you as you walk the earth. See with the eyes of a child and the merry playfulness of what you see emerges. Take your toys and go from the playground of suspicion and greed; go home to be the child of the universe you truly are, one of wonder, joy, and peace.

"The indescribable innocence and beneficence of Nature, of sun and wind and rain, of summer and winter—such health, such cheer, they afford forever, and such sympathy have they ever with our race that all Nature would be affected, and the sun's brightness fade, and the winds sigh humanely, the clouds rain tears, and the woods shed their leaves to put on mourning in midsummer, if any man for a just cause grieve. Shall I not have intelligence with the earth? Am I not partly leaves and vegetable mold myself?"

Hoping not to offend with my lofty talk.

I remain,
Henry

May 31, 2016 - A Perfect Day For A Perfect Day

The world is a fit theatre to-day in which any part may be acted. There is this moment proposed to me every kind of life that men lead anywhere, or that imagination can paint.

-Henry David Thoreau

Dear Henry,

It is a perfect morning here in Maine. A lemon-yellow sun rises in the eastern sky, the newest of green leaves rustle in a breeze. The warm earth is chock full of seeds from spring planting, seeds stretching at their edges, the original machinery of growth in process. The others, seedlings, are taking heart at the propitious conditions, straightening up and digging down for their destiny.

And what about me? The conditions are perfect for me as well. What will I make of this day? I have made plans to accomplish this or that. Something tells me that the plans are not as important as what seeps in and around them, giving me space and touch with the whole humming energy of being.

It is time to remind you, Henry, that the year of our conversation is only one month out from being concluded—at least in its everyday form. June will arrive tomorrow; our final month will tick down to July 1st. On that day, my personal calendar flips to a new year. The actual date for its conclusion won't change my tendency now, to talk to you much of the time; you have become a Forever Friend. I often say, "I wonder what Henry would make of that?" or cringe when I see something that you would be aghast with, or feel my heart warmed when I recognize something you would have responded to with great love and passion. In this way, I will always be speaking to you. It is a good thing.

So, let's get this perfect day started. I have begun by writing to you and taking stock of what is possible through your eyes. No matter what the day brings, no matter what I choose, it will be the perfect thing for going forward in my life. It will be my life. And now my life includes your life as well.

Fortunate, I am.

Cynthia

Summer 2016 - June

June is cautious. Her glance is the fleeting smile of promise and denial. Her moods are sunny today, but tomorrow will steep itself in fog that rolls in from the still cold depths of the sea. June celebrates growth. Strong, pulsing spears break ground to rise into the soft, warm air she breathes. Her vibrance radiates hope. Her dreams are of gardens, full blown and fragrant, and of leisure and love, and the seed within.

June 1, 2016 - An Empty Calendar

Dear Henry,

A new month stretches before us: June. Here in the northeast, warm June weather can still be subdued by the cold breath of the Atlantic's chilled seas. The ocean, only a few miles away from where I write, is 50 degrees today; any onshore wind brings its cold breath. But there is great promise in the bright sun.

Being the first day of the month, the prospect of June seems uncomplicated, all the allotted thirty days' worth of its delicious time floating free. Much will happen to fill in the squares on the calendar from here, confining and using up the freedom that delights me. I would stand guard on my time, keep the black ink of encroachment from weighing down June's airy calendar.

It is only when we forget all our learning that we begin to know…

-Henry David Thoreau, Journal

I would love to come upon a day with no expectations or preexisting conception of what it would be, to swim in the delight and amazement the simplest of experiences provide, to sit for a half hour watching the wind at play in the trees and grass. I have been educated against such a waste of time by all my previous years on earth and I can sustain such joys only so long. The interior talk of what needs to be done, what is waiting to be done, begins, and I enter the headlong rush of the thoughtless day.

A man receives only what he is ready to receive…

-Henry David Thoreau, Journal

May this June be an experiment in keeping my calendar light, empty, no fear of spaces unfilled. In your honor, Henry, may it be so.

Cynthia

June 2, 2016 - The Wood Thrush Is Singing

Dear Henry,

In West Kennebunk, the silvery flute of a bird calls from the green sward of pine early on summer mornings. The trill is so penetrating, I now associate the song of that bird with a verdant, new, and hopeful feeling that rises within me from the notes, especially coupled with rain's crystal effects. I hear it from a small forest behind the house where trees live (although this is changing). The fluted song of the wood thrush invites me to step off the porch into the green cathedral of woods. It offers delight, innocence, and discovery. I think you had this bird in mind when you said:

Whenever a man hears it, he is young, and Nature is in her spring; wherever he hears it, it is a new world and a free country, and the gates of Heaven are not shut against him.

I happen to know this bird to be your very favorite. In the everyday magic of the internet, today, I will offer the Wood Thrush's song. I'm sure he sings for you where you are by command but here, we need an address.

https://youtu.be/mcR6XrnD7Yc

This morning, the bird's text sounded clear and sweet through my open window. I have heard it for years, but never stopped long enough to find out who this bird was that so enchanted me, until today. Now I know this bird as the Wood Thrush.

It could be said that the notes of this lovely song are a 'wake up' call in the grandest of applications. Every now and then, I get a glimpse of the road I might walk were I free of mind-games and strode the open, sunlit, innocent paths that are there for me. This bird's call is an invitation to that path. It sets my feet on the blessed Earth.

Until tomorrow, Henry.

Cynthia

I am not afraid that I shall exaggerate the value and significance of life, but that I shall not be up to the occasion that it is.

-Henry David Thoreau, Letter

June 3, 2016 – Book Ends

Dear Henry,

Driving through fields and hills of West Kennebunk yesterday afternoon, I came upon crossroads that led to Winnow Hill. I have written of this narrow road in the hinterlands of the area before. Old farmhouses and barns built in the 1800s stand strong on Winnow Road. The vista from there is broad, offering nostalgia from the past; one that I never pass without offering a silent thanks to the settlers of this area on whose shoulders we all stand.

Today, as I passed the sign, I remembered that I had been here and recorded the scene for a letter to you in the early days of our correspondence, July 4th, 2015.

New England plays such a strong role in the emergence of this freedom we all enjoy. Though we rant and rave about the circumstances that rise in the maintenance of such a tricky blessing as freedom, the Freedom remains whole.

At this spot, almost a year ago, I stopped my vehicle to get out and take a picture, using its image as the starting point for an essay on the meaning of things. When I doubled back to reread that entry, I liked what I read.

But, in musings yesterday, I came to a different interpretation for this precious scene. As I stood and viewed its Spring emergence, it appeared before me shimmering in the afternoon sun.

Being here now, this view of Winnow Hill means that a year has passed, that almost 365 days have flown by, that people I love have passed on from the earth plane to the next level of understanding and living, that many seasons of a year have come and gone.

In spite of tremendous change at a cellular level, I am the same in body here, standing at a crossroads in the middle of the road looking for an opening into understanding through and with you, though you are Spirit. We stand together, Henry. I'm so proud to be your friend.

If for a moment we make way with our petty selves, wish no ill to anything, apprehend no ill, cease to be but as the crystal which reflects a ray—what shall we not reflect?

-Henry David Thoreau, Letter

I receive the melancholy blessing of the scene in a different mood today. It says time is flying and, though things look the same, characters are going off stage and returning, the props and arc of this drama are in flux, stagehands moving them around us. But the play is the thing!

The sky above is the same blue as it was in 2015, white swirls of clouds aloft, the grass the same nascent green. The play will go on until the curtain falls.

Only 27 days left until the end of our project.

Reflection begins.

Cynthia,
With gratitude

Live in each season as it passes; breathe the air, drink the drink, taste the fruit, and resign yourself to the influences of each.

-Henry David Thoreau, Journal

June 4, 2016 - Rhubarb Season

Dear Henry,

The air has a soft foggy quality this morning; everything is as still as can possibly be, no breeze, no noise. The day ahead will be warm and dry as we in Maine are in between two weather fronts. We await a real soaking rain tomorrow, which gladdens our hearts as we are dry deep in the soil and need a good watering.

On earth now, our weather is badly out of balance, with perpetually arid states getting deluged in water their land can't absorb. A lot is going on down here in that sense; whole regions are experiencing dangerous weather. Good old Maine stays green, though, all the time. Green and gray are our colors.

I was at the garden a few days ago harvesting rhubarb growing three to four feet in height from a clump just under the bird house down by the fence. The first crop emerges from cold March ground when nothing else will venture out. Rhubarb pays no attention to cold. Large, dark green leaves surge up to the sun on strong, red stems more than two inches in girth. It is a delight to see the return of the rhubarb. Fragrant pies and jams immediately come to mind. There are even rhubarb tonics.

Harvesting this feisty crop is a good job when done. One must reach in and pull, never cut, the stalk from the bottom, near the soil. It dislodges with a snap, and you have your prize. You probably know all of this, Henry, but I love the feel of that release when it comes away in my hands. The next process is to cut away the large, poisonous leaves. At the garden, we compost any plant material we can to fertilize next year's crops, so the leaves find their way back to the garden soil again.

Home you go to wash and cut the stalks into chunks which go into a pot with strawberries, blueberries (another Maine specialty), and sugar to bubble to a lovely purple jammy consistency. When poured into clear glass containers the jam is lowered into boiling water for a twenty-minute bath.

Then jars are set to cool, all the while listening for the lovely ping of the canning lid telling you that they are ready to be put away for a winter day or for giving as a gift. When the lid is lifted, the sharp sweet jewel-like taste of summer rewards you again. The price of rhubarb conserve is the love of doing it.

No question about what to do with your day in a garden. Tending plants once planted is daily meditation. We in Maine are waiting for consistent warmth to break the intermittent cold spells that still plague us in June.

I wonder if you grew rhubarb, Henry? I bet you did. And gave it to the women to tend. I wish I knew.

Live in each season as it passes; breathe the air, drink the drink, taste the fruit, and resign yourself to the influences of each.

-Henry David Thoreau, Journal

The fog burned off while I was writing to you.

Cynthia

June 5, 2016 - Grandfather

Dear Henry,

I trust in the morning light to bring something to the writing table when I come to my letter. A year's correspondence is no little thing if it is to be of some consequence. This morning's thoughts were all about grandfathers, no telling why. It must have been whispered in the wind as I slept.

Grandfathers are lofty, like mountains, friendly and accepting of their offspring, much as I imagine God is. They can be depended on, are never too busy for a game or a chat, or, in my case, a story. I was fortunate in my grandfather; he was all those things. He lived with us well into his old age and was always available to me. As I write this today, I know that I was special to him as well as that I shared his last years as I lived my first years. He died when I was nine.

A lobster fisherman from Prince Edward Island, an Acadian descendant, he left his lobster industry and boarded a train to Maine with his four children when his wife, Theresa McKinnon Gaudette, died of tuberculosis in the early 1900's.

There is much sorrow in this story of the sad little family traveling away from their beautiful island home. I suppose that is all my grandfather, Dugald J Gaudette, could think to do, Henry. He needed the help of family to raise his children, all ages below 11, and Maine was where his extended family lived.

He read to me at the drop of a hat and let me follow him around while he worked in his garden showing me all the mystery going on there. No wonder I love the brown earth of gardens today; I walk in his footsteps still. Grampy was generous as well, ready to give a little girl the 25 cents it took to get admission to the movies which I loved (and still do). At the tender age of five, I walked downtown in Rumford, Maine, slapped my quarter down and watched whatever was playing. My mother did not approve.

He smoked a pipe and used wintergreen oil for aching muscles, so he smelled heavenly, of a smokey, minty mix that meant love to me.

Grampy was the first person I was aware of dying. I remember standing by his bed when I was nine and asking him if he was dying. He looked at me with his calm, beautiful old face, its blue eyes still snapping with life, he told me, without a trace of fear, that he was in that process. He was a brave man; he died a few days later at the age of 96. He is never far from my thoughts, even to this day.

So, Henry, this letter is in honor of that man who was such an important figure in my life, a tribute. I could wish all of us such a blessing. He taught me how to *be* in old age.

I think that is enough for now.

The poem below is one I wrote for him a few years ago.

Until tomorrow,
Cynthia

The Old Fisherman God

The Old Fisherman God
she walks in his giant shadow
down brown rows of the summer garden.
red claws swinging at his side,
hands that once held back the sea.
straight and true he walks, as he walked
to the boat, from Lot 1 Tignish
as the first breeze of a new day
ruffled the cold sea.

his bony frame loves the earth already.
she watches him stoop, comb.
rake the rich loam,
bring up a harvest of
worms that drip from his hands.
the sharp glint of his old gaze
meets her blue fire delight. their eyes,
the same Atlantic hue,
he offers her the wriggling miracle.
in small, cupped hands,
she lifts the marvel to her nose-
brown incense burning in summer air.

she cannot know
that this garden is his last,
that soon, he will leave her behind.

he turns now to bless
her with his smile.

in the sun of this morning,
he stands as she will see him,

just ahead of her, in the gardens of her life.

-Cynthia Fraser Graves

You think that I am impoverishing myself withdrawing from men, but in my solitude I have woven for myself a silken web or chrysalis, and, nymph-like, shall ere long burst forth a more perfect creature, fitted for a higher society.

-Henry David Thoreau, Journal

June 6, 2016 - Advice

Good Tidings, Cynthia

I feel, too, the approach of our parting. I have loved listening to your tales and thoughts from earth for this space of time. If I were to give advice to such a faithful correspondent, it would sound like wind in the trees or rainfall at night when you were tucked up safely, listening, seeming as if you dreamed the messages you found in your heart in the morning.

Since the universe constantly and obediently answers to your conceptions, guard your thoughts. Spend yourself conceiving what it is you want, or want to be, and then give yourself the space to create that image. Be deliberate about this, my friend, there is nothing more vital in your life.

There is continual change in anything alive; change occurs every second. Do not be lulled into thinking that change is not taking place, or that it takes a long time to enact; its fruition may take some time to bring about, but the moment it is wished for heartily, it begins, and is as relentless as the coming of a season upon the woods. That change will sweep you with it. Habituate with those whom you emulate, or, better still, do not habituate at all. Go into solitude with yourself as does the butterfly, to break forth into a beautiful new being.

Rise early, be about your desires, take direction from no one but yourself, listen in deepest quiet to your heart. You do not know how many years, or days even, that you have left here. Be about your business, not the busyness of friends or society. This may cause many to fall away from your company, and so much the better. The only joy that outlives the moment is that silent stream deep within you mirroring an eternal source found nowhere on earth, only hinted of in Nature. Go there often. Do not fear lone-ness.

Enough. I closed my ears to advice when on earth. I trust that the unearthly source of these words will not spawn the same reluctance within you.

Your Friend,
Henry

June 7, 2016 - A Tide Of Iris

Dear Friend,

Your recent letter proffering such sweet and gently spoken advice has been read, noted, and put away somewhere near so I can refer to it when the direction I travel becomes vague and I need a friend's vision to guide me. I thank you in more than words; I send a burst of gratefulness in your direction.

My corner of the world is awash in Iris; a great tide of them sweeps over gardens, fields, and meadows. On my walk today, I crossed a meadow out near Winnow Hill. I have told you about the section of West Kennebunk where time has paused, and echoes of the past still stir in the wind. Purple flags of Iris have overtaken the meadow, but only for the short period of a week or two, depending on weather. The meadow is bejeweled in lovely flowers. Seeing them by the hundreds is a good enough reason for a walk.

How they got there, in that meadow by the hundreds, is a mystery I should like to investigate—go right to the plants themselves for their address. They are soon to be replaced by another tide rising, but not yet cresting; Queen Anne's Lace, of which I wrote of exhaustively when we began this conversation (Daucas Carota, the wild carrot). This cycle of blooms is another reminder of the full circle of a year coming to its end.

The Iris, so named in honor of the Greek word for rainbow, is prized for its leggy stalk and elevated blooms of fantastic hues. The irises in my garden are friends to me; I watch them emerge, hoping the temperatures will stay moderate so they don't rush to blossom, enjoying the first ruffle of blue taffeta petals as they break the shell of the green bud. The danger is in a pelting rain when they are in full blossom. They become bedraggled in such a forceful downpour. I say the tints of my irises, coming year after year to my garden, is such a magnanimous gesture on their part. A warm afternoon sitting on the front porch focused on the breeze among the flowers is restorative.

The true harvest of my daily life is somewhat as intangible and indescribable as the tints of morning or evening. It is a little stardust caught, a segment of the rainbow which I have clutched.

-Henry David Thoreau, Walden

And all the blooming world thinks the same. The iris is extolled in oriental art, in Vincent van Gogh's capture of them. Irises, painted in 1889, after you left the planet, Henry. I have no doubt that you knew of Iris in your walks. Today, thousands of fields are devoted to preserving the hundreds of existing species of this flower.

Enjoy these blooms while you can. The purple tide recedes as days go by.

Until tomorrow,
Cynthia

Where is the "unexplored land" but in our own untried enterprises?

-Henry David Thoreau, Letters

June 8, 2016 - Back To Walden Pond

Henry,

Oh! What a rain last night! At one time, the torrent fell in streams, not drops. Everything out of doors is sopping, saturated, and in dire need of the sun that is just now dawning through the trees and grass with its light.

I grow nostalgic beside the moon, a waxing crescent on this day, 15% visible. I see and fear the ending of our conversation arriving, dimly, down the road, not far. When I turn around to look back at the road we have traveled, I see that it all began at Walden Pond. For both you and me, it began with the book you so graciously attended to writing during your years there.

Whenever it came time in the school year to share the ideas of transcendentalism in my classroom, I was so happy. I became calm, invigorated, afire with your words, Henry. I could speak them into that fertile space of the classroom, bless my students with them and in so doing, bless myself. Do you know that once, reading Civil Disobedience with a class of third year high school students, they became so taken with your notion of justice that they refused to go to lunch, staged a protest outside the doors of the cafeteria, would not go in to be treated like cattle, as they felt that they were in the lunch line? It was wonderful! So, you see, the energy you left us is still potent.

Last spring, I think you will remember, I visited your cabin on Walden's calm shores, walked your path with the pilgrims present for that day. I left my stone on your cairn, stood at your grave. I will do that again this year. I know you better now, have read your words, pondered them, taken them as seeds into my own life, been nourished, listened as you have spoken to me personally. You have given me the priceless gifts of courage, inspiration, a seeing that comes from within, a voice, and, most of all, friendship. Some might ask how that could be between the disembodied and one still walking the earth. I know now, it can and IS done. Let any who wish to doubt do so at their loss.

In 1881, Walt Whitman visited your cabin.

Did you know that, Henry? He wrote of the visit,

Then to Walden Pond, that beautifully embowered sheet of water, and spent over an hour there. On the spot in the woods where you Thoreau had solitary house is now quite a cairn of stones, to mark the place; I too carried one and deposited on the heap.

And John Muir, the Scottish naturalist and preservationist, a man of your own heart visited Walden and wrote:

No wonder Thoreau lived here two years. I could have enjoyed living here two hundred or two thousand. It is only about one and a half or two miles from Concord, a mere saunter, and how people should regard Thoreau as a hermit on account of his little delightful stay here I cannot guess.

You started a breeze that has blown into a global wind. How could I keep from singing' your words, they are part of the air I breathe? I will come to Walden again this summer, carry another stone to your memorial, stand in silence at your grave.

As I write of my plans, the winds are tossing trees all around me and the sun has returned in full. You are as much in these things as you are there in Concord, thank God for that.

Cynthia

June 9, 2016 - A Letter To Mr. D.R.

Henry,

Today is a cold, blustery fallish day in the middle of June. The winds are out of the northwest with 30 mph gusts and temperatures will only climb to the low sixties. The chimes on my porch are ringing in the gale with all the trees in the yard in constant motion. Gardeners are especially disappointed with this coolness as the seedlings need warmth and do not respond well to this weather. Broccoli and cabbages might enjoy today, and kale, but the others—tomatoes and eggplant especially—will not. It snowed last night on Mt. Washington just down the road in New Hampshire.

On the 4th of November 1860, you wrote a letter to a Mr. D.R., chiding him for wanting more correspondence with you. This post, less than two years' time from your death, gives us a glimpse of your thinking. You said:

You know that I never promised to correspond with you, and so, when I do I do more than I promised. Such are my pursuits and habits, that I rarely go abroad; and it is quite a habit with me to decline invitations to do so.

-Henry David Thoreau, Letters

Going further, you tell Mr. D.R. that not having written for a year was *"not a very venial offense."* You tell the fellow not to look to you for a *"regular diet, but at most, only as acorns, which too, are not to be despised..."* You inform him that this life is not for complaining but for satisfaction, and hint that he be about his own, and that you take not rebuke from his tone, only misunderstanding.

Brightly etched in this letter of November 4, 1860, the careful shepherding of your time comes to us, clear and enviable. I see you busy with each day, meeting it in personal terms rather than being lost in its demands. You tell us in this letter that your, *"out-door harvest this fall has been one Canada lynx, a fierce-looking fellow, which, it seems, we have hereabouts; eleven barrels of apples from trees of my own planting; and a large crop of white-oak acorns, which I did not raise."*

Henry, I apologize for reading your private correspondence. I find it irresistible to pull aside the curtain and see you at the table beside the fire in that wan November light, writing to Mr. D.R. There is a connection between you, the letter writer, and me, the letter writer, and acorns and apples, simple gifts I can gather in this day.

Back to my time, Henry, until tomorrow.

Cynthia

June 10, 2016 - Acorns Abounding

Dear Henry,

The grove we live within is comprised of oak trees mostly—and of course the ubiquitous pines. Oak trees thrive down the drive and out back, all around and overhead. In the fall, the sound of acorns plummeting to the ground reverberates on the roof, the driveway, anything metal left out, and is almost comical in its thumping and pinging regularity. It goes on for a few weeks, leaving little capped nuts strewn all over the lawn and walkways, causing no little bother when stepped on unawares.

Because of this great harvest, we have squirrels and chipmunks running all over, a city of them with great industry on display, all in the guise of preparations for the upcoming winter season. No matter how far away we may think winter is, these creatures are at it already. There are a few chipmunks (it might be the same one over and over, hard to tell) who take the right to invade the garage to forage in the bags of bird seed stored there. I have seen a little fellow sitting IN the bag, eyes glazed with joy.

I write this letter to tell you I had never conceived of this harvest—acorns—as food. This is a totally new and delightful idea to me. In doing some reading about acorns, I was educated to the fact that these small nuts have played a very large and important role in the subsistence of the Native American population, as well as being a food source for the first settlers on this land we now tread. I am so far from living on the land that the acorn harvest has come and gone all the years of my life and I had no notion of the value of what was under my feet.

I searched for proof that you took advantage of this generous gift of the forest and found talk of you making acorn flour for bread and many other delicious sounding possibilities.

The process is one that takes real patience, and passion. Acorn flour is nutritious, with a nutty, deep flavor that reminds one of caramel, or so I read. I, for one, will attempt to harvest my acorns this year. As I work the process, I might feel the company of those who worked the acorn under open skies around a fire deep in the woods...grateful for the life it afforded them.

What else is hiding just below the surface of what things seem to be??

With gratitude to you and the Source,
Cynthia

Sometimes, in a summer morning, having taken my accustomed bath, I sat in my sunny doorway from sunrise to noon, rapt in a reverie, amidst the pines and hickories and sumachs, in undisturbed solitude and stillness while the birds sang around or flitted noiselessly through the house, until with the sun falling in my west window, I was reminded of the lapse of time.

-Henry David Thoreau, Walden

June 11, 2016 - The Summer Solstice Window

Good morning, Henry.

On this morning, as I walked with my coffee to my writing room, a ray of sunlight beamed in through the northernmost window of my home, waking me up to the fact that the sun has reached the position in the sky that announces the Summer Solstice. The sun comes to the window at this time of the year, but then, only for a short stay.

By Autumnal Equinox, sunrise will search me out through windows two rooms over, lending a very different aspect to everything, a Fall aspect if you will. At the December Solstice, the sun rises directly into the panes of glass of the front door like winter knocking for entry. The sun's presence was enough to send me to my desk to write of it.

A sense of place on this tilting, spinning earth home of ours is composed of many things. We create the feeling of home with our senses. Here in Maine, the sense of smell renders pine and evergreen notes, ocean air, salty, tangy, often a weedy smell of tide flats, mixed with mountain-clean air and the winds of Europe flowing in off the blue Atlantic a few miles away.

Sound renders forest songs, blowing gales from Canada echoing the lonely keening of those miles and miles of woods. The ocean breaking on the granite jagged coast and the pure quiet night solitude laced with the sound of wolves from the uninhabited stretches.

Delightful...

Taste of food in Maine tends toward the plain but sacred: blueberries, apples, rhubarb; sharp tastes from foods gathered in the short growing season that makes every berry precious. Lobster and haddock, clams, scallops, are the harvest of the seas.

Being in Maine means feeling cool (if not cold), Henry. The seasons here are distinct with real borders between. Living here all my life, I know where we are in each season's clock by looking out the window. The delicate messages of time are written in my front yard. Even on the 4th of July, I see summer ticking toward fall. There are three to four hot days per year when temperatures go over 90 degrees in daylight hours but never at night. The feeling here is one of less complicated living, people like things the same.

As for sight, well, that's harder to articulate. It's green here, green, green, green, in summer at least. A few years ago, Henry, I spent six weeks of the summer at the University of Texas studying Native American culture. It was hot (103 degrees and above), brown and dry. Not realizing what hot meant, I set out to walk to the library one day, a measly mile. I barely made it, almost succumbing to the heat!!

Coming home from Texas at the end of my six weeks stay, I flew into Portland, Maine. As the plane banked over the area, what was spread below me was so green, so lovely, so kind and constant, I teared up for the gift of it. And on the edge of that green waved the blue Atlantic.

In winter, the white and cold of snow everywhere makes of home a refuge, a place to take stock and come through the long white months to spring newness. The banner of wild fall color is a tonic for the heart, beauty waving from every tree around you.

I realized in my homecomings that I am a child of this place. I know it like one knows their parents.

Well, Henry, I intended none of this when I rose. That flash of light from the summer solstice window brought it all into my mind and heart, a prism touching sacred places with gratitude.

I offer it to you who loved your home as I do mine.

Cynthia

June 12, 2016, Earth Time - Dear Cynthia

"The delicate messages of time are written in my front yard."

-Cynthia Fraser Graves

Cynthia,

There are those who are well traveled, whose bags are always packed, who seem to only wait in between great trips here and there, who, on coming back, are still where they traveled, seeing not where they are, making the common ground of their region a foreign land for want of inspection, lulled by a familiarity that blinds them. I was not one of them. In my Journal of November 12, 1853, I recorded my thoughts on that subject:

"I cannot but regard it as a kindness in those who have the steering of me that, by want of pecuniary wealth, I have been nailed to this my native region so long and steadily and made to study and love this spot of earth more and more."

So, I was enchanted with your treatise on your love and veneration of the patch of earth you have built your life upon. As one who noted the qualities of dew, the antics of ants, the ebb and flow of currents in my beloved Concord River, I concur heartily, and applaud the life lived small, lived close to the minute, for that is often close to the source. The trips I embarked upon in my days always left me more ready to return to my kingdom, a wiser king for the contrast.

And so, I ask, what is your front yard telling you today, my friend? Traveling on Earth through the great, mysterious Cosmos, you, and all those living, are the receivers of great gifts every moment of your existence; sunlight, giving the gift of energy and light, starlight, illuminating the front yard of earth. It is true that your very body contains carbon from these stars you see, you are part of the Universe. And, wind, the great air purifier, always at work, its passage like music. Rain and dew that offer you moisture. Your front yard is quite extensive when you consider all that is going on there, so much, it would take years of concentrated observation to begin to see and realize it. We take it all for granted.

My advice is to take the journey out of your own front door today, see the whole with the eyes of wonder that require only a shift in perspective. Your front yard is a University above the Ivy League standards. It offers discovery to the aware, the interested, as is your street, your town, your state and so on. Live it with lively interest; let nothing stop you from seeing the wonder in it all.

For my part, I am happy to be a small part of this, your dialogue with mystery.

The fog is clearing in West Kennebunk, the wind is waiting in the wings. Enjoy this unique day, Cynthia. That is my wish for you.

Henry, with warmth

June 13, 2016 - Sea Rose And Sea Lavender Season

Dear Henry,

June is the month for sea roses on the coast in Maine. Classified as an invasive species, their fragrance and beauty make them very popular despite this. Approaching any of the beaches around the Kennebunks in June, one is sure to get overwhelmed with the scent and sight of them. Hardy and energetic, they rise at the edges of the sea, border sand dunes, salt marshes, rocky shores, roadsides, as well as gardens and shrubbery.

My favorite sea rose site is a harbor in Wells, Maine. At this time of year, the roses thrive and announce themselves with heady fragrance as you approach the little beach and marsh beyond. The perfume they exhale is worth burying your nose in the bloom, and both colors, bright pink and snowy white, have different notes. My favorite is the white, its sweetness is tempered by a bit of a woody, aromatic scent.

On an observation deck by the tidal river running parallel to the beach, you are assaulted with the sweetness of the roses as they bask in the rare light reflected off the Atlantic which doubles their potency. On your right is a view of the spits of marsh land floating between tendrils of sea water, always pushing inward, that beckon to kayaks and canoes that can float forever on incoming tides. As you had the flow and voice of your Concord River, Henry, I have my Atlantic flood and marsh, the caroling of birds overhead, and rose breath in the air.

Among the many species of grasses to be found on a walk along the paths on the border of the marsh, Sea Lavender is the most unique. The sighting of this is a matter of timing as it only in blooms for a few weeks. It is so much coveted that it has been picked almost to extinction along the Maine coast. The few stems of this delicate flower I allow myself feel like a prize for my walk.

Though the roses are in bloom most of the summer, they are never so sweet as in June. This is when they peak, mounding up from the impossible sandy soil and rocks as if all they need to thrive is sea air. They can take the cold at the water's edge and mark the change of seasons with their green rise, giving us hope in the long, cool spring.

By July, the bright red nubs of rose hips have started to form where the flowers were. Rose hips have an extra high store of vitamin C and, when made into jams, jellies, or rose hip tea, are believed to be beneficial to digestion and circulation.

The hips are edible and contain the seeds for new crops of the beautiful bush. They seem an endless gift to me. Their strong roots hold down the shifting sands of beaches and marsh borders. They are encouraged because of this.

Why speak of the thorns on these jewels of flowers. Yes, the stem is sharp and can wound but it's worth the risk to bring the bright jewels into the house for a day or two. Like so many of the emblems of the gardens, sea roses mark the passage of time. We are poised on the edge of what seems the turn of summer. After a month or so of cool temperatures, the tide of warm air approaches us. Weather forecasters tell us that the ocean has warmed up a bit and we can expect air temperatures of 70's and 80's to crest over us all week. That tells me to "gather ye rosebuds while ye may" as Robert Herrick suggested, for heat will ripen the roses to hips. Today is the day to go for a good visit with the banks of roses at the Harbor.

While there, I will ring the Ceremonial bell in a small memorial grove. It is dedicated to all those who have lost loved ones. It is, therefore, a memorial for us all. I listen to hear the bell ring over the sea, the chime blending with wind holding a scent of roses.

Monday thoughts, Henry, full of gratitude.

Cynthia

June 14, 2016 - Cranberries, Pigs, And Flag Day

Good morning, Henry,

It's Flag Day here, in America, commemorating the adoption of the flag, June 14th, 1777. If one could get an elevated perspective over the cities and towns in this country, streets would run red, white, and blue with waving flags.

In West Kennebunk, Maine, the town that doesn't even exist outside the post office, flags are affixed to lamp poles and buildings waving in the late spring breeze this glorious sunny morning. Parades will be held all over the country as they have been held each year since 1901. We need a coming together this year, Henry, we of the USA in the wake of a great tragedy in Florida. No details needed, just the request for assistance of any celestial kind possible to eviscerate the hate that destroys so cruelly, still.

This morning, I opened your Journal to read and connect with you and I happened on the entry of August 8, 1856, to find you chasing the family pig. Having just sat to supper, news of the pig's escape came to the table and you and your father rose to the chase. Henry, I learned so much about you and your neighborhood in that romp through gardens, patches of wood, streets, an army of helpers with you, small boys, neighbors with ruined flower gardens, plus the Irish family headed by Michael. It was a hearty spectacle for this early in the day, but I enjoyed it thoroughly. In the end, the pig snapped at everyone and needed to be wheeled home in a wheelbarrow. I had a good laugh. Oh, you had the life indeed. Your comment at the end was:

So, I get home at dark, wet through and supperless, covered with mud and wheel-grease, without any flowers.

Later in the month, August 30th, I read that you were sock and shoeless in the bog in Beck's Swamp, just south of Bedford Road, a beloved restorative place for you, walking in water on the sphagnum moss pocketing ripening cranberries. In the glowing enjoyment of this experience, you said:

With windows partly open, with continent concentrated thoughts, I dream. I get my new experiences still not at the opera listening to the Swedish Nightingale, but at Beck Stow's Swamp listening to the native wood thrush.

And here is our Wood Thrush. I am with you there as well, picking red berries, chasing pigs, and dreaming. These few pages encourage me to artistry and possibility, and to the humor that grows all around.

My day contains your day, Henry. There are two of us now.

Thank You, for the 351st time,
Cynthia

June 15, 2016 - Rhode Island Road Trip And Inspiration

Henry,

I am speeding along at 70 mph on a road trip to Providence, Rhode Island. This city, Providence, is a very special place to me as it is home to the Eastside Market, a place that provided a setting for my novel, Dusk on Route 1. In this scene, the central character, Pamela Iverson, has a mystical experience in the Floral Department which jettisons her out of a dead-end life consumed in unresolved grief and re-positions her for a rescue of mysterious proportions during a blizzard on the coast of Maine. Phew! Seems like a lot. I venerate this spot, the one that has stirred my muse. I'm sure you understand the gratitude of this visit.

We have been constant companions, you, and I, through your words left behind, through a waking, conscious walking with you as I move in time here, and in my growing affection for you. You have become my teacher, Henry; in the stillness of my heart, you instruct me with the template of your life. In plain words, Henry, you inspire me. As I drive along in this car, I can see your burning footsteps around me, leading me in a way I would not have gone without your life.

One of our great contemporary writers, Joyce Carol Oates, has written the introduction to The Writings of Henry D. Thoreau by Princeton Press. In her introduction, she talks about how strongly your writings resonated with her at fifteen, and how the sense of boundless energy in them gave her confidence. There are countless legions of us who have looked to you for advice in our confused living on earth. A paean rings out from all over the globe in gratitude to your brave life.

I often think of trying to describe to you the details of life today, to translate what things are like now into understandable symbols for you. I end up not even attempting the task for there is nothing to be gained from conveying complex, meaningless jungles of developing technology. I would rather walk with you on your quiet saunters, go into the woods berrying, or sail off on the fluvial Concord in your barque.

The sun is up; it is warm and seasonable for June. A grand day to go to Providence. I will be talking of you today… Looking for you as well.

The word inspiration can be easily reconfigured to read in-spirit. We are friends in-spirit.

Cynthia

June 16, 2016 - Our Thoughts Are Prayers, And We Are Always Praying

Dear Henry,

Good morning from planet Earth. The sun is rising faithfully into a partly cloudy sky. A perfect day in the offing, temperature 75 degrees mid-afternoon; there will be no rain and light winds. The stage is set.

On March 15, 1852, at 35 years of age, you wrote the following:

I go forth to make new demands on life. I wish to begin this summer well; to do something in it worthy of it and of me; to transcend my daily routine and that of my townsmen; to have my immortality now; that it be in the quality of my daily life; to pay the greatest price, the greatest tax, of any man in Concord, and enjoy the most!!… I pray that the life of this spring and summer may ever lie fair in my memory. May I dare as I have never done… May I purify myself anew as with fire and water, soul and body.

-Henry David Thoreau, Journal

This prayer, for that is what it is, conceived and written in your journal in 1852, was sent forth with the one requirement of all answered prayer: strong emotion, desire. Desire to become a vessel for the always moving, always seeking spirit within all things. No monk praying in any abbey or on a deserted plain ever prayed so fervently or well as you, Henry.

You were granted what you prayed for. Your life was what you petitioned the heavens to experience; you had your immortality in the years of your life, lived deeply in a way that we try to emulate still today.

Your prayer was the best kind; the kind that doesn't confine the answer to finite things with an expiration date, but to the very substance of knowing, the gift of love, the intense feeling of deep affection for all there is.

What few realize is that our thoughts are prayers, all of them, all the time. Those thoughts we send out with emotion and repetition become active in the world as surely as do our actions affect material things. We are always praying, whether we know it or not, whether we believe it or not... So beware of what you think on, of the arrows of prayer you shoot into air! They come to earth answered. You knew this, Henry. Worry is to be contained at all costs. It is a rosary of fear.

As I approached my desk today, I found an empty sheet of paper, no notion of what to write about. You were waiting with a subject worthy of a morning's thoughts.

As always, in gratitude,
Cynthia

The White Mountains, likewise, were smooth mole hills to my expectation.

-Henry David Thoreau, Journal

June 17, 2016 - Expectations

Good morning, Henry,

I am trying to remember what my expectations were for this year's conversation with you. I remember being excited about the project and anxious at the same time. Anxious that I would not be able to find something of interest to write about each day. During those first few months, I had not learned to trust the connection that I now do. I trust it to come forward when asked with a clear subject for the day. At this time, over 350 days later, I can approach my keyboard knowing that I rely on whatever or whomever is present to aid me in my pledge to write. I expect this and it has not failed me yet. It has been a great lesson in facing fear.

Whatever I expected, the process has yielded a double and triple return. The gifts from this year are rolling in like the fall harvest. To enumerate them is to lessen them, but I will try.

Whenever I see your name or your image, Henry, anywhere in the day, in the world, it is like seeing an old friend I know well. Spending the year reading and thinking about your life and your words, communicating with you in this way has forged a new bond, a real one that will endure. I can visit you at will, come to your door at Walden and knock softly. You will open it to me.

Certainly, I have practiced my writing. The *YearWithHenry* process has left me a better writer and that is for sure. I see its effect in all I attempt. And I am in touch with many people through this daily letter, people who now know you in a more intimate and current way.

I have new faith in myself, faith that I set goals that seem impossible (writing to you every morning seemed impossible then) and carry them out no matter the difficulties or doubt involved. I wrote to you from Ireland, from an island on the Maine coast, nothing kept me from my promise to you and to myself.

But chief among the gifts is your voice within me. I hear it whenever I stop running and become quiet. Your wisdom, your words, your life is now etched so within; it lights my way as if I had been your confidant and friend in life. The lens of my seeing has been refined in the process of this year. I rely on it not to dull, but to sharpen my going forward.

Expectation is a tricky aspect of forecasting. It can be a limiting force in the sense that we do not allow the whole measure of life to happen by expecting too little. Or disappoint ourselves by expecting too much. It is only ourselves that we may have expectations for; there is no control of others. In my year with you, Henry, I expected the rarest and most intimate of gifts; friendship with you. With your befriending me, I have (with almost thirteen days to go) exceeded it. Bless you!

With Gratitude,
Cynthia

June 19, 2016 - The Strawberry Moon Lights The Solstice

Dear Friend,

I am at my comfortable writing table this morning instead of trying to write to you careening around the curves of the unpredictable roads of New Hampshire.

The graduation we attended in Concord, New Hampshire, yesterday was a beautiful event. The weather was perfect, pure sun, light winds, vivid crimson of the graduates' gowns telegraphing the great energy and joy of these young people as they marched to Pomp and Circumstance, bringing the memory of their graduation back to each one of us in the sea of observers. The ceremony was heightened by the presence on the platform of the current Principal of Concord, New Hampshire High School, Gene Connolly, whose diagnosis of ALS will force him to take retirement this year. The outpouring of love for this man was palpable, tears flowing everywhere. The students sang a version of Lean on Me (readily available in the ether) for their beloved leader. In almost all the speeches, he was extolled for having been at the doors of the school every morning, welcoming each and every student to school for that day, a noble man, indeed. I had my hankie out as well, Henry. Hats were in the air in his honor. A great model of optimism these kids have for the future.

So, this beginning, mirrored in high schools all over this great country, is in season. And the season, in just a day now, will quietly, solemnly enter a new phase: summer. On this day, June 19th, we are one day away from the Strawberry Full Moon of June, so named because this is the time of year this glorious berry ripens to its full sweetness. Strawberry fields all around here have just put out signs that the fruit is ready. I will be in the Strawberry fields this week, baskets in hand, kneeling on brown dirt, picking for all I am worth.

This year, Henry, the full moon and the Summer Solstice coincide. Tomorrow, at 6:34 EDT, the sun will silently reach its highest point in the sky as the full moon crests above it. At Stonehenge, a ceremonial greeting for the season will be enacted as it has been for centuries. This is a very powerful conjunction of events. If one were able to bask in its effects and give it the attention it deserves, I bet you could feel the energy of it on your skin. These energies do reach us. Our lives are so busy now, though, the whole event might slip by unobserved. I will try to attend to this as the rare blessing it is.

All these beginnings going on at the same time overwhelm me a bit. We are called to action by them. Not to mention the wild green growth fizzing in gardens all around. It is an energetic time of year, Henry. May we keep our head and hearts focused on the quiet, inner voice in all these delightful distractions of Mother Earth's costume. Fall is queuing up down the road in a few months. That season will be as welcome as this, a time to rest and reflect. But that is not the mood now!

In Gratitude,
Cynthia

June 20, 2016 - Dear Cynthia, Sacramental Time

To faithful Cynthia,

This is a rare day as each day is rare, rising in your consciousness faithfully with the sun, whether you are awake and prepared for it or not, each day holding something to be given. But to be given, it must be received.

You and I share a love for and an enjoyment of plain days, days without prescriptive requirements. I refer here to Sundays when, in my time, one was required to go to church and spend the day listening to someone tell you how to live; someone who rarely knew how to live themselves. The 'good' life was seen as one un-lived, suffocating in the circular tread of respectability like an ox in harness trudges the grinder of a mill.

In my view, the hills and valleys of Concord and other horizons I traveled offered coffers of the jewels of existence, to be grasped by only lifting the lid of my vision. The idea that grace, the free and unmerited favor of God was imparted only within the doors of a church, was repugnant to me.

My life was my religion; its sacraments, experienced daily, were close at hand, indistinguishable outwardly from the living of life. Bathing, especially in Walden Pond, became a ritual of cleansing myself, chiefly inwardly, the cool, clean water rinsing any baseness from my nature.

"Sometimes, in a summer morning, having taken my accustomed bath, I sat in my sunny doorway from sunrise till noon, rapt in a revery, amidst the pines and hickories and sumachs, in undisturbed solitude and stillness, while the birds sing around flitted noiseless through the house, until by the sun falling in at my west window, or the noise of some traveller's wagon on the distant highway, I was reminded of the lapse of time. I grew in those seasons like corn in the night, and they were far better than any work of the hands would have been. They were not time subtracted from my life, but so much over and above my usual allowance. I realized what the Orientals mean by contemplation and the forsaking of works. For the most part, I minded not how the hours went. The day advanced as if to light some work of mine; it was morning, and lo, now it is evening, and nothing memorable is accomplished."

Forgive me for quoting myself, I cannot think how to say it better than I already have. After bathing came a silent communion in the church of a thicket I passed by, or walking meditation as I strolled up and down the byways.

I rose early, religiously, may I say, to reap the sun's first and most potent rays. I was abstemious with my diet, treating my body as a temple; I worked hard, with optimism and gratitude, feeling the human strength within me as a wand of power to create. I was careful with my word, speaking not against any man or woman, choosing my vocabulary from the book of love, if sometimes altering the text. I was a champion of justice as I saw it and paid the tax it cost.

To sum it up, Cynthia, I was a plain man, the plainest of the plain. And yet, I was caressed with the free-flowing grace of connection to my source in a blessed way. My solitude was my gift. I chose to see it so.

But I am far afield of what I came to say. Today is a rare Monday. Today, the slippage of the cosmos will deliver your planet into a new position in the sun's affection. Today, Summer begins for the Northern Hemisphere, lit by a full moon, the Strawberry Moon. Let the light of this moon shine on you as it rises. Your skies will be open and free tonight in Maine, the light of this moon will flow abundantly *onto West Kennebunk's Blueberry plains. Dance in its glow if you dare, and I hope you do. I will be watching.*

Henry

June 21, 2016 - Half As High As My Head

Good morning, Henry,

First, my thanks for your last letter. Because of it, I felt you beside me in the glow of that precious moon. The last time this confluence of moon and solstice lit the world was in the summer of 1967, the Summer of Love, which culminated in a huge celebratory gathering known as Woodstock.

As I stood in the moon's light last night, solitary in my quiet front yard, I saw the same moon that inspires the whole world and felt connected to others, known and unknown, who surely looked up to its quiet beauty and inspiration. Its light spread peace.

But that is not my text for today. As I drifted along on the barque of your Journal, I came upon this vignette concerning the publication of A Week on the Concord and Merrimack Rivers by James Munroe and Company, talked of in October 28, 1853:

For a year or two past, my publisher, falsely so called, has been writing from time to time to ask what disposition should be made of the copies of "A Week on the Concord and Merrimack Rivers" still on hand, and at last suggesting that he had use for the room they occupied in his cellar. So I had them all sent to me here, and they have arrived to-day by express, filling the man's wagon—706 copies out of an edition of 1000 which I bought of Munroe four years ago and have been ever since paying for, and have not quite paid for yet. The wares are sent to me at last, and I have an opportunity to examine my purchase. They are something more substantial than fame, as my back knows, which has borne them up two flights of stairs to a place similar to that to which they trace their origin. Of the remaining two hundred and ninety and odd, seventy-five were given away, the rest sold. I have now a library of nearly nine hundred volumes, over seven hundred of which I wrote myself. Is it not well that the author should behold the fruits of his labor? My works are piled up on one side of my chamber half as high as my head, my opera omnia. This is authorship; these are the work of my brain. There was just one piece of good luck in the venture. The unbound were tied up by the printer four years ago in stout paper wrappers, and inscribed: H.D. Thoreau's, Concord River, 50 cops.

So Munroe had only to cross out "River" and write "Mass" and deliver them to the expressman at once. I can see now what I write for, the result of my labors.

Nevertheless, despite this result, sitting beside the inert mass of my works, I take up my pen to-night to record what thought or experience I may have had, with as much satisfaction as ever. Indeed, I believe that this result is more inspiring and better for me than if a thousand had bought my wares. It affects my privacy less and leaves me freer.

I love the humor with which you write this. Sitting in your attic room, your books piled around you having come back home to the place they were penned, and you are glad of that, saying even that the notoriety their popularity might have lent you would be invasive to your secluded life's preference. Oh Henry, how indomitable you are, to be inspired by the return of unbought books, to take up your pen in your chamber, surrounded by stacks and look at them lovingly as the "result of my labors."

I'm confessing Henry. I too have a closet full of my first book, Never Count Crow; love and loss in Kennebunk, Maine. I purchased many (1,500) copies when it was published, sold some, gave many away, and have the remainder now stashed in *my* closet.

I love the intersections of your experience and mine. I, too, love having these copies to give, or just to open on a day and go back in time to my own thoughts. It seems magic to me that this story is in print…not lost to memories that fade. I am publishing again, a story I wrote over a period of twelve years and one I love. If no one else reads it, I will still love this work.

If you could have known the success of your precious book coming to you in the future, it might have disturbed your "privacy" and kept you from the life waiting on the next morning. It was your great heart and optimism that sailed your ship.

And, again, Henry, from one writer to another: thank you!

Cynthia

June 22, 2016 - Meadows

My Friend,

I woke with meadows on my mind this morning. Currently, many paths from my home bring me through meadows that stretch in all directions, open sunny areas like great puddles of color and movement rippling under the weathers. Wildflowers bloom, each at their appointed time among grasses swaying in breeze currents that rarely quell. Already this season we have beheld early waves of lupine, spires of pink and purple pointing up. Then, flags of wild iris, purple in color raising a purple haze over the land. Just now, white and pink yarrow accompanied by daisies stand the wind along with tribes of endless grasses.

There is nothing so beautiful as meadow grasses in motion, like the sea waving into shore but the pattern is that of wind, not of waves. I watch the wind's footsteps in the bend and swirl of stalks. Varieties like Bluejoint, Flat-topped White Aster, Tall Meadow-Rue, Tussock Sedge, Timothy (my personal favorite), perennial varieties that return each year to hold the meadow from floating away and to provide areas for nesting, food gathering, and shelter for wildlife.

The wide array of wildflowers makes them of great importance to insects, bees, and other pollinating species, keeping the whole ecosystem afloat. I once walked in a meadow during the afternoon when timothy bloomed in front of me, the whole meadow becoming purple. I wondered what earth I walked.

In my neighborhood, farmland meadows rise on lands left alone. Old, deserted barns add to the sweet nostalgia they present. In a few of these expanses, cemeteries—fenced off with whitewashed boards, bearing the name of the family interred—rule the space. Grass around this consecrated land sound the perfect note of respect, constantly rustling or silent under winter snows.

As you drive the roads bordering the beach here in Kennebunk, sea inspired meadows stretch under out. In these green-blue inlets, sea roses proliferate, fragrance coming so sweet on sea breezes you can hardly pass without stopping to inhale. Tide pools rise and reflect sky in little mirrors.

In fall, these same meadows bear Queen Anne's Lace and yellow ragweed among other signatures. The final bloom of the season, the aster, takes to the earth last. In its flower, we read of the arrival of the cold seasons.

And the circle of seasons goes on. You are not so far back in the chain of time that I cannot find you if I look.

What was your favorite setting, Henry? I would like to know.

Cynthia

June 24, 2016 - In Memoriam

Good morning, Henry,

I write with a heavy heart today. I lost a friend to the hidden life behind the Veil. All day, my friend was before me, in my mind, though I knew not the seriousness of her condition. I felt I had to call her, see her; urgency was strong.

But the moment of her departure came silently, and she walked bravely through the door that opened for her. All things, all actions, all thoughts of my day are rippling in the breeze that ushered from that door; the world looks different, feels diminished.

A woman of quality has left the earth, one of great love and compassion; a woman of jolly sense of humor that lent us much laughter. I could no more be me without her loving influence than I could forget her. I am grateful without measure for the kindness of her friendship, her caring advice and I can only hope I was worthy of it.

This feeling of palpable loss has come to remind me of all those in the bouquet of my friends, my teachers. How I depend on them in my daily goings on. They are gifts; I carry them with me in spirit to my advantage. Even when I do not think of them, they are there, the background of my experience on this earth. They come to stand in my memory from every age I have ever been, every place I have lived. They are quite a crowd by now.

And you, Henry, figure chiefly in this ring of constant communion. I have you as a friend, your words come like thoughts into the meadows of my mind. I retrace your life on earth, learn from you. In this past year, this friendship with you has become sacred.

I take this present moment, which is all I have, to put words to the river of gratitude that flows in my heart to each friend, no matter the flavor of their feelings for me.

Thank you.

This day I will live to honor these gifts.

In Memory of Denise Skillings, my friend forever,
Cynthia

June 25, 2016 - Stillness

Dear Henry,

Stillness is not the same as quiet. Stillness is a place, a seat of observation that, once achieved, calls you back with its deep, reedy flute. Its qualities are some of the same as quiet, but they come from inside where no one disturbs them, where conflict disappears, where an untroubled serenity reigns, where some august power is available to engage with us, a new vision.

Stillness is not a thought. Stillness, at its very center, entertains no thought. The mind stops the locomotion of the ego's voice and new music is heard: still-ness. The spell of this hush allows no judgement or analysis, no list of things to be done. In its presence, eyes may open to a new terrain, one where form disappears.

Stillness waits at the center of each and every one of us to be discovered. Stillness is priceless. Always a whisper guides us in its direction. As you said, Henry:

It is only when we forget all our learning that we begin to know.

Everyone is equal in this place, practiced or not.

Once welcomed in, it is where we wish to live, innocence itself transforming every moment into wonder. It is a way of walking in this world relieving us of the burden and ennui of judgement.

You knew of this stillness, Henry, searched for it, found it sitting in the door of your cabin at Walden, found it on your daily walks, found it within yourself.

I found it in your words, though words were not what you were about, but what you wanted to escape. When this stillness falls over you, you will know it. It is the *"balm of Gilead"*, the pearl of great price. Its cost is willingness and practice. But, beware; you will not stay as you are; it will change you.

It is not words I wish to hear or utter but relations I seek to stand in...

-Henry David Thoreau, Journal

As a friend of mine said recently about approaching this practice: "Run, don't walk."

Five days left,
In gratitude,
Cynthia

June 26, 2016 - Sheltering

Dear Friend,

This day, I closed my eyes and went with you on your saunter through the fields around Concord. It was May 29th, 1857. A storm overtook us, coming from an innocent blue sky, so we sheltered under a "lichen clad rocky roof, half-way up the Cliff, freshly leaving ash and hickory trees above" with a view out to Fair Haven Bay.

As the time passed while we sat and we watched artistry of the rain roll over the surface of water dividing it into different textured patches, droplets leaping off the surface as they hit. It was a proper gauge to the weight and heft of that fall.

Confined, our only other companion a mosquito, every sound was magnified in this chamber. The storm lightened a little, hinting at release, until thunder from over the hill said otherwise. Then winds came and the rushing roar of rain increased. The drama of our capture spiked with forked flashes of lightning piercing earth around the pond. Rain deluged in earnest. Birds, sounding alarm, flew for cover in this renewed intensity. We were afeared the rocks would be struck and tumble down on us in the fierceness of this storm.

After an hour and a half or so of confinement, clouds thinned, birds rushed to sing their good nights as the day was fled, and we were released to walk home pondering the deepened sight of an old scene made new from the vantage point of this refuge in the Cliff. In this forced encounter with a rainstorm, we are refreshed and renewed. We inhabited the storm. We were not protected from it.

As we stepped along toward home, our footfalls were lighter for the past hour's entertainment. You began to sing "Tom Bowling", your favorite song, always reminding you of your lost brother, John. A slight rainbow arced over us as we walked.

The blue sky is never more celestial to our eyes than when it is first seen here and there between the clouds at the end of a storm—a sign of speedy fair weather... I sang "Tom Bowling" there in the midst of the rain and the dampness seemed to be favorable to my voice. There was a slight rainbow on my way home.

-Henry David Thoreau, Journal

Remembering through your words,
Cynthia

June 27, 2016 - Retrospective

Good morning,

Henry, four days remain before we mark the culmination of our year together. This may sound presumptuous, but in my experience, it is exactly what the reality has been. Your presence has been real, questioning, palpable, watchful, instructive, energizing. It has been the same as if you were on a trip and sent messages back to me through whatever mode of communication you could use, mail, telegraph, the report of a fellow traveler... The two of us talking through the ether at will.

On my part, I lived my life each day thinking ahead in its events to: "What would Henry want to know? If we were to meet, what would I tell him?" Those questions lent me new eyes, sent me scurrying to sources I *must* research, places I *must* go to find, to seek answers to my own questions. Each small event in the natural world has seemed worthy of celebrating. My eyes are opened to new and sacred perspectives; the slant of sun on a pine wood, ants walking within the sophisticated lives they lead, the slow ripening of berries, the language of the wind... It goes on and on. I am never alone now.

I have risen every day, keeping my promise to you. The effects of this industry are life changing. Honestly, Henry, I doubt if I can really stop coming to this desk each day. What I have learned through my conversation with you, the effects of personal freedom that your energy embedded within me, is enormous. I question so many of the shackles of my previous living and there are far fewer moments wasted in the numbness of unconscious living.

Yesterday morning, Sunday here on Earth, I was up and making jam by 7 AM, then out walking a three-mile loop near my home, admiring ripening grasses in a field nearby. All the while I walked, your elegant banter circled in my heart.

Cynthia

June 28, 2016 - Industries Of The Wind

Dear Henry,

The sky is occluded and the ground wet from a shallow night rain. We need a deluge. When you dig a few inches down into soil, the gardens are dry. The next few days will offer a reprieve from the sunny, pleasant days. You can count on variety here in this state. Summer warmth is on, even under this gray cap, air feels balmy.

Just a few miles from where I write, the fields and meadows of Lyman, Arundel, and Dayton stretch out under the sky. A more pastoral and lovely scene in high summer could not be found anywhere. Consumption of this landscape by houses and businesses has been slow—although it has sped up in the last ten or twenty years. When I first came to live here, circa 1970, you could drive to Portland on back roads that wove in and out of villages of the last century, no traffic lights, few stores. One would see a green carpet of grass, gardens, with green forests all around. The town centers were of the New England pattern, church at the head, town hall, perhaps a general store, mostly white houses in attendance with farms a little farther out, all watered by the many brooks of the Kennebunk and Mousam Rivers, and all flowing down to the sea.

That drive is still there but the towns have changed somewhat. Many have traffic lights and the complexity and numbers of dwellings have increased now, but there is still no comparison to the heavily populated areas of this country. Arundel, Maine, will have approximately 440 cars pass the town hall each day.

But what I want to write of, Henry, is the gorgeous and kind rising of grasses in what still exists of these ancient fields and meadows. Within the seed heads of these grass families, there are enough seeds to plant the whole state with their species with more left over for the country as a whole. When harvested, the Poaceae, the family name for grass that feeds livestock, holds down the earth with their roots, provides staple foods from cereal crops, and provides building materials and fuels. Yet we walk over them and drive through them like they do not even exist.

It would imply the regeneration of mankind if they were to become elevated enough to truly worship sticks and stones... If I could, I would worship the parings of my nails.... I would fain improve every opportunity to wonder and worship, as a sunflower welcomes the light.

-Henry David Thoreau, Wild Apples

I agree, Henry.

The chief blessing of these grasses in my eyes is the poetry of their ballet in Maine's winds. I have a hard time keeping my eyes on the road with so much waving celebration going on. Right now, wildflowers grow in multitudes, costumed for the theme of summer. I know I have written of this before; this season of the rising of the grasses is ecstatic to me. There is a hypnotic effect in the show. One must stop and get out of the car for that to be close and available. That was your way.

Good day, Henry.

Cynthia

Only that day dawns to which we are awake. There is more day to dawn. The sun is but a morning star.

-Henry David Thoreau, Walden

June 29, 2016 - The Morning Star

It is pouring down rain as I rise this morning, the lovely sound of its falling, another morning song. Rain delights me. Something about its subdued mood, the muted colors under the clouds, the sanctioned withdrawal of things that can only be done out of doors in favor of interior pursuits like reading or writing, hours of uninterrupted concentration on a project seems good in all ways.

Then, there are umbrellas. I can open the little ceiling of color above me to walk out under the deluge of crystal drops sheening everything.

This morning, I read the story you told of sewing a pair of pants for yourself...

Within a week I have had made a pair of corduroy pants, which cost when done $1.60. They are of that peculiar clay-color, reflecting the light from portions of their surface. They have this advantage, that, beside being very strong, they will look about as well three months hence as now—or as ill, some would say. Most of my friends are disturbed by my wearing them. I can get four or five pairs for what one ordinary pair would cost in Boston, and each of the former will last two or three times as long under the same circumstances. The tailor said that the stuff was not *made in this country; that it was worn by the Irish at home, and now they would not look at it, but others would not wear it, durable and cheap as it is, because it is worn by the Irish. Moreover I like the color on other accounts. Anything but black clothes.*

-Henry David Thoreau, Journal

You are cutting, pieces arranged on the floor or table, pincushion, thread, scissors beside you, oil lamp lit and there you are, working with great concentration, probably for days, until you have your trousers. It mattered not to you that the gray corduroy fabric you sewed was judged as unworthy to wear. Your intention was above such small things.

Others in your town did not approve of your mode of dress and they brandished criticism of your lack of attention to the going threads and styles. Your reply was swift and without waver;

A man who has at length found something to do will not need to get a new suit to do it in.

My God, Henry, how I love you! And even more...

Beware of all enterprises that require new clothes, and not rather the new wearer of clothes.

Henry, in this, my last letter of this year's correspondence, the image of you sewing new trousers becomes an analogy of us, you and me, during these 365 days of letters.

I have taken on the job of creating something to wear as you did. What I have fashioned is a spiritual garment, something made of strong and durable stuff, something made of the experience of life itself. That it turned out to be your words I fashioned my costume from is most fortunate, for your words are natural and true and will last forever. A few scoffed at my industry as I cut and pieced, sewing my creation each morning according to a pattern I found in my mind and heart. The job was long, and at times I was beset by a fear that I was not up to the task, that I couldn't keep going when the end seemed so far away.

I now know that there is really no end to this conversation. I will have the rewards of this project to wear for the rest of my life. I will always have been a person who listened to you, sat at your feet and was taught and loved by the shining Mr. Henry David Thoreau. I have such a good ear for your voice that it is always in my hearing, offering me your perspective of and advice in my days on earth.

I have my trousers, Henry. I am the 'new wearer of clothes.'

Until tomorrow,
Cynthia

June 30, 2016 - Dear Cynthia, In The Beginning

Dearest Cynthia,

"Be true to your work, your word, and your friend."

This is a day for celebration! The year's journey is complete; 365 days ago, you set a goal, one that would have you at your desk early each day parsing my thoughts and my life along with yours. I have been with you through it all, through the uncertainties and doubts about the value and validity of what you were attempting; through the discoveries and triumphs you have earned; through the physical and mental anguish this responsibility at times cost, and I say today, "Well Done!"

There is now a new book of discovery and direction, one that we, you and I, have co-authored, one written of a year's experiences from the perspective of one who sees beyond the surface of things to the mystical nature within, who holds no fear of stepping out of the accepted to stand in the temple of mystery that is this life.

On the day I invited you to come with me for the year, as I whispered into your ear, you heard me, believed that such a thing was possible, took up the cause without hesitation and began. This is courage, my friend. And every day since, you have found a new topic to see with new eyes.

Now, the year is complete. I have reissued your first letter here in honor of this day… I trust you will stop by now and then when something takes your interest or delight to share it with me.

I am always waiting here, in my cabin in the woods, even though the hours of earthly days have ceased tolling for me. The idea that those passed over are now absent and unavailable is a misapprehension. We are present in the thoughts and feelings we share with those focused on us, able to connect and communicate in the realm of shared knowing, as you witnessed that day in Princeton when I spoke, and you heard. I will be with you in many ways now, one of those ways being our shared correspondence. Don't let anyone tell you I was not here!!

I send warmest regards and will be waiting (though time is absent here) to hear from you whenever you wish it.

Your confidant and fast friend,

Henry David Thoreau

July 1, 2015 - Day One, Again

Dear Henry,

We will walk on our own feet; we will work with our own hands; we will speak our own minds... A nation of men will for the first time exist, because each believes himself inspired by the Divine Soul which also inspires all men.

-Henry David Thoreau

When I was slogging away in my high school classroom day after day, struggling to instill an appreciation for the genres, writers, and concepts of the American literary canon, the clouds always parted and the sun came out when I arrived at Transcendentalism. The air in the classroom became charged with new, hopeful energy and interest. During one year, I took on the task of being your spokesperson, and a prescient group of students boycotted the lunch line because of the inequities that had been exposed there by the tenets of the living art of you and Ralph Waldo Emerson. I got into trouble on your account, Henry, and I relished being your stand-in deeply.

Your words have life within. "*God is Omnipresent, Man is divine, Intuition lives within us.*" Simply saying them aloud challenges any dogma to the contrary, making rules unbearable. I was christened a devotee in those days and remain one today; these inspiring beliefs making a great difference in my life then, and now.

Henry, you didn't surprise me on that Sunday stroll in Princeton, NJ, when I came upon your image, and you spoke to me. The glimmer of encouragement lit your literary stare from that cover, and I heard your invitation as clearly as if you had been standing beside me. I smiled my acceptance, and that is the trust upon which I now act.

For tomorrow's blog, I will include a story I would tell you, eyes alight with discovery, over a cup of tea on a drizzly summer afternoon. I know, Henry, in some way unimaginable, you will hear me here and now in West Kennebunk, Maine, on this warm July afternoon.

My pledge is made. My intention set. I will drop a missive into the ethers every day for one whole year. 365 days. The rest, I trust to you.

With great affection,
Cynthia

Summer 2016 - July

Torpid July, indolent and hot, lays back on the land and languidly smiles. She calls forth spectacles of towering grey storms that sweep along waterways with tongues of lightning striking those who doubt her. She is sweet mornings but sultry and stubborn noontides, exacting a price for those who would linger in her presence. July sports with growing things, bringing them to reveal their souls, then sapping their composure. She is conniving and needs taming. July wears the delicate gem of the firefly in her deep night-scented hair.

July 7, 2016 - The Perfect Summer Day

Dear Henry,

I miss writing to you, Henry. That truth has dogged me down these last seven days. I see a cardinal or a tree in full bloom and I want to tell you about it; feel the velvet of a tomato leaf and smell the lavender scent from my weeding around it and I make a note to write to you about it. Hear a thunderstorm at night and want you to know.

The blue dome of sweet, scented summer air is cresting over us here in Maine. I sit on a bench in the sunlight of late mornings and early afternoons. Like the matrons of our town snapping green beans, I warm myself in the age-old way, having a conversation with the wind that stirs the trees on my acre plus of earth. These trees seem like persons to me, faithful friends watching and guarding my comings and goings as they have for many years now. I feel a flood of gladness and peace whenever I am conscious of them.

This vision, this new seeing, is a gift received of you. Since our year together, rather than diversion, I seek silence. In the landscapes of my life, I see it like it was a color or shape; I relax in its calm hold letting everything drain from my mind to ride that bubble of quiet.

At night, bats come out of their secret lairs to flap around the yard silently lending a thrill to those of us waiting in the dusk. Later, fireflies populate the air like fairies, blinking off and on in random patterns on black, velvet air.

As you know, Henry, New England has very distinct seasons. The days of these seasons tick away like little clocks, each moving us along on the proscenium of the year. We are in early summer now, everything is still green from spring's rain, summer flowers are rising to perfection, the warmth of the air has reached its zenith with a little more heat to achieve in late July. Perfect, Henry, just perfect.

I think on a day like this you would be stretched out on a hummock, off the path, whistling while you collected an assortment of grasses that grow around where you rest, braiding them into a wreath to grace your bedstead tonight, lending its scent to your dreams. You are composing an essay or poem as you rest, prompted by something in the wind, a scent of new mown grass perhaps, or the flight of a bird as it arrows its way across your sight lines.

It is as I told you when we parted; we cannot part. You are here as real as can be whenever I stop and look for you behind things, in the aslant glance of Emily Dickenson's rhyme.

No one could ever dissuade me from this knowing.

I will write again soon. Reply when it suits you.

Your friend,
Cynthia

Summer 2016 - August

August walks in on the simmering sweetness of summer's landscape. Her perfume is delicious: ripening berries, full throated flowers, clear, charged summer air. She is content. In her fathomless clarity she gifts us with invigorating strength and ripening for ourselves. August demands boldness and fleetness as her nights begin to chill. Her song is the ticking of summer's clock. Earth presents this month with diadems of turquoise and coral sunsets to bedeck the cloak of her shimmering days.

August 28, 2016 - Postscript

Henry,

We have traveled all the way through the summer without speaking with each other except in the way one does internally. July's soft nights, full of sweet air and fireflies, have given way to the clear, dry perspective of an August that holds the colors of plants and flowers so sharp they hurt to look at.

As I write, the wind is in constant song out the open door, all the trees swaying to its news of another season's completion. The tomatoes have been so successful this year, great red gems of perfect proportion dangling from vines that cannot support them anymore and so are drying up in the effort, lowering them to the brown earth they have sprung from. This crop is somehow always the standard.

The berries I have watched come on from white flowers in spring. Now, they offer themselves to the coveys of birds that flirt all over the neighborhood, landing on trailing boughs to lighten them of their precious load. If this sunny spell keeps up long enough, the berries will ferment, and the birds will be drunk from it. I have seen it happen before. On my walk, I pass by these berries almost daily and always think about how they would please you. As traffic passes these boughs, they are not noticeable, even to the red stain of them falling onto the roadside and smashing beneath the trees.

There is so much to tell you of that there is almost nothing I can grab hold to begin. Just let this note inform you of the fact that I have not forgotten our correspondence of the past year; just the reverse, Henry, it means more to me every day since and, always moving at my back is the intention to begin again with news of the wind, or the crops and neighbors, or what I am led to think on by what I see and know you would have an interest in.

I send you my most affectionate regards and hope that my long absence has not brought you to mistrust my words as insincere. I am renewed in our conversations.

Cynthia

August 29, 2016 - The Angelus Rings

West Kennebunk, Maine

Dear Henry,

I stand on the island of noon in 2016, looking across a simmering berry field, fruits all but dried to brown nubs, their sweetness stolen by the sun. I am thinking about olden days, days when laborers in the fields, kitchens, and mills of that hand-to-mouth world stopped at noon, rested under shade trees, drank water from a nearby stream, ate bread and cheese and were glad of it.

From the mountaintop of this distant summer's instant, I hear the Angelus Bells rippling at the crest of noon, twelve chimes that spread in the air of the past asking for remembrance of all of our departed, remembrance that behind the power of the plants and clouds, behind the sun and rain, within the wind, a presence blesses us all in the moment, this moment, any moment, all moments.

Your friend in time,
Cynthia

August 30, 2016 - Red Gems

West Kennebunk, Maine

Dear Henry,

I simply had to share news of my tomatoes with you today. These red gems will be sauced by this evening, spiced, and simmered to rich perfection. Next, the canning process will proceed, steam rising from boiling water in which six or seven quarts of the rich red velvet sauce will be submerged. When cooled, they will be set out on shelves as treasures to uncover in the cold weather to come. Just to say that a lot of important rituals took place in the sacred kitchen out of notice of the male workday world.

September will be knocking at the door in one day and New England is still in the loving grasp of warm, sunny days with winds that keep the air fresh and cool at the edges if warm in the center. Tomatoes still grow and ripen as if it were mid-August. It is a fortunate summer, Henry.

Cynthia

2017 And After - Tatters Of Letters

Dear Henry,

It is so poignant to look back on our year together in time. Writing to you and being heard was a pinnacle from which my understanding and vision deepened, broadened, and coalesced into those things that one comes to know though they are not supported by the going cultural beliefs of the day. Running against the tide in the way we did was exhilarating, enlivening... Not easily stopped.

See the letters below as the reluctance to step out of the tide of that connection.

And, beloved friend, I have never stepped out totally. I still hear you in a bird call, or a storm. Your message has not changed...

Be Alert... Aware... It is not the academic bastions I address.... It is the person out in the fields, the one looking for the wind in trees, the one smelling apple blossoms. I address you, my friend. We are One in this approach to love and knowing. I will never leave you.

You will never hear a Goodbye from me, Henry. These tatters of letters that I continue with prove that I will be writing to you until I arrive at your cabin for a good talk, sometime anon.

With love,
Cynthia

November 26, 2018 - Phantom Geese

Dear Henry,

There is something in the air today... Something calling me back to my conversations with you. I miss your voice, miss the overarching silence that comes

291

over me at times when I know you are listening, waiting, and the charged vibration when you bent close felt very sweet and particular to me. You lent me a certain view of things, one I would not spawn on my own. I need to see through your eyes, spectral though they might be.

Just now, I was tapping out a formulaic piece for a book query and I heard the chatter of geese overhead. Oh, the music in that sound! Henry, it just took me off my task in an instant… I rushed out on the front porch, and there they were, the stirring V's of sentinels in the sky, talking with each other, comparing notes on just when to turn and when as they swung an abrupt left and headed south right over my home. I would say there were forty or so.

Today's weather here in West Kennebunk is rare. November this year has unleashed deep winter, surprising us all. We already have over a foot of snow and temperatures on Thanksgiving morning were in the single digits. This puts us all in mind of the old-time fierce winters when -30 degrees was not impossible… But this early? So, today the temperatures are up almost to 40 degrees and, with rain in the offing, there is a slight fog or snow-smoke out under the maples, oaks, and pine trees. The skies are filled with a hazy grayness so that everything in the landscape is colorless… Just the darker gray of tree trunks and rocks punctuate the scene.

When I looked up, the geese were etched in the gray sky, shapes a little bit darker gray, a ghostly apparition calling in gentle songs as they lit out for southern fields.

Henry, I know you have stood on the hills of Concord and on the banks of Walden and heard the farewell of these birds as winter approached. I know too that you have thrilled to their beauty and felt reticence to let them go.

We are united in that, you and I, and our friendship is a stitch that will hold through all time. One more of my poems, Henry.

Crewel

the stitch of three black crows across linen the color of fog,

blue wool wind swirls in grey trees,

heavy storm clouds billow- grey, mauve mounds.

in and out, in and out, earth appears, recognizable in brown.

stabs of green, tufts of white, pink silk blossoms

swell.

bargello lightning juts yellow stabs,

thunder echoes, black.

the silver needle

flashes,

rain.

November 29, 2018 - November Winds

Dear Henry,

November winds have whisked color away, left behind the salty gray and dark green boughs of Maine's forests under a white blanket of snow. This color scheme is weighted towards introspection. Well, yes, I grant you there is the ochre of tattered oak leaves sturdily attached to the mother tree, unwilling to let go. This acorn hue is meant for encouragement and nuance, for relief from the starkness of the long winter, but is not lightheartedness.

The deep cold of January and snowy weeks of February have been installed in some queue we cannot yet guess. Somewhere, just a little outside of our small vision, the sprightly palette of April crocuses, tulips, nascent green leaves, and blue skies also waits to surprise us. It waits for the hands of the artist to gild and love the world in spring, should it come.

Native Americans were wise enough to bless and praise the coming of all seasons as well as each day's light... Knowing that the coming of this light was not a certainty. There is graciousness to Time that seems unstoppable, but we are putting that graciousness to the test these days when gratitude for what IS wears thin.

Winter is approaching fast now. Gone are the warm days and nights of Indian summer. Winter takes the deepest of breaths. With each exhale, it transforms the world outside our windows, etching them with frost and icy flakes. A secret presence in the woods, this structure of cold stretches, sways, cries out on the coldest nights, bends, whispers at our windows, shows us the way to acceptance.

The earth is now a stem holding the blossom of a winter sky.

My deep and warm regards,
Cynthia

December 2, 2018 - Nativity

Dear Henry,

Last night, along with a throng of two thousand or more revelers, I stumbled along in the dark walking to the Franciscan Monastery in Kennebunkport, Maine. What we were all scurrying to attend was the Prelude Caroling held to welcome Advent and the Christmas season.

Each year the number of carolers for this weather-challenged event has grown and now the sea of people standing in the cold before the Shrine to Mary, the Mother of God, is so expansive that it fills the whole landscape of the Monastery and spills back out onto the street. Each participant is welcomed and given a candle. Led by a small band of musicians and raconteurs seated within a brightly lit grotto, singing starts tentatively at 6:30—but by its conclusion, the voices are full enough to fill the skies.

The weather this year, 2018 (if you can believe so much time has gone by, Henry), is quite mild; no rain or snow, no winds. There have been years when bitter cold blasts and snowfall have challenged the carolers. People gather, no matter what, more and more come to sing the traditional hymns—children along with their parents. I'm sure traditions are begun in some of these families, and that this event will go on for a good long line of Christmases.

Upon entering the area, carolers dip their dark candles into fire held by others and the light of the little flames spread speedily until we are all standing in glow. I didn't know the woman who shared her flame with me, but in the moment of sharing, we met. I asked if I could light my candle from hers; she smiled an acceptance, and I put her flame to good use. It was significant, Henry; it was felt at the heart.

Everyone in that field shared the unity of the moment, smiled, sang, gave others a hand standing on the uneven ground. A wave of light went out from that place, up and out over everyone there and, I am sure, beyond. I found myself wondering if you saw it somehow.

The climactic moment came after a telling of the Nativity story punctuated by hymns that celebrated each scene. We were led in a closing hymn that was sung in full throated harmony by all: Let There Be Peace on Earth. By this time our emotions were in full blossom; we were open and joined as an audience of like souls. When the first words of Let There Be Peace on Earth sounded, everyone raised candles and swayed with in deep moment.

Let there be peace on earth, and let it begin with me, Let there be peace on earth, the peace that was meant to be.

As I looked around me, I was in a swaying ocean of flame, all of us of one heart and mind. It was an awesome experience. There was no face not lit, not displaying a smile. As we left the shrine, we knew we had been present to something real, something powerful.

I thought of you out there in that field only yards from the Atlantic Ocean spilling on the land with the same tides as flowed in your day. Henry, how you would have loved the shared humanity part of the experience (if not the religiosity).
We are really all one anyway.

With regards on the 1st Day of Advent,
Cynthia

December 7, 2018 - Winter Solstice Begins

Dear Henry,

We had hoarfrost a few mornings ago. The mostly bare, frozen ground of December shimmered in the rays of a rising sun after frigid temperatures fell below 20 degrees at midnight. Hoar frost is the grayish-white crystalline deposit of frozen water vapor formed in clear still weather on vegetation when the air around is warmer than the earth: fences, trees, grass, rocks, every surface was covered in diamonds. I have no doubt that you are well acquainted with the phenomenon, as your Journal tells us you walked out in all weathers, inspecting the work of nature and reporting back for your own reflection and posterity—and for your neighbors who had less curiosity and endurance and imagination than yourself.

He who sits still in a house all the time may be the greatest vagrant of all; but the saunterer, in the good sense, is no more vagrant than the meandering river, which is all the while sedulously seeking the shortest course to the sea.

Your words Henry.
And this afternoon, this minute in fact, the sun is sinking for the earliest sunset of 2018; 4:06. The sun will set at exactly this time for the next eight nights and then begin the long road back to spring. In the meantime, we come together before the fires when night falls, just as you did. The darkest month of all is waiting in the wings: January. the beginning, and the end... Both at the same time. The beginning of a new year, 2019, here in Maine.

With great hope,
Cynthia

April 1, 2022 - In Chartres This Morning

Dear Henry,

It's here! April has stepped upon the stage to beguile us with showers and flowers, raining here today to greet this month and the beginning of National Poetry Month. During this month, I will offer a poem and its details of creation from my own poems written over the fifty odd years I've been listening with a poet's ear; the first of this endeavor is not the first in the writing. This poem simply came up out of the lot first. In Chartres This Morning was written in Maine after returning from a trip to France in 2018, so this poem may even be seen as futuristic to 2016. Let's not let a time-warp slow us down...

In Chartres This Morning

In Chartres this morning, a cathedral still rises
from earth hammered flat by Roman boots.

Under the bright disc of a Gallic sun
oil of rosemary, the acrid sweetness of old roots trampled
underfoot rises in my steps.

Needles of spires jut up, prick the old sky, rip clouds in two,
point away from earth, away from silent stones
that wait in the dimness under buttressed walls.

Below the arch, a labyrinth spins in stone.
Multicolored shards of glass burn like candles
in sun, and in moon through the centuries,
lighting the living circle below.

Ask, Listen, Receive, Rejoice,
step in the ancient way.
Soon, the dumb stones themselves sing OM,
the sound of sounds lifting in the holy space.

Underneath the hollow church
an ancient well tunnels down to cool
water, Original water,
water flowing from the first spring that still
is shimmering below us,
now out of reach.

-Cynthia Fraser Graves

April 2, 2022 - God, The Iridescent Love Cloud

Dear Henry,

Many years before we began corresponding in this way, I wrote the following poem for my Mother, Ida Gaudette Fraser, when she was in her middle 90s. My Father had predeceased her by this point (2004), and she was marking time, so to speak, until death could release her from a life that was pretty much lived out. As the person who saw the most of her, I felt her state keenly. This poem describes my response.

God, The Iridescent Love-Cloud

God, the iridescent, trembling
fragrant love-cloud is calling my
Mother's name, calling her home
as if a spring dusk is falling
and supper is on the table
waiting.

In her childish way,
she is hiding, pretending
not to hear the motherly call in
for rest and safety.

On the edge of the woods,
she grasps her playthings, waits
and watches the stars whirl above
her hiding place.

But, alas, the day is gone and
her little friends have returned
to lit porches and open doors.
She alone bides now,
Crouching, tiring with her game,
hearing calls repeat now like prayers.

She does not know
how this much this trembling love-cloud
wants her, or how alone she is
in the empty yard.

-Cynthia Fraser Graves

April 3, 2022 - All About The Light

Dear Henry,

Poetry, at least poetry for me, seems to have telegraph lines established within. Poems come rattling along from somewhere, electric and quick, and I have to be quick to receive and print them, so they are visible.

The next poem is one that arrived simultaneously with the news of the death of a woman I didn't know very well, but who inspired in this poem.

All About the Light

Your priesthood is shattered, broken into shards of light,
broken as you stepped through the curtain
which death veils its chosen ones.

Your quivering light touched us all
those last secret nights, and this light grows,
grows like the endless seconds since your departure
will grow into minutes,
and your absence will grow
into hours, days, years we must
spend hidden in your now perfect sight.

Just behind air, you are watching and,
if, as the seers say, No Where is Now Here,
then, you are here with us,
available as breath and thought,
dreams and love that reach through
the fabric of time and place
longing to set us free.

You dance on the point of my pen as I write,
smiling the deep-eyed joy you loaned my soul.

Your earthly shadow called home,
you are now free to shape-shift into geese overhead,
tracking south on a fall day,
or into fireflies mimicking God
playing hide and seek,

or into me, reaching out to someone in need,
reading their heart to sing courage and love into a shawl
to warm them-
or write a poem in memory of one
who could not be contained for long by time.

-Cynthia Fraser Graves

May 10, 2022 - There Truly Is No End, Henry

Dear Henry,

I'm in a hotel room in New Hampshire. It's 10:21 AM on a Tuesday and I'm here because I had to make a space away from the everyday world to, in our way, come to the public part of our ongoing letters to each other. I cannot reach you if there is any obstruction. Therefore, I declare myself open to you again in that very privileged way I experienced during my YearWithHenry.

I know our conversations will never end for all the reasons cited between us. When you entered Earth's dimension the two or three times that I am aware of, what I knew to be true from the outset became—as they say on earth—carved in stone. You and I are fast friends and will eternally be so.

With that said, something that I feel deeply I need to do at the conclusion of the year of this rewrite and edit is to dedicate the work in hand before I send it off to the people who will rearrange spacing, check grammar, and spelling, and form... Those dear brilliant people without whom I would be lost.

Henry, I dedicate this book to you, to you my dear, dear friend. There is no one else I could conceive of that could bear the weight of this work that we have done together. I come to your cabin door and knock again... And see your bright smile for me as you open the portal. I long to spend the afternoon with you as you describe the thrift of a pinecone or rail against conventional dullness... Or teach me to make acorn flour.

The sound of your footsteps will never stop echoing in time.

In tribute to you, Henry, I use the words of a poet who lives in your town now, someone I'm sure you know: Sir Stephen Spender. Note Henry how this poet speaks of waving grasses as the simple but lovely communication center of the wind. I will always be listening for you there.

Near the snow, near the sun, in the highest fields,
See how these names are fêted by the waving grass
And by the streamers of white cloud
And whispers of wind in the listening sky.
The names of those who in their lives fought for life,

Who wore at their hearts the fire's centre.
Born of the sun, they travelled a short while toward the sun
And left the vivid air signed with their honour.

-Stephen Spender

Cynthia, with great love.